The

BIG THREE
and ME

BILLY CASPER

With James Parkinson and Lee Benson

Genesis Press, Inc.
P.O. Box 101
Columbus, MS 39703

ISBN: 13 DIGITS: 978-1-58571-628-9
ISBN: 10 DIGITS: 1-58571-628-6
Manufactured in the United States of America

First Edition 2012

Dedicated to my family . . . welcome to my family

CONTENTS

FOREWORD

Ask any one of us, and we will tell you: the 1960s was a golden age of golf. The public's interest in our sport grew by leaps and bounds. Television played a big part. The four majors—the Masters, the United States Open, the Open Championship and the PGA Championship— as well as a growing number of regular PGA Tour events, were all televised. Galleries were large and growing, new golf courses were being built all over the world, and an unprecedented number of people took to the links.

And we became known as The Big Three.

The name was a product of the marketing genius of Mark McCormack, who for a time represented each of us. The Big Three name did a lot for our careers and a lot for the game of golf. For a number of years in the sixties, and beyond, before every event, and especially the majors, much of the pre-tournament talk was about which one of us would win. There was even a Big Three made-for-TV golf event that one of us was guaranteed to win.

Inside the ropes, however, we were well aware of something the public at large didn't seem to know or appreciate. There was another player who was winning as often as we were, a player we kept an eye on and worried about just as much, if not more, than each other. His name was Billy Casper.

It could have been The Big Four.

It wasn't like Billy was unknown, certainly not in the golf world. Even a casual fan recognized his name. But for all that, he was often overlooked, even when he won.

Simply put, Billy Casper was a threat to win every golf tournament he entered. He beat us as many times as we beat him. You don't have to take our word for it. Look it up. Billy's fifty-one PGA career wins rank seventh all-time. He won two U.S. Opens and one Masters. He won at least one tournament a year for sixteen straight seasons, from 1956 through 1971, a record exceeded only by two of the undersigned (seventeen years each for Arnold and Jack). Perhaps Billy's most memorable victory came at the 1966 U.S. Open where he entered the final round three shots back of Arnold and one ahead of Jack—chased by one of us and chasing the other. He beat us both. Close to that one for dramatic finishes was the 1970 Masters where, after a tremendous duel on Augusta's back nine on Sunday, Gary came to the final green with a chance to join Billy and Gene Littler in the next day's playoff. Gary missed the putt, and Billy went on to win the playoff and the green jacket.

Billy Casper played on eight Ryder Cup teams. His 23½ points are the most by any American player in history.

Why our friend Billy Casper was so successful yet received so relatively little attention has many possible answers. Perhaps it was his conservative play. Perhaps it was a consistency that could almost lull you to sleep. It could be he made the game look too easy, especially on the greens, where anything inside ten feet was a gimmee. But, whatever it was, his stature as one of golf's all-time greats, whether widely heralded or not, is beyond doubt.

As Jack put it in his autobiography, "The trio should really have been a quartet."

—Arnold Palmer, Jack Nicklaus, Gary Player

Making the Case

Billy Casper and Jim Parkinson at The Olympic Club, August, 2011.

I was sixteen years old the first time I met Billy Casper, and it didn't go like I planned.

It was January of 1966 and Billy had just given a talk at the Mormon meetinghouse in Palm Springs, California. Afterward, he was greeting the audience in the part of the building most people would call the basketball court and Mormons call the cultural hall. As I waited my turn in line, I went over in my mind what I wanted to say, a short and sweet: "Mr. Casper, good luck in the Masters." But when we shook hands, I was so nervous I forgot the "Mr. Casper" part entirely and instead blurted out, "Good luck in the U.S. Open." A verbal shank.

As we walked to the car, I turned to my older brother Rick and said, "He's going to think I'm an idiot." To which Rick asked, "Why?" I answered, "Because I wished him good luck at the Open. Every golfer knows the Masters is in April and the U.S. Open is in June. He's going to think I'm not a golfer." Rick opened the door to my parents' Pontiac, reached over and unlocked my side, and said, "You are an idiot, Jimmy. Billy Casper doesn't care if you know when the majors are. He won't remember a thing you said."

If only I'd known then what was going to happen at the U.S. Open later that summer in San Francisco, I could have told Rick that what I said wasn't idiotic, it was a premonition.

BILLY CASPER HAD COME TO the desert for the 1966 Bob Hope Classic, and I was suddenly very interested in watching him play. Not only did I get to shake his hand, but we now belonged to the same church—him by choice, me by genetics. My family's ancestors had been with the first group of Mormon pioneers, members of the Church of Jesus Christ of Latter-day Saints, when they settled Salt Lake City in 1847. The Parkinsons were fifth generation Latter-day Saints, as pedigreed as they come. On the other hand, Billy and his family had joined the church just that month, as new as they come. We rank-and-file Mormons welcomed him with open arms—and a chapel filled for his talk. As anyone inside the church knows, the religion isn't nearly as weird as it is often perceived by the outside world. The rules may be a tad strict—abstaining from drinking and smoking and paying a ten percent tithe aren't negotiable—but day-to-day life isn't that different from anyone else. Nothing like a famous celebrity joining up to make us look more normal.

But my main interest in Billy Casper wasn't his conversion. It was his golf. As the Brits would say, I was keen on the game.

Our family had come to the Palm Springs area when my father moved us to the little town of Indio to start his medical practice. That was in 1957. I was seven years old. As good fortune would have it, a golf pro lived directly across the street. Roger Pettit ran the pro shop and gave free lessons to kids at Cochran Ranch, a golf course on Monroe Street just outside the Indio city limits owned by history's most famous aviatrix not named Amelia Earhart—Jackie Cochran. Cochran's course was open to the public, and, better yet, she let kids play for free. If they treated kids everywhere the way we were treated at Cochran Ranch I'm convinced everybody would play golf all their life.

By the age of sixteen I was a walking golf encyclopedia. I knew all the top players and all their stats, which meant I knew about Billy Casper. But still, until he became a Mormon I never paid that much attention to him. He had won the Hope the year before by a stroke over Arnold Palmer—and I had rooted for Arnie.

Casper didn't successfully defend his title in the 1966 Hope. I watched as he finished seventh. Doug Sanders won the tournament in a playoff—over Arnold Palmer. It was a precursor of things to come.

SIX MONTHS LATER, IN JUNE, I was at my friend Steve Farrer's place, just hanging out on a Sunday afternoon. From the living room, Steve's dad shouted, "Hey Jim, don't you like Billy Casper?"

"Yeah," I shouted back.

"Then you should come in here and see what's happening."

Mr. Farrer was watching the final round of the U.S. Open, played that year at The Olympic Club in San Francisco. I had watched the first nine holes on TV at my house, rooting for Casper. But when Arnold

Palmer took a seven-shot lead after the opening nine I turned off the television in disgust and headed to Steve's house.

But now his dad was saying, "Will you look at this!"

I walked into the TV room just in time to see Casper make a birdie putt that pulled him within three shots of Palmer's lead with three holes left to play. He had made up four strokes in the last six holes. He was still behind. But even though we didn't have high-definition in 1966, you couldn't miss the body language of the two players. Palmer's shoulders were slumped. Casper was dancing off the green.

Steve had six or seven brothers and sisters and they were running around the house making all kinds of noise but I managed to out-shout them all when Casper made another birdie and Palmer another bogey on the next hole. Then Casper parred the seventeenth and Palmer made yet another bogey. When they both parred the final hole they were tied, setting up an eighteen-hole playoff for the next day.

I had to go to my summer job, swamping grapes, on Monday, but when I got home I turned on the news and there was proof that God was in heaven and life was fair after all. Casper had won.

After that, I didn't do anything in golf that wasn't patterned after him. To this day, my pre-shot routine is Billy Casper's pre-shot routine—size up your shot, pull one club decisively out of the bag, take a three-quarter practice swing, and hit the ball.

Two weeks after he won the Open I met Casper again. He came to Salt Lake City to present trophies at the Mormon Church's All-Church Golf Tournament. I won my flight at Willow Creek Country Club. That got me an autographed golf ball and another handshake from Billy Casper.

"Congratulations," he said.

This time I kept it simple and just said, "Thanks."

Every Monday I'd look in the *Indio Daily News* to see how Casper had done that week. I had plenty to cheer about. He won a lot of golf tournaments in the late 1960s and finally won the Masters in 1970. I was on a Mormon mission in Argentina by then. After that I came home, got married, finished college, attended law school, and went to work practicing law. Billy continued to come to the desert every year to play in the Hope, on the sunset side of his career, and that's how both Rick and I got to know him as a friend.

I could cite you his record chapter and verse. In twenty seasons he was PGA Player of the Year twice—and it would have been three times if they'd given an award in 1968. He collected five Vardon Trophies for low scoring average. He won three majors—the 1959 and 1966 U.S. Opens and the 1970 Masters. He won nearly two million dollars in official earnings; and he finished first in fifty-one PGA tournaments, the sixth highest total in history when he retired, behind only Sam Snead (82), Jack Nicklaus (73), Ben Hogan (64), Arnold Palmer (62) and Byron Nelson (52). (Tiger Woods has since won seventy-one tournaments, and counting.)

By any measure, Billy Casper's golf career rates among the most accomplished in the history of the game.

But as the years passed, and as he won still more tournaments on the over-50 Tour, I began to feel he never really got his due. When talking of the "greats," golf historians often pass Casper by entirely or give him only fleeting mention. He is at best an afterthought. When the talk is about his era, his "Big Three" contemporaries, Arnold Palmer, Jack Nicklaus and Gary Player, overwhelmingly overshadow him. I'll give you one example. In my library at home I have a history book about the Masters called "Augusta," written by Steve Eubanks. After lengthy, detailed accounts of the tournaments won by Palmer, Player and Nicklaus, this is how Eubanks describes the 1970 tournament: *"In the end it would be another Masters playoff in 1970, but this time the Big Three sat out. Gary Player was the only member of the triumvirate who had a legitimate shot, but his putt on the seventy-second hole to tie the leaders stayed high. Gene Littler and Billy Casper teed off on Monday. Casper won."* That's it. It's as if the tournament was largely irrelevant if Palmer, Nicklaus or Player didn't win.

The first tangible evidence of Casper neglect came in 1974, a year before he won his last tournament on the regular Tour. A group of golf historians, most of them writers, got together in Pinehurst, North Carolina, to vote on the charter class for the World Golf Hall of Fame. Eleven men made the cut: Harry Vardon, Walter Hagen, Francis Ouimet, Gene Sarazen, Bobby Jones, Byron Nelson, Sam Snead, Ben Hogan, and The Big Three: Arnold Palmer, Gary Player and Jack Nicklaus.

No one can argue that Casper should be included ahead of any of them, unless perhaps it was Ouimet, a lifetime amateur famous for his upset of Vardon and another British professional, Ted Ray, in the 1913 U.S. Open, the first real blow for American golfers against British superiority. I knew Casper's relative paucity of major victories—his total of three is equal to Ouimet and less than anyone else in the above group—was his Achilles heel. Even though he played in an age when concentrating on majors hadn't turned into the obsession it is today, it might be a plausible reason for voters to leave him out of the charter class.

What's not plausible is why another fourteen people entered the Hall of Fame ahead of him in 1975, 1976, and 1977. The credentials of these subsequent inductees are not in question. All certainly had Hall of Fame careers, but none of them had won nearly as many tournaments or lasted as long as Casper. Yet they all preceded him into golf immortality. Tommy Armour, for instance, who was inducted in 1976, won three majors and twenty-five tournaments on the PGA Tour—half what Casper won—and played in the 1920s and 1930s when the Tour was much less competitive.

Billy Casper didn't make it into the Hall of Fame until 1978, when he came in with a group that included Bing Crosby.

Other delayed honors or exclusions followed. When the Professional Golfers' Association of America gave Casper its Distinguished Service Award in 2010, it was a well-deserved tribute—but it came *two decades* after Jack Nicklaus and Arnold Palmer were so honored. And he is yet to be given the United States Golf Association's Bob Jones Award, an annual honor started in 1955 that recognizes distinguished sportsmanship in golf. The first recipient was Francis Ouimet. Gary Player received the award in 1966, Arnold Palmer in 1971, and Jack

Nicklaus in 1975. More than thirty-five years later, Casper, who is well known for his sportsmanship and whose charitable efforts have been extensive, has yet to receive the award, while players and contributors who weren't born by the time his career was finished have since been honored.

As a lawyer, this "case" has long intrigued me. Why, in a game where numbers mean everything—in the immortal words of Walter Hagen, "It's not how, it's how many"—have Casper's numbers been so over-looked? Why has a man who accomplished so much for so long been so unsung?

If what you're about to read sounds like an opening statement, I plead guilty. I am a lawyer and what follows is an overview of the evidence that makes the case for Billy Casper's greatness. The only witness I'm going to call is the record book. There will be no cross-examination because you can't cross-examine facts. And these are the facts:

LIFETIME WINNING AVERAGE
Throughout his career, Billy Casper won at a pace rarely equaled in contemporary golfing history.

Batting average is a baseball statistic. But if golf kept a statistic that counted wins like hits, Billy Casper would be in Ted Williams territory.

Casper played in 556 tournaments on the regular PGA Tour. He won fifty-one of those events. That computes to a lifetime winning aver-age, or batting average, of 9.2 percent.

Since 1950, among all players whose careers are complete, only one golfer has a higher lifetime winning average. Jack Nicklaus played in 594 tournaments and won seventy-three of them for a winning average of 12.3 percent.

As for the other members of The Big Three, Arnold Palmer won sixty-two times in 734 tournaments for an average of 8.4 percent and Gary Player won twenty-four times in 440 tournaments for a 5.5 per-cent average.

PGA Tour Lifetime Winning Percentage
Modern Era – Careers Completed 1950–Present

Player	Events	Wins-%	Top 10-%	Top 25-%
Jack Nicklaus	594	73-12.3%	286-48%	389-65%
Billy Casper	**556**	**51-9.2%**	**236-42%**	**380-68%**
Arnold Palmer	734	62-8.4%	245-33%	388-53%
Tom Watson	601	39-6.5%	219-37%	353-59%
Johnny Miller	385	25-6.5%	105-27%	190-49%
Lee Trevino	466	29-6.2%	166-36%	286-61%
Greg Norman	328	20-6.1%	129-39%	191-58%
Seve Ballesteros	150	9-6.0%	35-23%	63-42%
Ken Venturi	236	14-5.9%	77-33%	129-55%
Gary Player	440	24-5.5%	177-40%	281-64%
Tony Lema	226	11-4.9%	65-29%	143-63%
Gene Littler	616	29-4.7%	213-35%	382-62%
Doug Sanders	459	20-4.4%	146-32%	274-60%
Nick Price	482	18-3.7%	137-28%	238-49%
Tom Weiskopf	444	16-3.6%	136-31%	251-57%
Hubert Green	587	19-3.2%	91-16%	204-35%
Raymond Floyd	700	22-3.1%	163-23%	347-50%
Hale Irwin	659	20-3.0%	165-25%	303-46%
Lanny Wadkins	691	21-3.0%	139-20%	259-37%
Nick Faldo	301	9-3.0%	52-17%	113-38%

PGA Tour Winning Percentage of Top Current Players
(Through the 2011 Season)

Player	Events	Wins-%	Top 10-%	Top 25-%
Tiger Woods	274	71-25.9%	168-62%	222-81%
Phil Mickelson	443	39-8.8%	158-36%	244-55%
Vijay Singh	474	34-7.2%	175-37%	293-62%
Ernie Els	321	18-5.6%	116-36%	188-59%
Adam Scott	181	8-4.4%	48-27%	78-43%
Jim Furyk	458	16-3.5%	146-32%	254-56%
David Duval	372	13-3.5%	68-18%	122-33%
Retief Goosen	215	7-3.3%	60-28%	109-51%
Zach Johnson	213	7-3.3%	38-18%	93-44%
Davis Love III	643	20-3.1%	172-27%	306-48%
Sergio Garcia	227	7-3.1%	66-29%	118-52%

Tom Watson, with thirty-nine wins in 601 tournaments, and Johnny Miller, with twenty-five wins in 385 events, each won at a 6.5 percent pace. Lee Trevino won 6.2 percent of the time with twenty-nine wins in 466 tournaments, Greg Norman 6.1 percent of the time with twenty wins in 328 tournaments, Seve Ballesteros 6.0 percent of the time with nine wins in 150 tournaments, and Ken Venturi 5.9 percent of the time with fourteen wins in 236 tournaments.

These are the only players whose career started and ended after 1950 who won more than five percent of the tournaments they entered. (Statistics for golfers who played prior to 1950 are unreliable and in some cases not even available. Record keeping was lax or non-existent in the early years of the Tour and whole boxes of statistics were misplaced or lost when the PGA Tour separated from the PGA of America in 1968. Another problem with comparing the careers of players pre-1950 to more modern careers is that competition was so much leaner as the Tour was developing. Consider that in the 1945 season, Sam Snead, Byron Nelson and Ben Hogan won twenty-nine of the thirty tournaments played that year on the Tour. After 1950, winning golf tournaments became progressively more difficult.)

As the adjoining chart shows, many of golf's best-known names won less than five percent of the time over the full course of their careers. Just twenty players since 1950 have won more than three percent of the tournaments they've entered—and Casper tripled that.

As for current stars, through the 2011 season, the likes of Vijay Singh (7.2 percent), Ernie Els (5.6 percent), Adam Scott (4.4 percent), David Duval (3.5 percent), Jim Furyk (3.5 percent), Retief Goosen (3.3 percent), and Davis Love III (3.1 percent), are all well below Casper's standard. Even Phil Mickelson, yet to complete the downhill side of his career, cannot match Casper's 9.2 percent. Through the 2011 season Mickelson had played in 443 tournaments with thirty-nine wins for a winning average of 8.8 percent. (The PGA Tour lists numbers for tournaments entered and tournaments won for players past and present at www.pgatour.com.)

The only current player on the PGA Tour with a higher winning average than Casper is Tiger Woods, with seventy-one wins in 274 tournaments for a 25.9 percent average, by far the highest of anyone in the modern era, although Woods, too, is yet to play through his declining years.

Casper's record is all the more remarkable for how long it endured at such a high level. For more than two decades he was competitive virtually every time he teed it up. This consistency is reflected in the percentage of times he finished in the top 25 throughout his career. His 380 top-25 finishes works out to 68 percent, the best of anyone—higher even than Nicklaus's 65 percent. Player placed in the top-25 64 percent of the time during his career, Littler 62 percent, Trevino 61 percent, Watson 59 percent, and the go-for-broke Palmer 53 percent.

History is clear. In the Tour's modern era, no player in history whose career is complete placed among the top finishers so often and for so long as Billy Casper.

CASPER AND THE BIG THREE

In head to head competition, Billy Casper more than held his own with Palmer, Nicklaus and Player.

Superagent Mark McCormack branded Arnold Palmer, Jack Nicklaus and Gary Player "The Big Three" after Nicklaus turned professional and joined the PGA Tour in 1962. Casper wasn't included in the group for the simple reason that he wasn't a McCormack client.

In the nine years that The Big Three were The Big Three—from 1962 when Nicklaus turned pro and signed with McCormack until 1970 when he left McCormack—Casper was in their league, and then some, when it came to victories.

During the whole of that nine-year stretch, from 1962 through 1970, Casper and Nicklaus tied for most wins on Tour with thirty-three each. Palmer won thirty times during that span and Player eight.

From 1964 through 1970, Casper won twenty-seven times, Nicklaus twenty-five, Palmer fifteen and Player six.

THE BIG THREE AND CASPER
PGA TOUR WINS FROM 1962 – 1970*

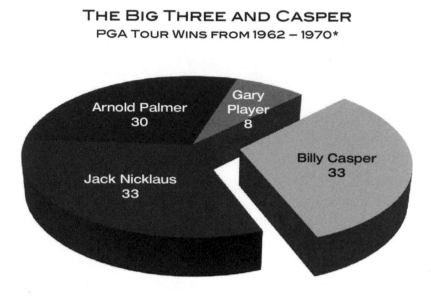

* The Big Three Era lasted from 1962 through 1970, a time when Arnold Palmer, Jack Nicklaus and Gary Player were in the prime of their careers and all three were represented by agent Mark McCormack.

From 1968 through 1970, Casper won thirteen tournaments and The Big Three won sixteen—Jack with eight, Arnie with five and Gary with three (and one of those victories counted double when Nicklaus and Palmer partnered to win the 1970 PGA National Four-Ball Championship).

In the 1968 season, Casper's six wins were one more than The Big Three managed combined—Arnie and Jack had two wins each and Gary had one.

You could make a case that Casper was the Big One.

Mark McCormack himself affirmed Casper's status as one of golf's real Big Three in 1968 when, with an eye toward helping his growing stable of international clients, he first came out with his statistics-based McCormack's World Golf Rankings, a concept that evolved into today's computerized Official World Golf Rankings.

When the initial rankings were released in 1968, The Big Three were not the big three. Nicklaus was ranked first, Palmer second, Casper third and Player fourth. In 1969 it was Nicklaus, Player, Casper and Palmer. In 1970 it was Nicklaus, Player, Casper and Lee Trevino, in that order, with Palmer out of the top foursome. Forgetting for a moment the issue of why Casper wasn't No. 1 in McCormack's ratings at any point during the three seasons when he won more tournaments, including the 1970 Masters, than anyone else on Tour, the record absolutely shows that even by Mark McCormack's own standard, Billy Casper was one of the world's top three players. He just wasn't marketed that way.

RYDER CUPS AND VARDON TROPHIES

Billy Casper's record in the Ryder Cup is the best of any American player in history. Only Tiger Woods has won more Vardon Trophies.

The Ryder Cup is often described as the biggest pressure-cooker in golf. Billy Casper handled Ryder Cup pressure as long and as well as anyone

Most Career Points, Ryder Cup
(United States Team)

Player	Points
Billy Casper	**23 ½**
Arnold Palmer	23
Lanny Wadkins	21 ½
Lee Trevino	20
Jack Nicklaus	18 ½
Gene Littler	18
Tom Kite	17
Hale Irwin	14
Raymond Floyd	13 ½
Phil Mickelson	13
Davis Love III	11 ½
Julius Boros	11
Tiger Woods	11

Through 2010 Ryder Cup

Vardon Trophy, Most Wins

Player	Wins
Tiger Woods	8
Billy Casper	**5**
Lee Trevino	5
Arnold Palmer	4
Sam Snead	4
Ben Hogan	3
Greg Norman	3
Tom Watson	3

in the history of the matches. In eight consecutive appearances as a player from 1961 through 1975, he accumulated 23½ points, the most ever by an American. Arnold Palmer is next on the all time list at 23, then Lanny Wadkins at 21½, Lee Trevino at 20 and Jack Nicklaus at 18½. Casper's six singles victories for the United States tie him with Palmer, Sam Snead and Trevino for most ever.

An enduring testament to Casper's steady, consistent play is his total of five Vardon Trophies—the award given annually to the Tour player with the lowest scoring average for the season. During a nine-year stretch from 1960 through 1968, Casper and Palmer took turns winning the low-scoring trophy. They each had four going into the 1968 season, when Casper broke their deadlock with what was then a record fifth Vardon Trophy. In the years since, Lee Trevino has also won five Vardons and Tiger Woods has collected eight.

THE PGA TOUR'S LIFETIME RANKINGS

The Tour's own research verifies Casper's stature among the greatest ever.

In 1988, the PGA Tour commissioned golf writer and historian Al Barkow to write a comprehensive history of the Tour. As part of this

Most PGA Tour Wins

Place	Player	Tournaments Won	Winning Span
1	Sam Snead	82	1936-1965
2	Jack Nicklaus	73	1962-1986
3	Tiger Woods	71	1996-2009
4	Ben Hogan	64	1938-1959
5	Arnold Palmer	62	1955-1973
6	Byron Nelson	52	1935-1951
7	**Billy Casper**	**51**	**1956-1975**
8	Walter Hagen	45	1914-1936
9	Cary Middlecoff	39	1945-1961
9	Tom Watson	39	1974-1998
9	Phil Mickelson	39	1991-2011
12	Gene Sarazen	38	1922-1941

As of 2011 Season
Source: PGA Tour

project, the PGA assembled all the tournament statistics it had access to in an effort to rank the greatest golfers in Tour history. "We sought a way to compare the players of yesterday with the big-money players of today, a way to bridge the eras," explained Tour commissioner Deane Beman in the Foreword to *The History of the PGA Tour.*

Three separate statistical standards were used to rank players. The first was called Percent of Purse and awarded points for the percentage of money a player won in any given tournament. The second was the Ryder Cup System, which awarded points in descending value for finishing in the top 10 of a tournament. The third was called the Lifetime Point System, and used a formula developed by Barkow that was a hybrid of the first two systems.

Using a combination of these three standards, the top 500 players who played the Tour during its first 75 years were identified. As of 1988, these were the top 20:

1. Sam Snead
2. Jack Nicklaus
3. Arnold Palmer
4. Ben Hogan
5. **Billy Casper**
6. Byron Nelson
7. Lloyd Mangrum
8. Gene Littler
9. Cary Middlecoff
10. Horton Smith
11. Gene Sarazen
12. Jimmy Demaret
13. Harry Cooper
14. Lee Trevino
15. Tom Watson
16. E.J. Harrison
17. Walter Hagen
18. Doug Ford
19. Gary Player
20. Julius Boros

SUMMATION

Billy Casper's numbers eloquently state his case.

Clearly, Billy Casper's record ranks him among the greatest the game has ever seen.

His better-known contemporaries in the golden age of golf left their undisputed legacies. Arnold Palmer's 1960 season alone—when he won the Masters and the U.S. Open and personally revived the British Open—deserves a place in golf's history alongside Bobby Jones's Grand Slam season of 1930, Tiger Woods' nine-win, three-majors season of 2000, and Ben Hogan's remarkable run in 1953, when he entered six tournaments and won five of them, including three of the four majors. Gary Player won 153 tournaments in his amazing career, with victories in every hemisphere and time zone—golf's first truly international superstar. Jack Nicklaus exceeded the records of both Bobby Jones and Ben Hogan and is widely and justifiably regarded as the most complete player of all time.

But year after year, Billy Casper held his own with them all.

And yet, he is best known for being unknown.

He's the man Johnny Miller described in *Golf Digest* as "the most underrated golfer of all time, hands down."

He's the man whose plaque at the World Golf Hall of Fame has this inscription:

"At the peak of his powers, he got more attention for his allergies, his conversion to Mormonism, his eleven children (six of them adopted) and his offbeat diet of buffalo meat and organically grown vegetables. The public would come to know very little of Billy Casper, making him arguably the best modern golfer who never received his due."

And how's that for rich irony? The Hall of Fame that brought him in late acknowledges that he was brought in late.

In Lorne Rubenstein and Jeff Neuman's entertaining book, *A Disorderly Compendium of Golf,* they have a chapter titled "Golf's Most Underrated Player?"

The entire chapter is about Casper.

How does that happen? How did one player's legendary career manage to slip so cleanly through the cracks?

Why is Billy Casper's legacy to be the forgotten fourth?

IN LATE 2010, MY CELL phone rang. It was my brother Rick.

"Jim," he said. "Billy would like to do a book."

These days Rick is Billy's dermatologist. They live not far from each other in Utah and get together socially now and then for a round of golf and dinner. On one of these occasions the subject of Casper's life story came up. Billy said it had never been written and he'd like to get it down on paper. Rick knew that I'd recently been involved in some publishing projects. One was a book I wrote called *Autodidactic,* about writing and the importance of education. Two other books had been a collaborative venture with my writer friend, Lee Benson. One was *Soldier Slaves,* a book about a lawsuit involving World War II soldiers imprisoned by the Japanese. Before that we worked together on *Blind Trust,* a book about my sister-in-law's adventures as a congresswoman when she discovered her husband was a fraud.

Lee had to do his homework to write about World War II and politics, but golf is more familiar ground. He spent the majority of his career as a sportswriter for the *Deseret News* in Salt Lake City. He's covered the British Open, the U.S. Open and the Masters. He interviewed and wrote about Billy Casper on the regular Tour and later on the Senior/Champions Tour. His first boss at the *Deseret News* was Hack Miller, the person who baptized Billy and his family into the Mormon Church in 1966.

Lee and I agreed to another collaboration: to assist Billy Casper in writing the story of his life.

We went to see Billy in Springville, a community in Utah located fifty miles south of Salt Lake City. He lives there in a pleasant but hardly ostentatious house in the foothills of the Rocky Mountains with Shirley, his wife of fifty-nine years. Shirley's sister Margee lives upstairs in a sister-in-law apartment. Shirley and Billy's youngest daughter, Sarah, a single mom raising three little boys who recently graduated cum laude from Utah Valley University, also lives with them, as well as four Yorkshire Terriers, Chaucer, Winston, Nixon, and Penelope. It's as if Shirley and Billy, both products of broken homes, are determined to never again be alone.

When you first enter the house you'd never know a legendary golfer lives there. But clues emerge if you wander into the den off the living room. There's a picture of Casper with Hogan, another with Sarazen, a signed note from Hagen, a first edition Herbert Warren Wind book with a personalized inscription inside the front cover: *For Billy Casper, with warm regards, Hal Wind.* On one wall is a frame containing the scorecard and a copy of the oversized check ($12,000) for winning the 1959 U.S. Open at Winged Foot. Next to it are the framed scorecards, all five of them, from the 1966 U.S. Open at The Olympic Club. In the corner of the room there's a poster from the 1995 Ryder Cup signed by every living Ryder Cup captain to that point, including Hogan, Snead and Nelson. On the far wall there's a plaque with fifty-one numbered golf balls, each one representing a Casper victory on Tour. Another nine golf balls on the plaque represent his Ryder Cup appearances as player and captain.

On the first day we meet to discuss the book project he's wearing a #80 San Diego Chargers jersey, a gift from his kids to commemorate his favorite NFL team and the age he'll be on his upcoming birthday.

Billy has thirty-four grandchildren and fifteen great grandchildren, and counting, which is what you can expect when you start with eleven children. He doesn't have an email account. He doesn't own a cell phone. "I've lived my life just fine without one, why would I need one now?" he tells his kids. He is unfailingly upbeat and has a phenomenal memory, which he enjoys showing off. He remembers names and golf courses and what iron he hit on the seventeenth hole during the third round at Riviera like it happened this week.

YES, HE AFFIRMS WHEN THE subject turns to a book project, he'd like to get his life story down on paper.

It's about time, I tell him. All the other guys who have won fifty tournaments have long since done it. Most of them several times. Jack wrote his definitive autobiography in 1997, Arnold in 1999. Both were bestsellers. Gary wrote the first version of his life story in 1974. And if they're not telling their story, somebody else is. The other day I was in the bookstore and saw a new book about Arnold Palmer by his dentist.

Lee and I show Casper a list of last year's Top 50 money-earners in golf. It's a compilation put out annually by *Golf Digest* that ranks the game's celebrities in order of the income they made on and off the course.

In the rankings, Tiger Woods, despite his domestic troubles, is still far and away No. 1 with $72 million earnings. Phil Mickelson is second at $36 million.

It's the No. 3 name on the list we want Casper to see. It's his old running mate, Arnold Palmer. The report says Arnie made $36 million in 2010, all of it off the course. Number five on the list is Jack Nicklaus at $25 million and Number eight is Gary Player at $15 million. Forty years later, The Big Three are still in the Top Ten, while Billy Casper is nowhere to be found.

I suggest that he's not in the income category of his old rivals because his priorities, with eleven kids, have always been different.

He agrees that his large family might have something to do with it, then a wry smile comes across his face and he adds, "And I am the genius who left Mark McCormack."

WE SHAKE HANDS TO SEAL our book deal. It's the same hand I shook forty-five years ago in that Palm Springs church when I wished Casper good luck at the U.S. Open and then drove away thinking that to him I'd always be the goofy sixteen-year-old who didn't know when the Masters was played.

It was my decision to commandeer the opening of this book to list Billy Casper's career accomplishments and statistics for the simple reason that he wouldn't. And for that matter, couldn't. He doesn't even know most of them. That became more and more obvious as we talked. When we showed him *The History of the PGA Tour* that in 1988 ranked him the fifth best Tour player of all time, it was the first time he'd looked at the list (even though the book had been in his bookcase for twenty years). He had no idea about his 9.2 percent lifetime winning average. When told that from 1964 through 1970 he won more tournaments than either Palmer, Player or Nicklaus, he responded, "Really?"

WHAT FOLLOWS IS A STORY that started in the Great Depression and kept appreciating from there. It's a love story about a boy and girl who met at a high school football game and never dated anyone else. It's a story about realizing impossible dreams because nobody told you they were impossible. It's a story about sticking to your game plan no matter what. It's a story about discovering you're allergic to everything you're eating at breakfast. It's a story about an elite athlete joining an unpopular church in the prime of his career. It's a story about winding up in a playoff at Augusta with your boyhood friend and rival. It's a story about a man who handled the pressure of hundreds of golf tournaments without breaking a sweat but got shingles when he was caddying for his son at qualifying school. It's a story about a man who values family above all else and who had to endure the heartbreak of watching another son sent to prison for 105 years. Through it all, it's a story about a man and the game that saved and then made his life—and the heights you can reach when you only concentrate on the next step.

It's a remarkable story about a remarkable man who did remarkable things that you've never heard before. That's the one benefit of being unsung.

—Jim Parkinson, 2012

1

Olympic

2

The eighteenth green at The Olympic Club, 1966 U.S. Open.

San Francisco, California
June 14, 1966

To begin my story, let me start in the middle . . .

It was nineteen sixty-six, the summer of peace and love, and San Francisco was still asleep when I drove across the Golden Gate Bridge that Monday morning. Sitting next to me, riding shotgun and also asleep, was my nine-year-old son Billy. In the trunk were my golf clubs. The fog hugged the ground as we passed Golden Gate Park, and about a million sleeping hippies, and kept going south alongside the ocean until we arrived at our destination: The Olympic Club, site of the sixty-sixth playing of the National Open.

The parking lot was mostly empty; the golf course still quiet in the mist. You could practically hear the Open rough growing. This was how I liked it—get to the course before it's crowded, when you can see what you're up against without a lot of distractions.

Ben Hogan was the reason I was there early. Ben Hogan was the reason I did a lot of things in golf the way I did them. It began with a lesson he gave me when he didn't know he was giving it.

I was fifteen years old when the San Diego Country Club, the place that raised me, hosted what the handbills called a "world championship" thirty-six-hole match between Ben Hogan and an Englishman named Dai Rees. Both Hogan and Rees had come to San Diego early to tune up on the course, but they went about it in completely different ways. Rees introduced himself to several members of the club and played practice rounds with them in order to gain whatever local knowledge he could pick up in a week. Hogan played alone. One day at dusk, as I was leaving the caddy shed, I noticed a golfer in the middle of the fifth fairway. He was wearing a flat linen cap and walking with a kind of clipped military precision. Even in the fading light I knew who it was.

I watched as Hogan dropped one ball on the right side of the fairway, another right center, another left center, and so on. He then proceeded to hit the balls toward the green, staring at each shot, watching where it landed and how it rolled. I couldn't figure out what the heck he was doing. But years later, after I played enough golf of my own, I got it. He was sorting out where he should land his ball for the next shot. He wanted to know where the fairway was the flattest, which part of the green accepted shots best, what parts of the course should be avoided. He was like a pool player, always setting up the next shot with the current one. He didn't want to just hit fairways and greens, he wanted to hit fairways and greens at precisely the right spot. Even though I was oblivious to it at the time, standing there in the twilight I was introduced to course management by the greatest course manager of them all.

At the end of the exhibition, Dai Rees left San Diego with more friends. Ben Hogan left with the $5,000 winner's check.

The more I played the more I appreciated the Ben Hogan approach to golf, which could be summed up in one word: control. There is so much about the game that is out of your control—the weather, the condition of the course, the other players, even sometimes your own swing—that you have to focus on what you can control. My main purpose in practice rounds wasn't my score, it was getting to know the golf course. Whenever I could, I preferred to arrive early and play alone, like Hogan.

I GOT IN TWENTY-SEVEN HOLES of course management that Monday morning at The Olympic Club's Lake Course, a layout with, oddly enough, no water hazards. The name comes from Lake Merced, which sits nearby but never comes into play. Water or no water, it's a beautiful, classic golf course that is part of the oldest athletic club in America. The Olympic Club was started in downtown San Francisco in 1860 as a gathering place for athletes and sportsmen. One of its earliest members was Mark Twain. It's so old it wasn't named for the modern Olympics, but the ancient Olympics. When the Olympics were revived in 1896, almost forty years after the San Francisco club got started, The Olympic Club lived up to its name by sending large numbers of its members to participate in the new Games. In the 1924 Olympics in Paris no fewer than twenty-four members on the United States team came from The Olympic Club.

The club expanded to include golf in 1918, when The Olympic Club bought the financially troubled Lakeside Golf Club course, located seven miles due south of Nob Hill. The existing eighteen holes were demolished, additional acreage was purchased, and two eighteen-hole courses were designed, the Lake and the Ocean. The Lake Course, which came to be the more prestigious of the two, might more accurately be called the Forest Course. It has forty thousand trees—mainly pines and cypress, with a scattering of eucalyptus, redwoods, cedars and a few palm trees—that are interrupted here and there by small greens and narrow, slanting fairways, which of course the USGA made narrower for the Open.

My history with the Lake Course involved just one round I played years earlier when I was in the Navy in San Diego and we came north for matches against military teams in the Bay Area. We played the course at Stanford University, another fine old layout, and the Lake Course at The Olympic Club in the same day.

In 1955, after I turned pro, I tried to qualify for the U.S. Open the first time it was played at Olympic, but missed by a shot in the sectional tournament in Los Angeles. Thus I wasn't there for one of the greatest upsets in golf history when unknown pro Jack Fleck shot 67 in the final round to tie Ben Hogan, who had finished hours earlier and was already in the clubhouse being asked by the press how it felt to win a record fifth national championship. Hogan never got to answer that question. In the next day's eighteen-hole playoff, Fleck won, 69 to 72.

(Before Jack Fleck, it seems Olympic already had a history of not giving anyone a free pass, no matter how legendary their name. It was here in 1939 that Ty Cobb, retired by then as a Hall-of-Fame baseball player, was soundly thrashed, 7 and 6, in the first flight of the club championship by a twelve-year-old kid. Cobb, so the Olympic lore goes, walked off the course and was hardly seen again for years. The kid was Bob Rosburg, who went on to win the PGA Championship in 1959 and become a Tour mainstay as well as my good friend.)

MISSING THAT U.S. OPEN IN the summer of 1955 delayed my debut as a touring pro—by seven days. The following week I played my first official tournament on the PGA Tour at the Western Open in Portland, Oregon. I tied for thirtieth, good for last-place money, and my wife Shirley and I left town towing our Spartan trailer and counting our winnings of thirty-three dollars and thirty-three cents.

It might not sound like much of a beginning, but we caught the start of the biggest wave in golf's history. In a decade, I watched as the golf Tour went from house trailers to jets, and I mean that literally. In 1955 players on the Tour towed their trailers from stop to stop like gypsies in a caravan. By 1966 we routinely flew to tournaments, some in their own planes.

Interest in the game just exploded. In 1954, the year before I arrived, the purse for the entire PGA Tour was $600,000. In 1958, just four years later, it was $1 million. By 1966 prize money was $3,700,000, a six hundred percent increase in twelve years. Thirtieth place in the Western Open didn't pay $33.33 anymore; it paid $1,000.

There were several key reasons for this dramatic upsurge. Americans had more leisure time than ever before, and were devoting a lot of it to golf. President Eisenhower became a golf nut in the 1950s, installing a putting green at the White House and playing every chance he got. The arrival of television brought golf into living rooms all over the country. This exposure in turn attracted large corporations as tournament sponsors, dramatically increasing the size of purses that in the past had been provided by cities and clubs that often struggled to come up with the money.

And a big part of it was Arnold Palmer, who started on the Tour in 1955, the same year I did. Arnie was our first great star on television. He played an exciting, aggressive golf game that America loved. John Wayne in spikes. Arnie's Army grew to be bigger than Eisenhower's. Everyone inside the Tour was well aware how popular he was and what that meant for the rest of us. Frank Beard, a Tour veteran who was there in the days before Palmer arrived, said, "I figure that for every dollar I make I owe twenty-five cents to Arnold Palmer," and no one in the locker room disagreed with him. (Although I don't recall anyone ever actually paying up.)

THE TOUR'S HEALTH WASN'T ALL that had improved by leaps and bounds by the mid-sixties. So had mine. For the first time I felt like I had gained the upper hand on allergies that for years had been seriously plaguing me and affecting my golf game. The credit was due to Dr. Theron G. Randolph, a Chicago physician years ahead of his time. He diagnosed what I was allergic to and identified the petrochemicals, pollens, pesticides, and foods I needed to avoid. He changed my diet to include a variety of wild game, including buffalo, which naturally turned me into Buffalo Billy in the press. It was time-consuming and it definitely wasn't inexpensive, making sure I had buffalo, caribou, elk, hippopotamus, bear and other exotic meats shipped to me wherever I played. But not only did my health improve tremendously as a result, for the first time in my life people started calling me svelte. I went from a high of 227 pounds—my weight when I won the U.S. Open in 1959—to a low of 165 pounds, and it was entirely without dieting, just eating differently. I got so thin I had to put pounds back on. By the time I arrived for the '66 Open at The Olympic Club, I weighed 185 pounds and felt like I was in the best condition of my life.

I WAS ALSO IN BETTER shape spiritually. Nineteen sixty-six was the year I found religion and joined The Church of Jesus Christ of Latter-day Saints, commonly known as the Mormons. Shirley had been interested in the Mormons since a visit to Salt Lake City, the church's headquarters, when I played in the Utah Open in 1959. By 1966, our two oldest children were approaching their teenage years, and I was impressed by the church's youth program. On New Year's Day Shirley and I were baptized, along with our daughter Linda and son Billy (our five-year-old son Bobby hadn't yet reached the required baptismal age of eight). Making the transition to a religion noted for its prohibitions against alcohol, tobacco, coffee and tea wasn't difficult for me. I'd already given up all of that.

In my first tournament as a Mormon I won the San Diego Open, a special victory to me since I'd been trying to win my hometown's PGA Tour event ever since I first competed in it as an amateur in 1952. We played the final round in rain and fierce 35-mph winds that were as tough as any conditions I ever encountered. But the weather blew away all my allergies and I shot 64 to come from behind by four to win by four. I took this as an omen that I was making correct decisions for my life.

Shortly after that win I left for Vietnam. The war was at its height and the State Department had set up a sixteen-day trip for me to entertain the troops with golf exhibitions and clinics. I slept in tents, got shot at, visited the Green Berets, and hit golf balls off an aircraft carrier at a Russian trawler in the Tonkin Gulf.

Shirley stayed at the Mormon mission headquarters in Hong Kong while I was in Vietnam. When I rejoined her there, the man presiding over the mission, Keith Garner, said, "Billy, Sunday is district conference; we would like Shirley to sing and you to speak. You'll have an interpreter so use short sentences." Then he added, "And don't talk about golf, they have no idea what golf is." Speaking from the pulpit is standard procedure for members of the Mormon Church, where the clergy isn't paid and the lay membership does the preaching. I learned quickly that they like to pick on new converts to break them in.

So Shirley sang and I was praying like mad during her song. I'd never spoken in a church before, any church. I'd barely *been* to church. When I got up to speak I used short sentences and it seemed to be going well so I started adding more words and I noticed the longer my sentences got the shorter the interpreter's sentences got. I really don't know what I said, but there I was, halfway around the world, talking about everything but golf.

I returned from Asia just in time for the Masters, where I placed tenth. Jack Nicklaus defeated Tommy Jacobs and Gay Brewer in a playoff and broke Arnold's streak of winning the green jacket in even-numbered years. He became the first person to win consecutive Masters. Palmer finished fourth. A lot of writers started to speculate as to whether the Age of Palmer, who was thirty-six, had given way to the Age of Nicklaus, who was twenty-six, and wondered if perhaps the U.S. Open might help clear up that debate. Nicklaus, as he often did for the majors, came to San Francisco a week early to get ready. With a chance at the Grand Slam, he got a lot of attention as a favorite, as did Palmer and the other member of Mark McCormack's Big Three, twenty-eight-year-old Gary Player, the defending Open champion. Nicklaus, Palmer and Player all had won a U.S. Open—Nicklaus in 1962, Palmer in 1960 and Player in 1965. I had one myself, in 1959 at Winged Foot. At Olympic, we were all chasing our second.

THE USGA RECEIVED A RECORD 2,577 entries for the 1966 U.S. Open. Out of those, one hundred and forty-four players, including both Jack Fleck (who survived qualifying) and fifty-four-year-old Ben Hogan (who got a special exemption), made it to the finals in San Francisco. It would be the second time the National Open was played at The Olympic Club. Unlike eleven years earlier, when I was eliminated in the qualifying rounds, this time I was lucky enough to be included in the final field.

ON TUESDAY I GOT IN another twenty-seven holes of practice, this time without my son Billy; I think I wore him out the day before. I used the time to become better acquainted with my caddy, Jim Stark, a member of the golf team at Stanford. You didn't bring your regular Tour caddy to the Open in those days; you were assigned one by the USGA. The idea was to give younger players a feel for the experience. Jim and I clicked from the start. I told him that I was a man of few words on the golf course. If I asked for yardage, I only wanted yardage, not which way the wind was blowing or other details or opinions. It was all part of my effort to stay in control and focused. I explained to Jim the science behind my pre-shot routine: select the club from the bag, line up the shot, take a three-quarter practice swing, address the ball, and hit the shot. It allowed me to blot everything else out of my mind and focus on the task at hand. I did it all very quickly, but if anything interrupted that routine—someone moving in the crowd, a camera click, a plane flying overhead, any distraction at all—I'd put the club back in the bag and start all over again. I'm sure people in the gallery thought I was nuts when I did that. But it was the only way I knew to maintain the absolute intensity I needed to play tournament golf.

I didn't spend much time on the practice tee at Olympic. I hit a few balls before I went on the course to warm up and that was it. In that way I was the complete opposite of Ben Hogan, and most of the other players on Tour, who could spend hour after hour at the range. My feeling was that you always had a perfect lie on the practice tee, so what was the sense of practicing there? I never felt like I was really learning anything by hitting shot after shot from a flat lie.

TUESDAY NIGHT I GAVE A "fireside" talk at a Mormon meetinghouse near the golf course. I don't know if I was any more coherent in San Francisco than I had been in Hong Kong, although this time there was no ban on speaking about golf. After the talk a woman came up to me and said she had a son in college who was a very fine player and he was thinking of becoming a professional. She wondered if she should encourage him.

I told her, well, if he doesn't try he'll always wonder if he could have made it so it's important that he tries. If it doesn't work out he can always turn to something else, especially if he gets his college degree.

She thanked me, shook my hand, and introduced herself as Sister Miller. She said her son's name was Johnny.

THE WEATHER WAS TYPICAL FOR June in San Francisco, foggy in the mornings, still cool but more comfortable with better visibility as the day wore on as the mist lifted. The galleries were full of people wearing sweaters when the tournament started on Thursday morning. I went off in a threesome with Kel Nagle, the Australian who won the British Open in 1960 and lost a playoff in the 1965 U.S. Open to Gary Player, and David Marr, one of my best friends on Tour. Everybody liked to play with Dave. We had some good battles. The year before, he was leading the Hartford Open and I caught him in the last round and won. But he got me back and then some the next week at the PGA Championship at Laurel Valley, where he made an up-and-down par on the last hole to beat Jack Nicklaus and me and win his first major.

Dave was easy-going, good-natured, and never at a loss for a good line. When reporters asked him if the fog at Olympic made the course play longer, he said it certainly did. When they asked "How much longer?" he answered, "About thirty minutes." That was Dave. One of his most memorable quips came at the 1964 Masters when he and Arnold Palmer stood on the final tee with Palmer holding a six-stroke lead over Dave and Jack Nicklaus. When Palmer asked if there was anything he could do to help, Dave answered, "Yeah. Make a 12."

I OPENED THE TOURNAMENT WITH a 69, one stroke under the Lake Course's par of 70. I had four birdies and three bogeys, including a five on the short but narrow 337-yard par-four closing hole. Despite the finishing bogey I walked off the final green with a sigh of relief. You can't win an Open on the first day, but you can shoot yourself out of one. The Lake Course was formidable under ordinary conditions, but with the USGA's standard Open makeover—longer rough, narrower fairways and faster greens—it could quickly turn catastrophic. I felt par was a good score for the day and a good goal for the week. When Olympic hosted the Open in 1955, Ben Hogan and Jack Fleck tied at the end of seventy-two holes with scores of 287, seven over par. Tommy Bolt and Sam Snead tied for third place at 292, twelve over par. Only three under-par rounds were shot during the entire tournament and all three were by Fleck, a 69 in round two, his magnificent 67 to draw even with Hogan in round four and the final 69 in the eighteen-hole playoff that beat Hogan's 72. Eleven years later the course had not changed. Only the trees had grown larger. The distance was virtually the same, 6,700 yards then to 6,727 yards now. After complaints about the length of the rough in '55, the USGA promised to limit the growth to a maximum of five inches this time around. But a five-inch rough is formidable enough. There was no reason to think par was going to be any easier to beat.

My 69 was good for fourth place, two shots behind the leader, Al Mengert, a club pro from Washington state who I had played with in my first tournament as a rookie in Portland eleven years earlier. Al found his putting touch on the way to a 67 that put him in front of Gene Littler and Don Massengale, who shot 68s. Arnold Palmer and Jack Nicklaus both scored one-over 71s. Gary Player flirted too often with the trees and finished with a 78.

In Friday's second round, playing again with Marr and Nagle but with an afternoon starting time, I had four birdies and two bogeys, including another five on the short eighteenth, for a two-under-par 68. Again I exhaled with relief. Knowing how much trouble was out there, I couldn't imagine too many totals under par and I was right. After thirty-six holes, Olympic had yielded eight rounds under par and I had two of them.

When I walked out of the scorer's tent I learned I had moved into a share of the halfway lead, although all the talk wasn't about the way I had quietly made my way around the course. All the talk was about Arnold Palmer bringing Olympic to its knees on Friday with a four-under-par 66 that could have easily been a 65 if not for his two-foot birdie putt lipping out on the final green.

Arnold had played in the morning and was long gone from the course when I signed for my 68, giving me a 137 total to match his 71-66. At even-par 140 were Phil Rodgers and Rives McBee, a relatively unknown pro from Texas who opened with a 76 and then equaled the

U.S. Open record with a 64 in the second round. Jack Nicklaus and that young Mormon amateur I'd never heard of, Johnny Miller, were another two shots back tied for fifth place at 142. The cut was 151, eleven over par. Jack Fleck was among its victims. But Hogan was safe. He shot 72-73—145 and was still in contention. Gene Littler was among those who barely survived, adding an 83 to his opening 68 after making nine on the par-four eleventh—a reminder of how fast the course could chew up a contender. Arnold and I were three shots clear of the field and the only players in the tournament under par.

As tough as the course was playing, after shooting his 66 Arnold could have reasonably expected to be clear of *everyone*. No one was close when he handed in his scorecard and left the grounds before the afternoon rounds were completed. It wasn't until early that evening, after all the scores were in, that he was apprised by his agent Mark McCormack that the scoring was indeed high and everyone was backing up—with the exception of one person. After all our years on Tour together, I suspect Arnold knew it was the kind of golf course I would treat with absolute deference, which accounts for his response to McCormack, "I'll bet the exception is Casper."

2

The Comeback

3

Dueling with Arnold at the 1966 U.S. Open.

San Francisco, California
June 18, 1966

No one ever mistook me for Arnold Palmer, or Arnold Palmer for me. We didn't look alike, we didn't talk alike, we didn't act alike, and we sure didn't play golf alike. He was East Coast from Pennsylvania; I was West Coast from San Diego. His father was an ever-present force in his life; my father said goodbye when I was fifteen. Arnie was a riverboat gambler; I wouldn't get on a riverboat. He was forever having to hitch his pants up as he walked down the fairway; I never had that problem.

But probably nothing sums it up better than this: When I won my first U.S. Open in 1959 at Winged Foot I purposely laid up on the third hole every round for four straight days. The third hole is a par three. I chipped close, one-putted, and made par each round and wound up winning the tournament by a single shot. When Arnold won his first U.S. Open the following year in 1960 at Cherry Hills he attempted to drive the first hole every round. The first hole is a par four. He missed the green for three straight rounds until finally on his last eighteen he succeeded. He made birdie and used the momentum to rally from seven shots behind and pass fourteen players to win the tournament by two strokes.

Pairing us together in the U.S. Open was like pairing yin and yang.

But here we were, anchoring the field as the final twosome, the co-leaders, the guys to beat, when the third round convened at Olympic on a foggy Saturday.

In one area, however, we were exactly alike and he knew it and I knew it. When you play golf for a living you soon realize that there are great talents and there are great competitors and they don't always, or even very often, come in the same package. Year after year, you'd see players come out on Tour with swings that were fundamentally flawless. Their technique was so perfect you wanted to take a picture of it. Your first thought was, might as well surrender and get it over with. There was no way they could lose with a swing like that. But the swing was only part of it. You had to be able to execute that swing when it mattered. The swing not only has to hold up under pressure, it has to *get better* under pressure. The players who stayed the longest, who thrived, couldn't just execute the swing when it mattered; they relished the opportunity to be able to do so. They loved to compete. They loved being in the thick of it on the final few holes. They didn't shy away from the pressure, they yearned for it. Much more than wanting to make a good swing, much more than wanting to post a good score, they wanted to win. That's what they lived for.

That was Arnold. He yearned to compete and he yearned to win. He wanted to win every single time he played. So did I. Our methods were not at all alike. His game plan was different than mine. He was aggressive; I was conservative. He aimed for pins; I aimed for position. His personality was different than mine. He thrived on crowd interaction; I tried to shut out the crowd. And no one ever confused our homemade swings. But we were after the same thing and it wasn't to perfect our mechanics or shoot a good score. It was to win.

Although he was twenty-one months older than I was, we both joined the Tour in 1955. He arrived at the start of the season in January and I arrived six months later in June. He'd mustered out of the Coast Guard the year before, about the same time I left the Navy. Arnold had won the U.S. Amateur in 1954 before turning pro. He grew up around golf. His father, Milfred, who everybody called Deacon, was the pro at Latrobe Country Club, a company course owned by a steel mill in western Pennsylvania. Deacon Palmer came from the time when a golf pro was the club caretaker, greenskeeper and janitor. Well into the 1930s, when Arnold was growing up, club pros were still not allowed in the front door of the country clubs that employed them, and neither were their families. That was Deacon Palmer's era. He taught himself how to play golf and in turn taught his son with a simple approach that Arnold summed up as "Hit it hard, go find it; hit it hard again."

Nobody hit it harder, and kept finding it, than Arnold Palmer. He had such tremendous power. If you picked up one of his clubs you could feel exactly where his fingers fit. He held them so tight his handprints were permanently grooved into the grips. He swung like a blacksmith. He wanted to make birdies every time. They could have put the flag in the top of a tree and Palmer would have tried to figure out how he could get his ball on one of the limbs so he could get a birdie.

And could he putt! His touch on the greens was often overlooked because of his power, but in his prime Arnold was a marvelous putter, especially in the clutch, when he absolutely had to have it. Like Bob Rosburg said, "The ball's scared of him. I guarantee he'll get it in the hole if he has to stare it in."

WE KEPT A RESPECTFUL YET competitive distance the first few years Arnold and I were on Tour. The first time we got to know each other on a closer level was when we became Ryder Cup teammates in 1961. In those days, the PGA had a rule that you had to wait five years before you were eligible to qualify. Both of us made the American team the first time we were eligible. Jerry Barber was the captain that year and decided to pair Arnold and me in the first Ryder Cup match either of us would ever play.

The competition was foursomes, the alternate shot format where you take turns hitting shots and one of you drives on the odd-numbered holes, the other on the even-numbered holes. Our opponents were two British veterans, Ken Bousfield and Dai Rees, who had finished second earlier that summer to Palmer in the British Open (and who had played in that exhibition in San Diego with Ben Hogan when I was a teenager). We were at Royal Lytham & St. Annes in England and Arnold and I went 1-up on the par-five seventh hole and the match stayed that way all the way to the seventeenth. Arnold was driving on the odd-numbered holes. Seventeen is a short par five with a narrow driving area. I said, "Arnold just take that 1-iron and hit it in the fairway and I'll knock it on the green." He stared at me, threw down his cigarette, gripped his driver, let it rip, and missed the fairway by maybe six inches. I hit an iron six feet from the hole and he holed the putt and we won, 2 and 1. That was my first experience in the Ryder Cup and my first experience teaming with Arnold Palmer. That afternoon Palmer and I teamed again, this time in four-ball (best-ball) against John Panton and Bernard Hunt. We won, 5 and 4. Arnold went on to win two singles matches the next day and I won my lone singles match on the way to a 14½-9½ U.S. victory. The two "greenhorns" left England undefeated.

OVER THE YEARS, ARNOLD AND I played in hundreds of the same tournaments on Tour and we had our share of showdowns, although not as many as you might think considering that by the time of the 1966 U.S. Open he had won forty-seven times and I had won twenty-nine times on Tour and yet somehow we'd never faced each other in a playoff. We finished one-two a number of times: In the 1958 Buick Open, where I won by one shot. In the 1962 Phoenix Open, where Arnold won by twelve shots. In the 1962 Tournament of Champions, where Arnold won by one. And the 1965 Bob Hope Desert Classic, where I won by one.

At the 1960 Masters, I was one of five players who trailed Arnold by a stroke going into the final round. Ken Venturi, Ben Hogan, Dow Finsterwald and Julius Boros were the others. I was paired with Arnold in the final twosome. I took myself out of contention early in the round on my way to an undistinguished two-over-par 74 and a fourth place finish. It didn't look like Arnold's day for a green jacket, either. Up ahead, Venturi had already posted a score of 70 and was in the clubhouse with a one-shot lead over Palmer with three holes to play. On the par-three sixteenth at Augusta, Arnold missed the green with his tee shot.

He was in a tough spot. He needed to get down in two and make birdie on seventeen or eighteen, neither one considered a birdie hole, to catch Venturi and force a playoff. I watched as he took out his putter at the sixteenth green and hit the ball so hard from the fringe that if he had missed the pin his second putt would have been from the sand trap. But the ball smacked into the flagstick and stopped right next to the hole. He tapped in for his par, followed that with a 27-foot birdie putt on seventeen and then, after a superb approach shot and after I putted out for my 74, he "stared" in a five-foot birdie putt on the eighteenth green to avoid a playoff entirely and win outright. No one needed to tell me what Arnold Palmer was capable of when a major championship was on the line. It was that Masters that really fueled his reputation for charging to wins. Two months later he cemented it at the U.S. Open in Denver. That's the tournament where he drove the opening green and made up those seven shots in the final round and won by two. After that, no lead was considered safe from an Arnie charge.

My reputation for coming from behind was not as fabled, but the truth was, that's how I won a majority of my tournaments. Rarely did I lead from Thursday through Sunday, and at the start of the final round my name was often not in first place. My tendency was to play steady and safe from the first hole to the seventy-second hole. I wasn't renowned as a charger, but whatever you called it, I tended to pass a lot of players along the way.

As we teed off in the final twosome for round three of the '66 Open— it was the first time the USGA paired the two lowest scorers in the third round—Arnold knew I would try to finesse the course. And I knew he would go for the kill. There would be no surprises.

Power prevailed in round three. I shot three-over 73 and stood at even par 210 after fifty-four holes. Arnold shot 70 for 207, giving him a three-shot edge going into Sunday. Only one stroke had separated us when we stood on the sixteenth tee, the long par-five, but Arnold made a 25-foot putt for birdie and then finished par-par while I made par on sixteen, bogeyed seventeen and after missing the fairway for a third straight day on the short and very narrow eighteenth had to scramble to save par. I dropped two shots to Arnold on the last three holes.

Par scores had remained as elusive as ever in the third round and I was alone in second place. Among the contenders, only Jack Nicklaus made up ground. He shot 69 and was one-over for the tournament at 211, a shot behind me and four behind Arnold. That meant Arnold and I would be the final twosome again on Sunday, directly behind Jack and Dave Marr.

My one abiding thought for round four was to stay in control of myself. Don't change anything. Play my own game. Years later, when Greg Norman had a big lead at the Masters going into the final round and said his plan for Sunday was to play as if he were one behind, I knew then that he wasn't going to win. You can't manipulate your game plan. You can't change by the round. You need to ride, as the old saying goes, on the horse that brung ya.

Saturday also reinforced to me how important it was to go into what I called my cocoon whenever I played in the same group with Palmer. He was such a gallery favorite, you had to be very patient playing with him. When he finished putting his fans would start moving even if you still had to putt. It was a fact of life. Inevitable. You had to let the marshals know beforehand and you had to steel yourself that it was going to happen so it wouldn't throw you off your game. In the U.S. Open, with the huge crowds, it was only more pronounced. By the time we finished round three, and Arnie was on the charge, thousands of people were following us. They surrounded each of the finishing holes since we were the last group and galleries were allowed to do that back then.

After the round I gave my statement to the press and quickly left the premises. I didn't hit any balls at the range, just got in the car and drove back to the private home in Greenbrae, a suburb north of San Francisco where we were staying with Ray Leininger, a Mormon bishop, and his family. I ate a late dinner with Shirley and the kids and got a good night's rest. The next morning Shirley grilled a bear steak for my breakfast, and once again I drove back toward the Golden Gate Bridge and the course next to the ocean.

A TOTAL OF 74,874 PEOPLE paid to watch the 1966 U.S. Open. It seemed every one of them was there on Sunday afternoon to witness Arnold Palmer hit his first tee shot. The Beatles wouldn't have drawn a bigger crowd. Arnie's Army was out in force and they were not disappointed. He birdied the first two holes, had four birdies on the front nine alongside just a single bogey and made the turn in 32 strokes.

At this rate he would shoot 64 and equal the U.S. Open record for lowest round.

Another record was also in reach and it wasn't just possible, it was probable. In 1948 Ben Hogan had won the U.S. Open at Riviera in Los Angeles with a 276 total, the lowest seventy-two-hole score in Open history. Palmer could tie that mark with a 37 on the back nine—two over par. The record would be his if he scored 36. Arnold already owned the British Open record for seventy-two holes with the 276 he shot at Troon in 1962. As he acknowledged later, the record set eighteen years earlier by Hogan—who at that very moment was up ahead at the eighteenth green applying the finishing touches to a round of 70 that gave him a 291 total and a twelfth place finish—crossed his mind. With no one challenging him from the present, why not chase the past? It gave him something to charge after.

I'd played the front nine in 36, one over par. I was still the closest of anyone in the field to Arnold, but that wasn't saying much. I was seven shots behind with nine holes to play.

You could practically feel the energy generated by Arnold's front nine. Every hole, the crowd got bigger—until it reached a certain critical mass and actually began to get smaller as some people, their views completely obscured, gave up and left the course for home so they could watch Arnie win on TV. I couldn't leave, but I was as ready to place the U.S. Open crown on Arnold Palmer's head as anyone. At that point I was two shots ahead of Jack Nicklaus and Tony Lema and as we stood on the tenth tee about to start the final nine, I said to Arnold, "I'd like to finish second."

He answered, "I'll do everything I can to help you."

It was a light-hearted exchange; mine an acknowledgment of his commanding lead and his an acknowledgment that of course he'd help me finish second—by finishing first. Over the years it has amused me when writers and commentators have suggested I was asking for help in some real way. It was just casual banter, no different than when Dave Marr asked Arnold to "Make a 12" when Palmer had a six-shot lead standing on the eighteenth tee at the 1964 Masters. At the time, his lead at Olympic seemed equally out of reach.

On the par-four tenth hole that feeling didn't change when I parred while Arnold missed the green, hit a wedge shot to ten feet and came up short on the putt and made bogey. He was still six ahead with eight holes to play.

After we both made routine pars at eleven and birdies at twelve the result seemed even more inevitable. Now I was down six with six to play.

On thirteen, a dangerous 191-yard par three with the pin tucked in the back, I hit first and landed safely in the middle of the green, continuing to take care not to do anything rash and jeopardize finishing second. As Palmer wrote in his autobiography, the birdie on twelve had steadied him and reawakened thoughts of Hogan's Open record, something he could now accomplish by shooting one-over par over the last six holes. He confessed that he was slightly irritated that I didn't shoot for the pin. In his view, I had nothing to lose, why didn't I go for it? But it would have been as hard for me to shoot at that pin as it was for him not to shoot at it.

He took out a 4-iron, aimed dead for the flag, and ended just off the green, but in deep U.S. Open rough. He hit a difficult chip shot to fifteen feet and two-putted for a bogey four to my two-putt par. I was now down five with five to play and still concentrating on Nicklaus and Lema, not Palmer. That focus only intensified after the par-four fourteenth, where we each hit the green in regulation and missed birdie putts from twenty-five feet. Arnold's came close. It hit the edge of the hole and spun out just left. I remained five down but now with only four to play against a man performing in front of his home crowd—because *every* crowd was Arnold Palmer's home crowd.

But golf is a game of swings.

Our tee shots on the short par-three fifteenth hole opened a small pinprick of light.

Again, I hit first. This time, sensing I was running out of time, I aimed at the flag, but made sure I had plenty of club and ended up on the green some thirty feet beyond the cup. Again, Arnold went right at the pin, which was tucked in the right front corner. His ball trickled into the adjacent sand trap.

All week my putting had been solid, as had Arnold's. To that point in the tournament, on U.S. Open greens slicker than the parking lot, he had three-putted once and I hadn't three-putted at all. Arnold blasted out of the trap to fifteen feet as I concentrated on the thirty feet of green I had remaining. The last I saw of my ball was when it disappeared straight down for birdie. Arnold two-putted from twelve feet for bogey. I was now three down with three to go.

BACK IN GREENBRAE, THE LEININGERS looked around and noticed that my five-year-old son Bobby wasn't in the room where they were watching the tournament on television. He hadn't gone to the course with his brother and sister because he wasn't yet old enough to walk the full eighteen holes, but now he was missing. Earlier, Bobby had left the room so he could say a prayer for his daddy to win. When he returned this time and they asked him where he'd been, he answered, "Saying a fresher prayer."

AT THAT POINT IT WAS still just a prayer. Arnold Palmer, winner of seven majors and forty-seven tournaments in eleven years, had a three shot lead with three holes to play to win the U.S. Open. I still had to give him a shot a hole. But. Wait. Wasn't Arnie up seven a minute ago? Hadn't he just dropped four shots in six holes and three in the last three? When you're competing, there is no louder noise than the silence of shifting momentum.

Arnie's Army was by no means defecting. The groans were tremendous when his par putt on fifteen came up short and stopped. But people who like a good underdog were perking up, jumping on my bandwagon. I began hearing shouts of encouragement: "C'mon Billy," "Charge, Casper," "You can do it." Standing in the gallery, Shirley, Billy and Linda heard it too. They coined a name for our newfound fans: Casper Converts.

My mind went to the trip I'd taken earlier that year to Vietnam, where I had visited eight remote Special Forces camps. The Special Forces soldiers were situated in the midst of the Viet Cong. Sometimes the enemy lived right outside their gates. They had to be ready for anything. Conditions could turn from peaceful to a full-on firefight at any moment. These men were trained to be ready for whatever happened, whenever it happened. Their readiness impressed me, and now I found myself comparing my situation to theirs. Like them, I had trained long and hard. Like them, I had prepared for these very circumstances. Now I needed to take advantage of that preparation and do what I knew how to do when I needed to do it.

It was a huge advantage to be able to hit first, and with the honors on sixteen I connected on a long, straight drive that landed in the center of the fairway, in good position to approach the green on the left-bending hole. At 604 sea-level yards, the par-five sixteenth was the longest hole on the course and one of the longest we played all year. In the years before metal heads, titanium shafts and souped-up golf balls, no human being, not even Arnold Palmer, could reach sixteen in two.

But that didn't stop him from trying. He swung hard with his driver, came around too fast and sent a smother hook left. Just how far left the ball might have traveled became a moot point when it collided with a pine tree's branches no more than 150 yards away and dropped straight down, completely out of sight. I doubt another ball had landed in that area all week. Most drives, even if they were hooking, went much farther. To make the lie worse, the left side of sixteen wasn't open to galleries. No one had walked through that area all week. Except for his caddy, Arnold was all alone for his second shot, far from any encouraging words, in untouched ankle-deep rough, forty yards sideways from the fairway, still a good 450 yards from the green.

Things went from bad to worse when he pulled out a 3-iron, aimed toward the distant green in an attempt to straighten out the dogleg, and plowed a furrow in the grass that any farmer's tractor would have been proud of, but that managed to move the ball just fifty more yards—and it was still in the rough. At that point he surrendered, did what he should have done in the first place and chipped out sideways to the fairway, to a spot barely beyond where my drive had landed. He was lying three; I was lying one. I was now one shot out of the lead in the U.S. Open, and right in front of me my opponent was falling apart.

Normally I would have hit a 4-wood from where I was standing. But there was nothing normal about where I stood. Years earlier, when I had a chance to win my first tournament during my first full year on Tour, veteran Ted Kroll gave me a piece of advice I never forgot: When you're in contention and the pressure is on, hit your straight club. Above all else, keep the ball in play.

Thanks to Ted Kroll I took out the 2-iron, my straight club. I made solid contact and the ball came to rest in the middle of the narrow fairway. Straight and safe. From 290 yards out, Arnold put every ounce of his strength into a 3-wood and made it to the trap in front of the green. A prodigious blast, but he lay four and was in the sand. My ball was in the fairway, 165 yards from the pin after two shots. The best chance for birdie meant landing on the left side of the green, below the hole. I tested the wind, took a deep breath, reached in my bag, and pulled out my 5-iron . . .

3

Pasture Golf

4

Building the San Diego Country Club in the 1920s.

Silver City, New Mexico
1935

The first golf club I ever hit was a 5-iron in Silver City, New Mexico. I was four years old. I don't remember how far the ball went, but I remember for sure the club was a 5-iron. Because that's the club my dad hit.

He had cut down another club for me to use because I was so short. But I would have none of it. I cried, kicked and generally pitched a fit until he let me use the same one he was using. I'm sure a therapist would have a fine time interpreting what all that meant but the only therapy I was interested in was that 5-iron.

I played my first golf course the same day I hit the 5-iron. It was a family-owned course. My father, William Earl Casper, the man for whom I am named, laid it out with his brother Virgil in a cow pasture on the family farm. The Casper Country Club consisted of three holes carved out of sun-baked dirt and clumps of cheat grass situated just down the road from the clubhouse, a.k.a. my grandfather's farmhouse.

Exactly why and how my dad and Virgil got interested in golf enough to build their own course is a story lost in time. They never explained and I never asked. I wish I had. They weren't professionals. They never had any instruction. Probably it had something to do with the Great Depression, a time when people made a lot of things at home because they couldn't afford them otherwise. It could be they were inspired by Bobby Jones, who in 1930, the year before I was born, won the original Grand Slam of the U.S. Open, U.S. Amateur, British Open and British Amateur all in the same year and was given his own ticker-tape parade down New York City's Fifth Avenue. It wasn't long after that that my dad and his brother built their course in the pasture.

They used what was available. In the Southwest they have red ants, so they dug up the anthills, got rid of the ants, and spread the fine sand to make the greens. They buried a tomato can for a cup. With the soil that was left they made the tees and then leveled them out with their shovels and rakes. You'd tee up on clumps of grass. The fairways were just wild grass and pastureland. I can't remember what par was. After they'd finish working on their father's farm, or on someone else's farm, they'd bring out their collection of mismatched golf clubs and see about setting another course record. By the time I was four I got to take my own rips.

We'd moved to New Mexico when I was three. The Great Depression definitely had something to do with that. My parents were both originally from the Silver City area but they relocated to San Diego after their teenage wedding in 1930—my mother, Isabel, was seventeen and my dad nineteen—to launch out on their own. I was born the following summer, on June 24, 1931, in the San Diego McCullough Hospital. The economic depression that began on "Black Tuesday," Oct. 29, 1929, was in full swing by then. After three years of struggle in San Diego my parents decided it was time to return home.

We moved in with my dad's mother and father. William Adolf Casper was from Hamburg, Germany, and Bertha Vogel Casper was from Bern, Switzerland. They made an interesting pair. He was a huge man, six-foot-four and at least four hundred pounds. She wasn't quite five feet tall and was very petite. Everyone called her "Little Grandma." My grandfather was a tyrant, a man hard to live with and harder to please. His children kept leaving because they couldn't get along with him, and then they'd come back, like my father did, because they knew he could help them make ends meet. Adolf was a man of some means. He owned the mercantile store in nearby Central and had a stake in a gold mine. On his farm he raised crops and livestock, both of which could be that night's dinner, an important thing in the 1930s. He cut a wide swath, figuratively and literally, and even as a young child I sensed how fortunate he was to have my grandmother to smooth things over for him. He was the dictator but she ran the show.

On my mother's side, I only knew my grandmother, Grandma Hattie Wilson. My grandfather Stanley died before I was born. He was a merchant marine whose travels took him around the world. As a result, my mother was born in Chile. As family legend had it, Grandpa

Stanley drowned while swimming in the mouth of the Golden Gate in San Francisco when the cross currents caught him and took him under. My grandmother eventually married a man named Green and moved back to New Mexico, but we never lived with them or spent much time with them.

How and when my parents met is another lost story. I never asked either one of them for the details and they never volunteered them. They took care of me in the big ways, made sure I had enough to eat and a place to sleep, but from the earliest times I can remember both of them were constantly working. You could not fault their work ethic, but there was never enough energy or inclination for much talking. They had no more children, I was it. As far back as I can remember, after providing the basics of surviving, they left the rest up to me. When I was four and five I was alone much of the time. I would walk around my grandfather's farm, just roam for miles. I had two pals, a couple of big farm dogs named Minnie and Blackie, that I spent way more time with than anyone in my family.

When I was six we moved back to San Diego. We lived in a small house—a shack, really—in the Sorrento Valley quite a ways north of downtown, where my father found work in a dairy. My mother got a job at the telephone company. A lot of people were poor during the Depression, including us. One of my clearest early memories of life in San Diego is going in the evening to the lima bean patches in the hills. My parents and I would pick what was left after the farmers had harvested the rest. I thought everybody did that. It was our version of fast food. To this day I love the taste of lima beans.

We were self-sustaining in many ways. We raised our own chickens and rabbits and ducks. I learned to fish in the stream that ran through the valley. But the dogs hadn't come with us and I was alone even more than in New Mexico. My father gave me chores at an early age. He put me in charge of the two ducks we owned. Every day I'd take them down to the creek but one day one of them wouldn't follow me back, so I got sore, threw a rock at him and killed him. When my dad asked where the duck was I told him a skunk got him. He saw right through me. I got a blistering for that. I always have been an awful liar.

We moved constantly. We lived in a trailer and hauled it to Mission Valley closer to town so my dad could work at another dairy. It was in an area near the stadium where the Chargers play football now, but back then it was nothing but wide-open fields and the San Diego River. Then we moved again. And again. I attended five elementary schools in three years. Changing schools is never easy for a kid, and I was a big kid for my age, which is a kind way of saying I was fat. The other kids invariably called me, the new kid, Fatso. It stung when they said it, but I'd get even when they had races. I would outrun everyone in the class. That would always surprise them. I was fat but I was fast. Anything to do with sports always came easy to me, which is more than I can say for my studies. By the time I got to third grade I was so far behind they made me take it over again.

When I was nine years old and World War II was already going strong in Europe we moved yet again, this time south of downtown San Diego to the community of Chula Vista. When I woke up the first morning I thought we'd gone back to New Mexico. Just up the street was a golf course. I had come full circle.

THE SAN DIEGO COUNTRY CLUB was organized in 1897 and arrived at its present location in 1921, at a time when 1.5 million Americans played golf, about one in every one hundred (today the number is closer to one in fifteen). The club's first location was in modern-day Balboa Park in the heart of San Diego, just up the hill from the bay. But in 1913 the government commandeered the land the golf course was on to make way for the 1915 Panama-California Exposition. That caused the members to move west to Point Loma on the coast, where they were welcomed by A.G. Spalding, the former Chicago Cubs pitcher and founder of Spalding Sporting Goods, who had built the Point Loma Golf Club in 1912. That stay was also short-lived, however, when Congress approved funds to build a training center for the United States Navy on nine of Point Loma's eighteen holes. Tired of depending on public land, the club members decided they would buy property and build their own private golf course. They settled on a piece of real estate farther south and out in the country in the sprawling farming enclave of Chula Vista, not far from the Mexican border. They hired golf course architect William Bell to design eighteen holes, and put down permanent roots.

WE DIDN'T GET ACQUAINTED ALL at once, the club and I. My parents were working around the clock. I was a kid trying to survive third grade. Again. But memories of the pasture in New Mexico lingered, and the golf course cast a huge inviting shadow, one that in time would engulf and preserve the best parts of my life. It would be where I would make lifelong friendships, where I would earn money, where I would discover the thrill and enjoyment of competing, where all sorts of people would look out for me and take care of me, where I would get a college scholarship (short-lived though it was), where I would learn the proper way to grip a golf club, where I would get started on my life's work. It would be the one place I could count on that was solid and stable and wasn't going anywhere. The San Diego Country Club wasn't my home away from home, as some have suggested. That was where my parents happened to be paying rent for the moment. The San Diego Country Club *was* home.

I started hanging around the golf course when I was nine, not doing much, just acting interested, making friends, hitting balls and putting on the greens when I could. When it got dark I had the greens all to myself and I just kept putting. I would memorize in my mind where the hole was and putt from various spots on the green completely blind. It wasn't out of any preconceived plan or strategy, I just enjoyed putting and didn't want to stop just because I couldn't see. It helped me develop at an early age a kind of sixth sense for the unseen parts of putting, the roll of the ball, the texture of the green, the importance of keeping the putter blade square, of getting the ball started in the right direction. I got so I could make as many putts when I couldn't see the hole as when I could see it.

My dad was still very much a golf enthusiast. On the rare occasions when he wasn't busy working we'd play some holes. Bing Crosby held a tournament in Rancho Santa Fe with a bunch of movie stars and golf pros called the Crosby Clambake and one year we went to see that. I don't remember much about it other than going with my dad. It was probably in 1940 or 1941. When America entered the war the tournament shut down. After the war it started back up, but Bing Crosby moved it to the Monterey Peninsula.

I began caddying right after I turned eleven, a year before I could legally carry bags. By that time I'd already developed good relationships with some of the members and they let me caddy for them whether it was legal or not. I caddied for one lady three days a week. I'd meet her on the second tee, carry her bag to the eighteenth tee, and she'd give me seventy-five cents for the round, full pay. Plus she'd buy balls from me for a quarter. That was a lot of money for a little kid in those days. I don't remember a single time when my parents gave me a penny.

My mom and dad were good, hard-working, industrious people. They didn't lay around the house. They didn't cheat others or break the law and they didn't complain about all the things they didn't have. They weren't partiers; neither of them drank alcohol or went to bars. It wasn't for religious reasons. They weren't churchgoers at all. It was for we-have-to-get-up-and-go-to-work-in-the-morning reasons. They got a good night's sleep every night and did it all over again the next day. It didn't leave much room for nurturing. I can never recall my mother giving me a hug. If I got out of line my father would take a belt to me, but that was the extent of what you'd call parental training. We didn't talk about anything in depth. My parents didn't fight openly. I can never remember them arguing in my presence. But when I was about twelve and they were about thirty they separated and shortly after that they said they were getting a divorce. It was probably more out of atrophy and attrition than anything else. They were just plain worn out. I don't recall anyone ever talking about the divorce either.

I ACTUALLY SPENT MORE TIME with my dad after the breakup. We developed a routine. On Saturdays he would come by the house in Castle Park in Chula Vista, where I remained with my mother, and we'd go to Old Town and play the Presidio Hills Golf Course, a little pitch and putt layout. Then we would play miniature golf before he brought me home. Also about this time my dad, who was now working for the San Diego Gas & Electric Company, joined the San Diego Country Club. The Depression and World War II made playing the country club course a bargain: $1 for a round or $9 for the month. (Earlier in his life, my father had lost an eye working at one of the dairies around Silver City when a piece of baling wire punctured the pupil. That got him a 4F medical exemption that kept him out of the war.) I could play the course by now, too, on caddy days. By the age of twelve I'd become a full-fledged caddy, so we'd play some holes together, my dad and I. Sometimes in the evenings when everybody was gone he'd hit balls out of an old shag bag on the seventeenth fairway and I'd run around and catch them with my baseball mitt. At the time I dreamed of one day being a great professional athlete—for the New York Yankees.

Beyond a strong work ethic, something else I got from my parents, or from somewhere in my family genetics, was natural hand-eye coordination. I never had any trouble seeing or handling a ball, whether it was a moving baseball, football, basketball, or tennis ball, or a stationary cue ball or golf ball. I was blessed with soft, rather small hands and good touch. It wasn't something I developed. It was just always there. I used to go to school and be in awe of kids who could do complicated math problems in their heads or spell a word without even thinking about it. I couldn't do that. But put a ball in front of me—any kind of ball, it didn't matter—and I could throw it, catch it and hit it without even having to think.

I couldn't hit the golf ball all that far when I was twelve but I could hit it fairly straight and I could putt like mad. I got so I could shoot in the mid 90s at San Diego Country Club and they gave me a handicap of twenty-four. My dad thought that was pretty good for my age so he entered me in my first tournament. It wasn't a junior event; it was open to any age. They held it at a course called Emerald Hills just east of downtown San Diego. There wasn't much grass on the fairways so distance wasn't a problem; I could run the ball like crazy. And the greens were all grass and well groomed so it felt like I was putting into a basketball hoop. My dad paid my entry fee and I went out the first day and shot 80—with a twenty-four handicap. That gave me a net 56! When my score was posted the people running the tournament found my dad and returned his entry fee. They felt justified in their assumption that we had padded my handicap. But we hadn't padded anything. I brought the same game to Emerald Hills that I played with at San Diego Country Club. I guess I was just on that day. There was something about the official atmosphere, the intensity of the competition, the importance of it all, that brought a different game out of me. It was a better game, a more focused game. I was as surprised as anyone at what I had done.

I AVOIDED GAINING A REPUTATION as San Diego's biggest sandbagger by leaving San Diego. My father decided to move back to Silver City and took me with him. There was no custody battle between my mother and father or any discussion at all that I remember about my leaving. One day my dad said, "Get in, we're going to New Mexico," and I got in and we drove off to the east. I had just finished sixth grade and happily bid grammar school good-bye.

I went to seventh grade in the little town of Central, near Silver City, and my dad went to work in his father's gold mine. We stayed at Adolf's house until there was some kind of conflict—if anything, my grandfather had only gotten more irascible—and then we moved to a place of our own. It was a guy's life all the way. Silver City is right at the foot of the Black Range of the Rocky Mountains and I went hunting and fishing there with my dad and helped him set his trap line for coyotes. We'd shoot pine squirrels and cook them in this Dutch oven he had. Pine squirrels live on pine nuts and they are delicious to eat. I played second base on an adult men's softball team and played a lot of baseball. The old three-hole golf course had more or less disintegrated back to a cow pasture—my dad had been away in San Diego, Virgil had moved to Albuquerque to start a roofing business and his other brother, Adolf, had moved to San Francisco—but there were two nine-hole golf courses nearby, one in Fort Baird and one in Silver City, that we sometimes played. There was almost no grass on the fairways because the elk, deer, cows and horses would eat it down to the dirt. The greens were a combination of oil and sand and you had to rake out the hoof prints of the animals before you putted. It made San Diego Country Club seem like some far-off Shangri-La.

But as always, working took precedence over playing games and when seventh grade ended so did our time in New Mexico. My dad got a job with a company called Boyles Bros. that was headquartered in Salt Lake City. They were a diamond-drilling outfit that cut veins deep into the earth looking for ore. We went from Silver City to a little mining camp high in the Sierra Nevadas outside Bishop, California. We lived at 10,000 feet and while Dad worked in the mines they allowed me to work as a flunky in the kitchen. I mopped floors and kept the place clean and got a paycheck every two weeks. Between meals I'd go down to the lake and fish. I didn't have a rod or reel, just a pole with some line, but it was some of the greatest trout fishing in the country. I'd catch fish and wait till my dad got off work. School? Nobody worried about school. I was well on my way to becoming the next Tom Sawyer or Huckleberry Finn, not Sam Snead or Ben Hogan.

When that mine job ended we moved on to San Francisco, where Dad continued to work for Boyles Bros. We lived with my Uncle Adolf and Aunt Bonnie and their son Billy Louis. Somehow my mother caught wind that I wasn't going to school so one day right after Christmas in 1946 there she was, on Uncle Adolf's doorstep with a bus ticket in her hand. We rode back together to San Diego. She brought me home to a little house on 4th Avenue in Chula Vista, just around the corner from the junior high school. But it wasn't the schoolhouse that made it a homecoming. Near my mother's house the San Diego Country Club, my sanctuary, still stood like a sentinel, and welcomed this wayfarer home from the road.

4

Homecoming

5

San Diego junior golfers in 1948: that's me standing on the far right;
Gene Littler is wearing the snazzy shirt on the first row,
second from the left.

Chula Vista, California
January, 1947

No one took much notice of my return to San Diego, with two exceptions: my mother and the school system. Neither knew quite what to do with me. My mother had her hands full with her job at the phone company and was used to coming and going as she pleased. As for the school officials, I completely stumped them. They were at a loss where I fit. Eventually, the same administrators who determined I needed to take third grade twice decided I should now rejoin my age group and go into ninth grade, even though the year was already half over. How they came to that decision I do not know. They did not include me in the discussion, but I was not in disagreement. Somehow I managed to skip eighth grade entirely.

Due in no small part, I'm sure, to my rather inconsistent attendance history, I was never much more than an indifferent student. I'd learned I could do what I needed to do to get by and that's about all I did. I displayed an aptitude for geography and math, two subjects that would prove handy for a professional golfer, but not for many other classes.

But if I wasn't book smart I was street smart. I had been taking care of myself for as long as I could remember. After I moved back to Chula Vista, my mother was gone when I got up in the morning and didn't come home until late in the evening. My father ceased being a presence in my life. He moved to Alaska with his job and I didn't see or hear from him again for years. I couldn't just run wild. I needed to be home at night in my own bed, but that was about it. Otherwise I was on my own. I had no real reins on me, no restrictions, no monitoring. I was in control of pretty much everything. If I didn't do it, it didn't get done. I made my own breakfast most every morning—my favorite was chocolate tapioca pudding—and usually fixed my own supper as well.

Fortunately, I found myself in a place conducive to such teenage independence. Someone was looking out for me when I landed back in

Chula Vista—the same higher power that has looked out for me all my life through so many tender mercies. For a boy in my situation, with my particular interests and my rather obsessive nature, you could have searched the earth and not found better circumstances for me at a better place in time.

Half-a-million people lived in San Diego by the end of World War II, but the harbor was ten miles away and there was still a buffer, a kind of protective hedge, between the city and what would later become known as the suburbs. Chula Vista was wide-open spaces in those days. Fields and lemon groves stretched all the way to Mexico just eight miles to the south. Sometimes I'd be looking for golf balls at the club and I'd run into Mexicans who had just crossed the river. We'd eye each other and go our own way, both of us heading for something we hoped was better but not at all sure what it was going to be.

It was a good time to dream. People had emerged from World War II to realize the war had gotten rid of both Hitler and the Depression. Although I was largely oblivious to it, I'd spent the first fifteen years of my life living through the greatest economic downturn in America's history, followed by the greatest war in America's history. What wasn't there to celebrate? With all the stress finally gone, you could almost hear the country exhale in relief. Freedom never felt so good.

I could have gotten into plenty of trouble with all my personal freedom, or turned into a complete slug. Fortunately, there wasn't much to entice a kid to stay inactive or indoors in 1947. TV had barely been invented. There were no video games, no World Wide Web, none of the kinds of distractions that could keep a teenager on the couch for very long. The consistently pleasant weather sure didn't chase you inside. The only difference between winter and summer was how many holes you could play before it got dark. Nowadays parents who want their kids to become professional golfers send them to a special golf academy in a place with a nice temperate climate where they can play golf every day after they get their requisite studies out of the way. I went to that kind of place too: Chula Vista, California.

I was also fortunate to grow up at a time when alcohol was the only mood-altering substance a kid could get his hands on. Drugs were mostly in the future, especially for teenagers. I did a little drinking but not much. For some reason, thank goodness, I didn't enjoy it. I tried smoking too and really hated that. I could have gotten hooked. My dad was a smoker and my mother smoked early on and heaven knows a lot of golfers smoked back then, probably the majority of them. But I didn't smoke and I didn't drink, something I was grateful for later on. And I didn't get into much mischief or trouble. One thing that kept me on the straight and narrow was that age-old deterrent: fear of getting found out. I knew so many people from the club—cooks, dishwashers, waiters, greenskeepers, members, fellow caddies, the golf pro and his staff—and they all knew who I was. Instinctively I just knew I couldn't go around town making a fool out of myself. I didn't want to disappoint people who cared about me, and who I cared about as much in return.

I got my old caddying job back at the club as soon as I returned to town. They treated me like I never left. I quickly fell into a comfortable routine, caddying after school and on weekends, hanging around the caddy pen, practicing my putting and chipping, playing some holes on the course every time I got the chance. The caddy pen was its own clubhouse. Plenty of grownups carried bags as well as kids. When we weren't caddying we'd putt for quarters in the dirt or we'd play cards. My dad had taught me how to play cards when we were on the road together, and I was good at it. Our most popular game in the caddy pen was called Tonk. We'd play Tonk till it got so dark you had to quit because you couldn't see the suit of the cards. Putting contests and cards was how I augmented my income.

But being an independent and relatively responsible teenager didn't make me a model of self-discipline. I tended to spend money as fast as I made it. And in sharp contrast to later in my life, I wasn't concerned at all about a balanced diet. I could eat anything and everything in those days, and on many days I'd try. Sometimes after earning some money at the golf course I'd make my way through Chula Vista stopping at every place that served ice cream sundaes. I'd start at one end of town and eat myself to the other end. I might hit eight places by the time I was finished. Then I'd wonder why I was fat.

At other times a bunch of us would leave the club and make our way downtown hitting golf balls. The game was to see how many strokes it would take to get to Chub's Pool Hall. We'd tee off from the first tee at the San Diego Country Club and we'd play to the second spittoon on the south wall of the pool hall. Most of the land was lemon orchards so you'd try to bounce the ball off the asphalt streets to keep it going, then just keep hitting it off the dirt. It was probably three miles to the pool hall. Once you got to town you'd play down the alley in back of the main street, over the library, then through the card room in the back, where they played poker, and finally into the pool hall itself. As I recall, it was about a par thirty. When we were finished we'd play pool.

I reprised my routine of putting after dark on the club's putting green, and chipping too. You could find a lot of amusement just with golf clubs; at the time I didn't realize it was also career development.

I was on my way home from the golf course at dusk in early February when I saw the man standing on the fifth fairway, about two hundred yards from the tee. At first I thought he was playing the hole but then I noticed he had several balls scattered across the grass, which he proceeded to hit toward the green.

I had heard of Ben Hogan but knew almost nothing about him. I was fifteen years old. Just a year earlier I'd been living in a mining camp in the Sierra Nevadas. I knew why Hogan was in San Diego from the posters hanging on telephone poles and bulletin boards around town. On the weekend he was going to play in the thirty-six-hole exhibition match at San Diego C.C. against Englishman Dai Rees, another professional golfer I didn't know much about. The winner would get $5,000, an enormous sum of money in 1947. A local businessman, Anderson

Borthwick, who was also the country club president, put up the purse. From what I was seeing, Hogan was not taking the match lightly.

At thirty-four, this was Hogan in his physical prime, still two years away from the car accident that would nearly kill him. The year before he had won thirteen times on the PGA Tour, was the leading money winner, and to start the 1947 season he had already won the first two tournaments of the season, at Los Angeles and Phoenix. And here he was on the fifth fairway at San Diego Country Club, putting in overtime for an unofficial event, sizing up the golf course in the near dark.

It could have been anyone out there hitting shots. But there was something about the way the man moved, the purposeful manner in which he hit his shots, how he held his follow-through, the exact repetition of every pre-swing routine, that made me sense that this wasn't just someone out to play golf. This was someone out to control golf.

I walked the two blocks home mesmerized; I just wasn't sure why.

On the weekend, Hogan shot five-under par over thirty-six holes and defeated Dai Rees by eleven shots.

GETTING BACK TO GOLF FOR me was like riding a bicycle. In the nearly two years I had been away I'd played only a handful of times in New Mexico, and none at all at the mining camp in the Sierras or in San Francisco. But when I got back to the club I returned to playing like I always had, unscripted and freewheeling. As precise as Hogan was, I was that un-precise. I swung the club entirely by feel. My father had his phases of enthusiasm for the game and was actually quite a good player but he was as unschooled as I was. He never had any lessons. Neither one of us had a set of matched clubs. I scrounged up whatever collection I could put together and was constantly throwing out clubs whenever I came across something that looked better.

But God had given me a natural ability to swing a golf club. Over time this caught the attention of people who did know the game. One day not long after I'd returned to Chula Vista, I was caddying for Roy Pickford, a wealthy businessman who owned a hotel in Coronado and several more hotels in Washington, D.C. After the round, Mr. Pickford said that if I would like to take some lessons from the pro he would pay for them. Now and then I played golf with Tommy Pickford, Roy's son and a good player who was a bit older than me. Tommy had noticed that I played golf using a full-fingered grip—I held the club like a baseball bat. He knew I didn't have a lot of money and without my knowing it he asked his dad if he would pay for lessons so I could learn a proper grip. When I accepted his kind offer, Mr. Pickford went straight to the pro shop and paid for five lessons. That's how I found myself on the practice tee with head professional Charlie Heaney for the first formal golf instruction of my life.

Heaney gave me a total of five lessons, one per day, Monday through Friday. He showed me how to lay my little finger over the first knuckle of my left hand to form the Vardon overlapping grip, named after legendary English champion Harry Vardon. I may have known who Ben Hogan was but I'd never heard of Vardon or his grip. The pro explained that it was the preferred way good golfers held the club and I should use it too. It felt alien and uncomfortable at first but Heaney wouldn't let me backslide. Every day for an hour we worked on the basics, and then he insisted that I practice on my own. When he turned me loose after the final lesson he made me promise that I wouldn't play the course for a week or two, that I would stay on the range and practice, and give what I'd learned time to sink in.

Anytime you change your hands it's difficult and I had to stick with it, but after hitting more shots on the range than any time in my life I finally went out and played the course. The lowest score I'd ever shot was a 69. I don't remember shooting much *over* 69 for the next several rounds. I wasn't spraying the ball nearly as much as before. I had so much more control. It was like I'd been driving a racecar and somebody showed me it had a fifth gear.

The funny thing is, I still fancied myself a baseball player. I loved baseball; I played second base and outfield on the high school team and could hit for power. I could hit pop flies higher than anybody I knew.

But if you were serious about baseball you needed to play American Legion ball and that meant Wednesday nights and every Saturday and Sunday and those were my caddying days. Economics dictated a hard reality. I simply couldn't afford baseball.

By the fall of '47 I was ready for high school whether or not high school was ready for me. Thanks to golf I had made many friends in a short period of time and I didn't feel like a stranger. The attention I was starting to get from golf helped too, although not always. When the County Amateur came along my sophomore year the qualifying round was played during the week. Since the tournament was at my home course, the San Diego Country Club, I couldn't pass up the opportunity. I made a command decision to miss school that day—and shot 72 to wind up as low medalist. The headline in the paper the next morning said "Casper Shoots 72, Leads Qualifying." When I got to school Mr. Stein, the vice principal, called me into his office. "Billy that was a nice round of golf," he said. Flattered, I said, "Thank you." Then he said, "You're welcome, you have five detentions for ditching school."

I was in the charter class of Chula Vista High School. For years Sweetwater High School took in all of South Bay, but when I was a sophomore a new school was created to account for the postwar growth. We didn't even have a building at first. While our schoolhouse was under construction we were bused about ten miles to Brown Field and met in Navy barracks left over from World War II. When we finally moved into our new building, still another high school, Mar Vista, had been created in the south bay and the Mar Vista kids moved in with us while their school was being built. We met in the morning and they met in the afternoon.

The schedule got me up early and out of school early, which freed up even more time for golf. When I wasn't caddying I was playing. I was on the high school team and the country club was our home course, which meant we could play as often as we liked as long as it didn't interfere with the members. I'm sure I played more rounds than most of the members, maybe more than any of them. Many of my friends caddied or worked other jobs at the golf course. There was my best friend Don Chase, Jack Peacock, Jack Stokes, Ed White, Basil Van Boom, and the Monahan brothers, Mike and Tommy. Tommy and I played out of the same golf bag for a while. He had better clubs than I did and he let me use them. For someone who came from a broken home and grew up in circumstances that could only be described as under-privileged, I certainly was privileged.

In many ways the times were simpler back then, easier. I don't recall a lot of racial tension. The border was very accessible. My friend Jack Peacock and I used to drive down to Tijuana on Friday nights to watch Jai Alai. Sometimes we'd go to a Mexican beach, fool around in the surf, build a bonfire and sleep overnight in a tent. We moved around very freely.

UNLIMITED PLAYING PRIVILEGES, THE NEW grip, inspiration from Hogan, all of it helped my golf game tremendously. At the same time, Al Abrego, Lou Smith, Norrie West, John Brown, Frank Alessio and others were starting up San Diego's junior golf program. These men and women were the best friends a young golfer ever had. Al Abrego ran the little eighteen-hole, par-three course in Old Town called Presidio Hills, and there wasn't anything he wouldn't do to help kids who took an interest in golf. His attitude was typical of so many others.

For years, San Diego area juniors had competed as an extension of the junior golf program in Los Angeles. Some good players came out of the county. Bill Nary, for example, was a fine professional who did well on the early PGA Tour, along with others. But after the war, the local golf leaders began organizing clinics and tournaments in San Diego for San Diego kids. What developed into the San Diego County Junior Golf Association became a model for the nation. San Diego has not only developed champions the likes of Gene Littler, Mickey Wright, Phil Rodgers, Craig Stadler, Scott Simpson, Pat Perez, Chris Riley and Phil Mickelson, but thousands of others who learned to love the game early and developed a lifelong interest in golf. It was my good fortune to come along just as the groundwork for local junior golf was being laid.

Between junior tournaments and high school golf I did not lack for competition and my game just took off. When I was a high school sophomore I finished first in the Harvey Fleming School Fund tournament and was awarded a $600 college scholarship. Then I won the tournament again as a junior and got another $600 for college. As a sophomore I finished second in the Southern California Interscholastic Federation finals and as a junior I took first place, giving Chula Vista High its first-ever SCIF championship. In junior golf I won such tournaments as the Ray Cook Memorial, the Rowcliffe Trophy and the Inglewood Invitational. In April of 1949 I shot the lowest round of my life, a 66 at San Diego Country Club, bettering the 68 I'd shot four months earlier.

But there was someone I couldn't beat. Gene Littler was eleven months older than I was and easily the best young player in San Diego. I first met him in junior golf and then in high school tournaments. He was the first player around my age I ever saw that I honestly didn't think I could beat.

When I was sixteen and seventeen, I played Littler in the San Diego County Amateur two straight years, and each time he beat me 2 and 1. I finally won the County Am when I was eighteen—and Littler wasn't in the tournament. He was off playing in some national junior event.

Gene lived in La Jolla, an affluent area on the opposite side of San Diego from Chula Vista. His father was an accountant for a construction company when the post-war building boom began. His parents joined La Jolla Country Club and put a golf club in their son's hands early in his life. Gene was one of those kids who got all his growth early. He was already at his full height and weight, around five-foot-nine and 170 pounds, by the time he was in high school. As an athlete he did it all. He was a gymnast and he threw the shot put for the track team. But golf was the sport that came most naturally to him. He had a swing that looked effortless. People called him "Gene the Machine." He was also very even-tempered. He was just this nice, mild-mannered kid who would beat your brains out and you couldn't even hate him for it.

IN THE SUMMER OF 1949, after Gene graduated from La Jolla High School and I finished my junior year at Chula Vista High, the two of us went to Los Angeles, sponsored by San Diego junior golf supporters. There we qualified along with Bud Holscher of Santa Monica to play in the National Junior Amateur, a championship put on by the United States Junior Chamber of Commerce that attracted hundreds of qualifiers from across the country.

That year the tournament was held at Houston Country Club in Houston, Texas. In the 128-man qualifier, Gene finished first, I finished second and Bud fourth. That cinched the state team title for California and got all three of us into match play with good seedings. We made it to the semifinals, where I faced Holscher and Gene played Bob Atkinson from Portland, Oregon. Gene defeated Atkinson 7 and 5, Bud beat me 2 and 1, and then finished off Gene in the thirty-six-hole final, 6 and 5.

The tournament was considered the junior version of the U.S. Amateur and got a lot of attention in the newspapers in Southern California. Gene and I came home labeled San Diego's "Twin Terrors" by the press. It was the first time I received any exposure for my golf outside of Chula Vista.

On that high note I started my senior year of high school. I had little to complain about. I had plenty of friends and as much fame and fortune as a high school kid could ever expect. I was in the school choir. They even gave me a featured spot in the bass section. I was a member of a social club called the Olympian Hi-Y Club and on the baseball team as well as the golf team. A real big man on campus.

But deep down something was missing and I knew it and it gnawed at me constantly. I felt it strongest when I came home from school to an empty house or stayed late at the golf course to avoid going home. For all the good people and good things around me, I was still very alone. I didn't really have a family.

In October, Don Chase and I went to a high school football game, Chula Vista versus Sweetwater, our archrival, at the Sweetwater field just north of Chula Vista. As we sat down in the visitor's section, I heard a girl screaming and hollering in the row behind me. I glanced back and saw a petite girl with curly dark brown hair and a face so cute it was difficult to comprehend that all that volume was coming out of her. I was instantly smitten. What I did next is what any red-blooded American boy would do. I took it as an open invitation to start needling her.

5

Shirley

6

The week she graduated from high school and I turned twenty-one,
Shirley and I walked down the aisle.

Chula Vista, California
October, 1949

She was sitting with her girlfriend halfway up in the bleachers. I was sitting with my friend, Don Chase, one bench below. Every time the girls cheered, we would mimic them by repeating the same cheer. It was the best way we could think of to get their attention. I was sure I'd never seen the good-looking girl on the left. I would have remembered her. She was about 5-foot-3, couldn't have weighed a hundred pounds and was screaming louder than anyone in the stands.

I don't recall who won the football game that night. What I do recall is going to the dance afterward, hoping that girl would be there, afraid she wouldn't be. When I finally saw her standing in the corner I walked right over and asked if she'd like to dance. She said yes. As we started around the dance floor we had a chance to introduce ourselves. She said her name was Shirley Franklin, she'd just moved to Chula Vista from Seattle, this was her first year at Chula Vista High, and she was a sophomore.

We danced every dance, the disc jockey played "Blue Moon" by Mel Torme', which on the spot became our song, and when the last dance was over I asked her if I could take her out. She asked when, I said the next night. Well, she said, she'd have to ask her mother. Late the next afternoon, a Saturday, Don Chase and his date Betty picked me up at my house and we all drove to Shirley's house on the other side of town. I remember her mother looked at me and said, "That's an old man!"

Still, after sizing me up, Mrs. Rader gave her approval and the four of us went to a movie. Afterward I asked Shirley if she'd like to go steady. She said yes to that, too. I don't know what qualifies as love at first sight, but I went home knowing I'd met the girl of my dreams. The next day, after getting a good night's rest following the very first date of her life, Shirley told her best friend Mary Ann that she'd just met the man she was going to marry.

We knew nothing about each other. She didn't know about my golf, or anything at all about golf for that matter. All we knew was that from the start we felt comfortable and safe around one another and that was enough for us. Her story was similar to mine. Her father was a dairy farmer and her parents had married early—Shirley's mother had been just sixteen. She grew up an only child. The family moved a lot during the Depression, looking for work. They were poor as dirt. Her parents divorced when Shirley was still young and after that she lived with her mother. She lost contact with her father when she moved to California but before she left Washington she had a relationship with him that revolved mainly around sports. He was a big University of Washington fan so he would take her to football and basketball games at the university, much like my dad took me to the golf course when I was younger. As a result, even though she grew up in an age when women didn't participate much, Shirley loved watching sports, an enthusiasm she would never lose.

Her family's roots went deep in Washington. Her mother, Dorothy, was one-eighth Snohomish Indian, making Shirley one-sixteenth Native American. The rest of her was a mix of English and Scottish. When Shirley was eleven her mother married a naval officer named Bert Rader who was stationed at Whitby Island in the Puget Sound. In the summer of 1949 Lieutenant Rader's assignment was changed to San Diego. As far as I was concerned, Shirley Franklin arrived in Chula Vista in the nick of time. It was my senior year.

We had each spent our childhood alone and I think that's what drew us to each other so close so fast. Here was somebody to hang onto. Shirley filled not only the girlfriend need for me but in a way the mother and the parent need as well, and I filled those same needs for her. One day she was just there and she stepped into this big void in my life and filled it and kept filling it. To this day, I don't know what I would have done without her.

We were more or less immediately inseparable. We ate lunch together, we went to movies and dances on the weekends, we both sang in the school choir (the only class we had together). She lived across town, on the north side of Chula Vista, and I'd ride the bus as far as it would take me and then walk the rest of the way to see her.

Ours wasn't the only romance going on. My mother had been seeing a man, Ray Williams, and soon after I met Shirley, she informed me that she and Ray had decided to get married. Ray had a son from a previous marriage but he didn't live with his dad, so it would be just the three of us. There was no honeymoon or big wedding party. They got married and Ray moved in, simple as that. The new arrangement didn't last for long, though. Ray worked for General Electric and soon after the marriage the company transferred him to Ontario, just outside Los Angeles. My mother arranged with the phone company for her own transfer to the Los Angeles area—she had plenty of seniority by now—so she could be with her new husband.

There was no part of me that wanted to move. I was in my senior year of high school. I didn't want to leave my friends, I didn't want to leave the golf and baseball teams. And more than anything, I didn't want to leave Shirley. I told my mother I wasn't going and to be honest I wasn't surprised when she didn't put up much of a fuss. I had long been accustomed to being on my own and taking care of myself; she knew it and I knew it. When cousins on her side of the family who lived in Chula Vista agreed to take me in, she and Ray packed up their things and left for L.A. without me.

It was only a short while before the cousins also moved away. After that my friend Jack Peacock asked his parents if I could stay with them and they said yes. The Peacocks had a house just off the fifteenth tee of the San Diego Country Club. I wound up closer than ever to the golf course.

The fact that I was this hotshot golfer did not faze Shirley. She shrugged and called it a minor sport. She had a job at a dress shop on 3rd Avenue that kept her busy and I can't recall her ever watching me play golf in high school. But if we didn't talk much about golf, we talked about everything else, including marriage. Especially marriage.

Our mothers, both of them teenage brides, were appropriately alarmed. My mother asked me to wait until I was at least twenty-one to get married and Shirley's mother made her promise that she'd finish high school before she even thought about tying the knot. That gave them a two-year reprieve at least.

In the meantime, a man I caddied for at the club, Win Day, approached me about going to college at his alma mater, Notre Dame University. Mr. Day loved two things: golf and Notre Dame. He had been captain of the Notre Dame golf team for three years in the 1930s and made it to the quarterfinals of the U.S. Amateur twice. He was president of the Notre Dame Alumni Club in San Diego. He had watched me play golf and felt sure I could get a scholarship and make the team. I'd never been to South Bend, Indiana, but of course I'd heard about Notre Dame and its legendary football team. Our local college, San Diego State, was also interested in me. Gene Littler and Bud Holscher were already there. But I was flattered that a big-name school outside of California wanted me as well. Shirley and I attended an alumni reception in San Diego that amounted to a recruiting session and I said I would consider very seriously making Notre Dame my college of choice.

That summer the deal was clinched when San Diego junior golf boosters drove me to Lindbergh Field and put me on a plane for Chicago. I was entered in the Western Junior Amateur, a prestigious junior golf tournament held at the Notre Dame golf course. I shot under par in the qualifying and was co-medalist. I was really on my game that week, playing some of the best golf of my life, and was sure I was heading to the match-play finals when I stroked a 35-foot putt on the eighteenth green that was going straight at the cup. But it lipped out and I was eliminated in the semifinals. It was the day before my nineteenth birthday, and the last stroke I would ever hit as a junior golfer.

I met the Notre Dame golf coach, Father George Holdrieth, while I was there and he confirmed that I was welcome to come back in the fall and enroll in school and join the team. The weather was fine, the golf course was terrific, the campus was straight out of a movie set. What wasn't to like? They showed me the athletic dorm where I would stay, just a couple of club lengths from the cafeteria and the golf course. I returned to San Diego and told Shirley I'd made up my mind. I was going to play for Notre Dame. She was all for it. She said she would miss me but wanted me to go because she felt it was the best thing for me and for our future.

Anyone who has ever played golf with me knows my strong suit isn't waiting. I'm just not very good at being patient. One afternoon Shirley and I got on the city bus and took it to downtown San Diego. We got off and stopped at a little jewelry shop near the harbor, at a spot where the Horton Plaza mall would be built years later. I'd saved up forty-five dollars from caddying and dropped it on the counter and bought Shirley a diamond ring. That was it. My proposal. If I was going off to school in Indiana, I wanted to take care of business at home before I left.

Actually, a ring with a diamond somewhere in it is a better description. When we showed it to my mother she said, "Wait a minute, let me get my magnifying glass." But it didn't matter. Shirley said yes. We were engaged and we were going to be married. Some day. I just had to make it to twenty-one and Shirley had to get through two more years of high school.

All this stability was having a good effect on my golf game. I shot a 63 in competition, my lowest eighteen-hole score ever, at the Municipal Course in San Diego, and I finally won the tournament I wanted most, the San Diego County Amateur, with a 6 and 4 victory over Frank Morey, Jr. in the thirty-six hole final at Rancho Santa Fe.

In the fall I got on the train and reported to Notre Dame, where I finished third in an open tournament that September that included several veteran members of the Notre Dame golf team. My future teammates—or so I thought.

I settled into college life. I was on the athletic floor of Zahm Hall, the freshman dorm at Notre Dame. My roommate was a big guy, a football player. He was the hall monitor because he was tall enough that he could look in the transom windows and make sure everyone was accounted for at curfew. I met the guys on the golf team and went to the football office and had my picture taken for the yearbook.

But then I was introduced to an alien concept I'd only seen in movies and read about in books: winter. And not just winter. Midwest winter. It seemed like it arrived overnight. Suddenly I was fighting for survival on an alien, frozen planet. How did people manage? I'd seen snow before when I was living with my dad at the mining camp in California but I didn't have enough clothes with me to handle that Indiana cold that goes right through you.

I was two thousand miles from home, still an indifferent student on my best day, and I couldn't play golf until the greens thawed in the spring. Each day I would sit in my room and hit wedge shots at the wall until the plaster peeled off. I probably drove whoever was in the next room as crazy as I was. Plus I missed Shirley terribly. For the first time in my life I was homesick.

One morning in December I got up, threw my stuff in a bag and left. I just couldn't take it any longer. I went to the train station and bought a one-way ticket back to California. I didn't tell anyone, I just fled. It was all terribly immature. I'd made a mistake by coming and then I made a mistake by leaving the way I did. I never played an official round of golf for the Notre Dame golf team, never finished a single class, and squandered all my Fleming scholarship funds in the process. It was a colossal waste of time, money and energy. I wasn't the first freshman in his first term to come to the realization that college wasn't for him, but I lacked the discipline to see the situation through until the end of the semester. I'd never really learned discipline when I was young and now I was displaying that in spades. The only silver lining to the Notre Dame fiasco was that it taught me the importance of thinking things through before committing to them. I like to think I never again handled anything that poorly or impetuously.

Shirley got a jolt when she opened her door in Chula Vista and there I was. I hadn't told anyone I was coming back out of fear they would try to talk me out of it. But she welcomed me with open arms, as glad to see me as I was to see her. I made it clear I wasn't going to return to school. I'd definitely gotten college out of my system.

I quickly slipped back into my comfortable old routine, playing golf and caddying at the club, this time without any school to get in the way. But I knew that lifestyle couldn't last for long. While I was giving Notre Dame a try, a border dispute in Korea had progressed into full-fledged civil war, pitting the communists in the north against the freedom lovers in the south. The United States began sending troops to South Korea by the thousands. I was nineteen and a half years old, healthy as a horse, unmarried, and not going to school. Candidates for the draft didn't come any more prime than that.

Weighing my options, I decided my best alternative was to join the Navy. I didn't have far to go. I got on the same bus Shirley and I had taken to the jewelry store and got off a couple of stops farther on at the recruiting station in San Diego. I went inside and signed my name on the dotted line for a four-year commitment. Within the month, I was to report to basic training.

LIKE MY FRESHMAN YEAR AT Notre Dame, boot camp got cut short. But this time not because I went AWOL. When the Navy found out about my golf background they assigned me to Special Services—Navy talk for working at the base golf course, a nine-hole three-par facility called Sail Ho that was part of the San Diego Naval Training Center, a place where thousands of sailors got their basic training. In the mornings I'd take classes so I could satisfy my own basic training requirements and in the afternoon I'd report to the golf shop so those thousands of recruits could have a little R & R. We had a staff of several golf pros turned sailors and we sold gear out of the shop, kept the locker rooms straightened up, gave lessons to officers, enlisted men and their dependents, and took care of the driving range. We operated pretty much like any normal golf operation, except this one was owned and run by the United States Navy.

I was assigned a bunk in the barracks but I can't remember ever sleeping in it. There were three or four old couches at the lounge in the back of the golf shop and I'd just stay over and sleep in one of those. I would shower and change clothes in the locker room. I basically just moved in. Now my home literally was a golf course. In the evening, after the range was picked up, as soon as they played Taps, I'd get on the bus and ride to Chula Vista to see Shirley. I did that almost every night. It was usually quite late when I got back to the base and I'd grab my blanket and curl up on that couch in the Sail Ho lounge. I never had any trouble getting to sleep.

ONE NIGHT I TOOK SHIRLEY to the movies. There was a new film playing at the Vogue Theatre in Chula Vista I wanted us to see together.

The movie was "Follow the Sun." It was about Ben Hogan and his remarkable comeback from the head-on car wreck in 1949 that almost killed him. Glenn Ford played Ben Hogan, Anne Baxter played Valerie Hogan, Ben's wife. The main focus of the film was Hogan's inspirational recovery from a tragedy that could have easily ended not just his golf career but also his life. Through great determination he willed himself out of his wheelchair and back on the golf course. In the movie's climax, he's playing Sam Snead in a playoff at the 1950 Los Angeles Open less than a year after the accident. (Hollywood rushed so quickly to make the movie that it was shot before Hogan won the U.S. Open in a dramatic playoff six months later in June.)

But Shirley and I weren't focused on the car wreck. We were focused on what Ben and Valerie did *before* the car wreck. The movie showed how they first decided to travel the professional golf circuit together as a young married couple, moving each week to the next tournament, seeing the country from one end to the other. They barely had a dime between them, but they decided to go for it. "We'll start out in California and we'll follow the sun," Glenn Ford/Ben Hogan says to Anne Baxter/ Valerie Hogan.

When the movie ended and the lights came back up, I looked at Shirley. "That's us," I said. "That's our life."

Shirley said, "I can't wait."

BUT SHE DID WAIT. And for once so did I. She jumped into her final year of high school and I settled into the golf course version of a sailor's life—and saw "Follow the Sun" another three times by myself.

Shirley never could stand still. She practically ran the high school. She was editor of the yearbook and sang in the choir and graduated near the top of her class. Not long after her senior year began, the Navy reassigned her stepfather to a base in the Bay Area and just as I had decided during my senior year, she told her parents she didn't want to leave Chula Vista. They weren't surprised. She was, after all, engaged to be married. So she lived with her friend Janet Strasser that year. Shirley was as accustomed to being on her own as I was. Our lives were parallels in so many ways.

Shirley graduated on June 12. I turned twenty-one on June 24. Four days after that, on June 28, 1952, a Saturday, we were married. The ceremony was held in a little Naval base chapel on 32nd Street in San Diego, the site of so many sailor weddings during the war years—but not many involving two kids from just down the street. Shirley knew the chapel well. It was where she attended church on Sundays and where she sang in the choir.

John Schilling, a Methodist minister and the senior chaplain at the base, married us. My best man was Don Chase, the friend who'd double-dated with us when Shirley and I went on our first date. His date from that night, Betty, was one of Shirley's bridesmaids. Her maid of honor was Janet Strasser. Russ Bullen was another groomsman. Shirley's mother was there with her stepfather. Her father, Lindsey Franklin, came down from Washington to give her away. My mother was there with my stepfather but my father was not. When our mothers left with their husbands for their homes after the wedding, it was just the two of us.

I took some of my leave time and we rode the bus up the coast to Laguna Beach for our honeymoon. We rented a room at the Laguna Beach Hotel. After two nights we rode the bus to Hollywood to visit my mother, then made our way back and settled into our new home: a one-bedroom apartment about the size of a sand trap on 3rd and E Street in Chula Vista. Rent was $40 a month.

Shirley still had her job at the dress shop and I remained in the employ of Uncle Sam. I made $54.50 every two weeks plus $25 a month from Special Services for helping run the golf operation at Sail Ho. Win Day, the San Diego Country Club member who recruited me to Notre Dame, owned a finance company called Local Loan and went to bat for us and helped us finance our first purchase as a married couple, a 1941 Plymouth. (Obviously he carried no hard feelings about how the Notre Dame experiment worked out.)

We were broke, in debt, in love, and living the American dream. I had three years left on my deal with the Navy, but we knew we were just biding our time until we would follow the sun.

6

Navy Golf

7

Wearing my Navy letter sweater.

San Diego, California
June, 1951

When I joined the Navy I fully expected to sooner or later, and probably sooner, find myself on a troop ship bound for some far-off corner of the globe, most probably Korea.

But that never happened.

As it turned out, serving my country was very good for my golf game.

The Korean conflict had San Diego full to overflowing with young servicemen. Not only did the military want to give them ample outlets to relieve their stress and nervous energy by providing golf courses, driving ranges, tennis courts, gymnasiums and ball fields, but there was also the issue of bragging rights. No one ever accused the military of not being competitive. The Air Force, the Marines, the Army, the Navy—they all fielded teams that competed against each other in all sorts of sports.

So it was not that long after my assignment to work at the golf facility at the Naval Training Center that I was also ordered to report to the base golf team. My commanding officers decided that the best way I could defend my country, and the Navy, was with a 2-iron. And I heartily agreed.

I played with and against many excellent golfers while I was in the Navy. It was not unlike what would later be called a mini-tour. We practiced and competed on excellent golf courses. The Agua Caliente course, later to become the Tijuana Country Club, a fine layout located just across the border in Mexico, was one of our "home" courses. Another was Rancho Santa Fe in the north county, one of the top courses in Southern California. When I was stationed at the Coronado Naval Air Station, long before the bridge was built to the mainland, the way we got to Rancho Santa Fe was by taking the San Diego Ferry. During my four years of active duty in the United States Navy, it was the only time I boarded a ship.

In addition to military golf, I could also use my shore leave to play civilian golf in and around San Diego. I continued to participate in a number of events such as the Tournament of Champions that I was accustomed to playing in every year. And I got to play in the first PGA Tour event in San Diego when the San Diego Open made its debut in January of 1952 at the San Diego Country Club.

The Tour was growing and expanding and a stop in San Diego was added to the western swing before the pros moved on to Arizona.

The tournament managed to kick up a little controversy even before it started. To boost ticket sales, the organizers invited Joe Louis, the boxing champion who had become an accomplished amateur golfer after retiring from the ring, to play on a sponsor's exemption courtesy of the San Diego County Chevrolet dealers.

Hearing that Joe Louis was in the tournament prompted two top African-American golf professionals, Ted Rhodes and Bill Spiller, to send in their entries. But both were denied spots in the field because of the PGA Tour's Caucasian-only rule. It had been five years since Jackie Robinson broke the color barrier in baseball, but *Brown v. Board of Education* was still two years away and the PGA was still a separate-but-equal organization in 1952. Blacks had their own tour, the United Golf Association, and as far as the PGA was concerned, that's where they belonged. (The Caucasian-only rule wasn't rescinded until 1961 as the Civil Rights crusades gained momentum.)

When PGA Tour commissioner Horton Smith turned away Rhodes and Spiller there wasn't much public debate, but when he ruled that Joe Louis was also out—as a result of not letting in the other African-Americans—that set off a national protest. Suddenly, the brand new San Diego Open had more publicity than it wanted. On his coast-to-coast radio-TV broadcast, Walter Winchell declared, "If Joe Louis could carry a gun in the U.S. Army, then he certainly can carry a golf club in San Diego."

So they let Joe Louis back in, but, believe it or not, not Ted Rhodes and Bill Spiller. I always thought it was a shame that Rhodes and Spiller passed away before Tiger Woods came along and won six San Diego Opens (through 2011). They would have enjoyed seeing that.

But in January of '52 I had my own concerns to worry about, mainly playing alongside touring pros for the first time in my life. Would I hold up? Did I have the game for it? Did I even belong in the tournament?

It helped that it was being held at San Diego Country Club, my old stomping grounds. There wasn't a player in the field who knew the course like I knew it. But I was a twenty-year-old amateur wading into the big-time, playing against people who did this for a living. My concern was sheer survival.

The PGA toughened the course by growing out the rough and lengthening some of the tees and I started shaky with an opening round of 75, three over par. The next day I improved slightly to 74 for a thirty-six-hole total of 149. Not great, but good enough to make the cut while dozens—including Joe Louis—did not. In my first PGA Tour event I lived to see the weekend.

I shot even-par 72 on Saturday and closed with 70 on Sunday. I was moving in the right direction. My 291 total put me in twenty-eighth place. If I'd been a pro I wouldn't have won any money. Lew Worsham and Harry Dee tied for twenty-sixth place and each got $25, last-place money. Everyone after that went away empty-handed. Pro golf was a tough business in 1952.

Ted Kroll, a man I would get to know very well a few years later, shot 276 to win by three strokes over Jimmy Demaret and collect $2,000 for first place.

I was second low amateur, behind my old friend and nemesis, Gene Littler, ever the pride of San Diego, who tied for seventh overall at 284. Gene, who like me had joined the Navy and was stationed in San Diego, where he was also playing plenty of Navy golf, would have won $426.67—two months' Navy pay—if he'd been playing as a professional and not as a lowly seaman.

A year later, Littler and I were both still swabbing decks, in a manner of speaking, and got another crack at the pros when the San Diego

Open returned for year two, still at the friendly confines of the San Diego Country Club.

This time Gene almost won, finishing tied for fourth at nine-under par 279, five shots behind the winner, Tommy Bolt, a man who had a swing every bit as sweet as Gene's. After rounds of 72-69-70 I was tied for eleventh place going into the final eighteen, but I closed with a 78 and a 289 total for thirty-first place. Again, I was second low amateur, behind Littler, and again, just out of reach of the pro money. But there was no calculating the value of the experience of playing against bona fide PGA Tour professionals without the added pressure of needing to make a check.

AFTER THAT, GENE AND I both qualified to play in the 1953 United States Amateur, held that year at the Oklahoma City Golf and Country Club. To get away for the week, we were able to secure a TAD assignment from the Navy—Temporary Additional Orders. We reported to the Navy recruiter in Oklahoma City and he signed our papers so we could be declared officially on-duty while we competed in the National Amateur.

I opened against Ted Roden of Odessa, Texas, and advanced fairly comfortably with a 4 and 3 victory. Then I met another Texan, Bobby Moncrief from Houston. He was a member of the University of Texas golf team. He made putts from everywhere to go 2-up on the opening nine and then, on the tenth hole, a horseshoe-shaped five par, he drove first and hit into the right rough. I drove down the center and hit my second shot right up the middle in front of the green. By now he'd hit into the trees and then into the trees again. He couldn't see the green on his fourth shot. He hit the ball completely blind and shouted up to me, "Do you see it? Do you see it?" I watched as his ball hit the green and ran straight into the hole. Yeah, I shouted back, I saw it. Moncrief beat me and I was eliminated from the U.S. Amateur.

Gene, meanwhile, was having no such difficulties. He sailed through every round. In the thirty-six-hole final he and his opponent, Dale Morey of North Carolina, were tied going into the last hole, where Gene sank a birdie putt to win the 1953 U.S. Amateur. The pride of San Diego was now the pride of America.

It capped quite a year for Gene. That summer he played on the U.S. amateur team that defeated Great Britain at the Walker Cup matches in Massachusetts. He also won both the California Open and the California Amateur, and, for good measure, he won the California Inter-Service championship in a playoff. I have personal knowledge of that because the playoff was against me. The tournament was held in Merced, California, and included golfers from all branches of the service stationed in the state. Gene and I had gotten rid of everyone else by the end of seventy-two holes, necessitating sudden death. Gene won with a par three on the fourth extra hole.

To cap one of the greatest runs by an amateur since the days of Bobby Jones, Gene came back home and beat the pros in the 1954 San Diego Open at Rancho Santa Fe. It was only the second time in PGA Tour history that an amateur won a tournament, and he made it look effortless. He won by four shots. (Once again, I was second low amateur.) If Gene had been a professional he'd have made $2,400. As it was, he collected a trophy and a handshake.

But his future was set. Not long after that, Gene succeeded in getting an early release from the Navy because of a persistent hay fever condition. The next day, to the surprise of no one, he announced he was turning pro and that he and his wife Shirley and their young son would be heading out to try their luck on the PGA Tour. He already had a sponsor, the Thunderbird Golf Club in Palm Springs, California.

I WAS ALSO ON THE move with my Shirley. With our combined incomes, such as they were, we upgraded from our first apartment in Chula Vista to a slightly roomier place down the street. It felt like we'd moved into the Taj Mahal. That's one advantage to starting small and moving up— you're always pleased by comparison. A short while later we moved yet again when the Navy finally decided to transfer me. After twenty-six months at the Naval Training Center, I was ordered all the way to the other end of San Diego Bay.

As always, golf was the reason. The Navy had set up a huge circular radio antenna at the communications station on Imperial Beach, just up the coast from the Mexican border at the southern tip of the Coronado strand, and Captain Tom Kurtz wanted me to build a driving range next to the antenna.

Shirley and I moved into base housing right on the beach. When we looked out our front window, we could watch the waves break practically underneath our feet. I had the Seabees at my command. Here I was, a lowly Seaman, telling them how to break ground and build a driving range. Once it was finished, I was in charge of the entire operation, dispensing range balls, giving lessons, and otherwise keeping the place ship-shape. When the captain came by, he'd visit the driving range first before he inspected the facility. He'd say, "Billy, get the balls ready. I'm coming back for a lesson." When I wasn't running the range, I played on the station's golf team.

By APRIL OF THE FOLLOWING year, a piece of very good news made me decide to leave my days as an amateur golfer behind forever. Shirley's doctor informed us she was pregnant. Turning professional would mean the end of any hopes of winning the U.S. Amateur or playing on the Walker Cup team, a very big deal back then. But instead of winning golf balls and head covers at local tournaments I could start taking home cash to provide for my growing family. Also, as a junior player and now as a member of the military I was used to playing courses all over San Diego County without having to pay green fees. With my Navy days drawing to a close, that was about to change. And professionals didn't pay green fees.

I won the San Diego County Open in my first tournament as a pro and added $150 to the family budget. I had won the same tournament the year before as an amateur and gone home with a pair of shoes from the golf shop. I decided I could get used to playing for pay.

After eleven months at the communications station I was transferred to the Naval Air Station in an area known as North Island on the far northwest end of Coronado. Shirley and I moved again, to a small house trailer we purchased on Imperial Beach. The trailer was so small it didn't have a bathroom. We used the facilities in the trailer park. At North Island I was assigned, as usual, to the golf operation, helping run the little nine-hole short course there and a driving range.

I could have hit at least a million balls in the service, and you'd think I would have, running all those driving ranges. But I didn't come close. I liked to play golf, the more holes the better, I never got tired of it, and I always spent time on my short game, my putting and chipping, but I was never one to spend a lot of time on the practice tee, incessantly beating balls. No one ever accused me of being a range rat. I used to tell people it was because I was afraid I might find something wrong with my swing. I was being funny, but there was some truth in that. Sometimes you can over-analyze and do more harm than good on the practice tee.

It was on the range at North Island that I first met Don Collett, a man who would become a cherished friend and have a great influence on my life.

Don *was* a range rat. He liked to hit balls during his lunch hour. He was a chief petty officer who worked in the journalism office and was captain of the Naval Air Skyraider golf team at North Island. We wound up teaming together in a lot of matches and never lost one of them. Don was an excellent all-around athlete. He had grown up in Utah and was on his way to play basketball at Utah State University when he was drafted toward the end of World War II. He wound up all-Navy in three sports: tennis, basketball and golf, a game he didn't take up until he was in the service. Ten years later, when I met him, he was a scratch golfer, and our coach, Glen Pritchett, appointed him captain of our eight-man team.

Of the many teams I was part of in the Navy, the Skyraiders was the most dominating. Bob Goetz, Leo Marchell, Bill Blanton, Charley

Bartlett, Glen Pritchett, Bill Bisdorf and Collett were my teammates and in the year we played together, we never lost a tournament, and we faced some tough competition. The Marines at Camp Pendleton had Tony Lema, the future British Open champion, on their team. The first time we played them was at Rancho Santa Fe, our home course, and we beat them pretty good. They said, just wait until you come to Camp Pendleton. A few weeks later we went to Pendleton for the rematch. One of our players shot 73, one shot 71—and the other six all shot in the 60s. The Marines didn't win a single point.

ALL GOOD THINGS MUST COME to an end, and the government-funded golf idyll I enjoyed courtesy of the United States Navy was no exception.

It all changed because of Billy Martin, the New York Yankees baseball player.

Martin had been drafted into the Army and, like many athletes, spent most of his time in the service playing sports. That wasn't the problem. The problem was that the newspapers picked up on what he was doing and wrote a story about Billy Martin getting preferential treatment. As a result he was assigned to regular duty, and so were a lot of other so-called pampered athletes.

With a little over six months to go in my four-year commitment, I was relieved of my golf duties at the driving range and transferred to the personnel office of FASRONFOUR, the Fleet Aircraft Carrier Service Unit, also located at North Island Naval Air Station. When an aircraft came into port it was my job to make sure everyone on board was issued proper identification credentials. I closed out my Navy career as a clerk.

BY THIS TIME OUR DAUGHTER Linda was already starting to crawl. She had been born on August 11, 1954 in the Chula Vista Hospital. We named her after the Linda Vista plateau that overlooks Mission Valley. Like all new parents, we suddenly had a different perspective, one that revolved around this tiny person you had no idea could absorb so much love—or concern. I'd worried before about how I was going to take care of my family, now I was really worried. I was about to leave the Navy and the steady, if skimpy, pay, and I had to do something to make a living. Both Shirley and I wanted that something to be golf, but the question was whether it was a path we could honestly afford.

Playing on the PGA Tour wasn't an inexpensive proposition. You couldn't just show up. There were a number of conditions. First, you had to have three professionals from your PGA section vouch for you by declaring that you were a qualified player and had the game to compete on Tour. Second, you needed to submit proof that you had a reserve of at least $5,000 in the bank—indicating that you could pay your expenses and not mar the image of the Tour by being a deadbeat. Third, once you were conditionally approved, you had to serve a six-month apprentice period during which time you could play in tournaments but couldn't make any money. If you didn't have a club to sponsor you, you needed to have your own nest egg until you got established.

Shirley and I weren't even close to having enough money to get started. We were still paying off our 1941 Plymouth and we had a baby to feed. The reality was that we had to save some money first. Through the Navy grapevine I heard that Rohr Aircraft, a big San Diego company that made airplane parts, was paying good money for people making rivets on the assembly line. I went to their offices and filled out a job application. I wrote on the application that I would be available as soon as I left the Navy. My plan was to get my seed money for the Tour by punching rivets.

One afternoon I started to tell Don Collett about my rivet-making idea. Don, who knew my golf game as well as anyone, held up his hand and stopped me. He said he was sure I could make it on the Tour, and in his opinion I shouldn't delay getting out there.

"I know a couple of fellas," he said.

A few days later Don and I met the "fellas," Dick Haas and Russ Corey, at San Diego Country Club. Dick was a Lincoln-Mercury car dealer in National City and Russ was a local building contractor. The four of us played a round of golf together. It was more or less an audition. I shot two-under 70 and holed a shot out of a bunker. I guess that and Don's talking convinced them I was worth the gamble. After the round we were in the grill, having a Coke, when Russ turned to me and said, "Billy, what's it going to take to put you on the Tour?"

I turned to Don, my new business manager, and said, "Well, what's it going to take?"

Don took a napkin and wrote what we figured I'd need to make it: a car, a house trailer, and $650 a month for expenses, plus a deposit in the bank to satisfy the PGA's minimum balance requirement.

Haas and Corey agreed to front the car, the trailer and the money and give me three years to pay it back—an investment that amounted to about thirty thousand dollars. In the meantime, they would get thirty percent of everything I won.

I looked at the napkin, then at Don, then at Dick and Russ. I knew it wasn't a great contract. I was giving away almost a third of my winnings and I had to pay everything back in a fairly short amount of time. But Dick and Russ were taking a huge risk. They had no collateral other than my golf game, and I knew it was the only way I could go on Tour instead of staying in San Diego and making rivets. Before any of us had a chance to think too long and hard, we shook on it.

Dick and Russ took the napkin and gave it to their attorney, who drew up a legal agreement that I signed. They would provide me with a new twenty-eight foot Spartan house trailer, a new 1955 Buick Road-master car to pull it, and deposit money in the bank to pay for gas, food, car repairs, anything else I needed, and they would also cover the security deposit.

I had my ticket out of San Diego.

NOT EVERYONE THOUGHT IT WAS a good idea. Traveling the country and playing golf was a risky way to make a living. Starting out in debt made it that much riskier. Only a handful on Tour made more than fifteen thousand dollars a year—a considerable sum at the time, but a sum considered to be what you needed to clear expenses and break even.

I'd enjoyed success locally, both as an amateur and as a professional, but I hadn't won any national titles as a junior and some considered my lack of practice time on the range as an indication of a poor work ethic. Besides that, no one looked at me and saw a lean, trim Ben Hogan. I was 5-foot-11 and weighed 215 pounds. I enjoyed hamburgers and milkshakes. Most of the newspaper stories used an adjective like "burly" or "stout" or "husky" to describe me. I was always some variation of "Big-bellied Billy Casper."

In short, there were those who thought I was fat and lazy.

And then there were the inevitable comparisons to Gene Littler. Was there room for two of us from San Diego on Tour? Would I always be in his shadow? It was like having a big brother you were never going to measure up to.

Shortly after I'd struck the deal, Bob Hummel, the head pro at San Diego Country Club, said to Don Collett: "You arranged for Billy Casper to go on the Tour? He couldn't carry Gene Littler's shoes."

Just before heading out, I played in the final round of the San Diego County Open with Paul Runyan, the head pro at La Jolla Country Club and Gene Littler's longtime mentor. In his younger years, Runyan had been a dominant player on Tour. He was leading money winner in 1934 and won twenty-nine tournaments in his career, including two PGA Championships. He was considered a keen judge of talent and what it took to survive on the pro Tour. After we played together, he was asked what he thought of my chances of making it. Word circled back to me what he said: "I don't know why Casper's going on Tour. With his game, he'll starve to death. Why doesn't he go out and get a nice job selling insurance?"

On that note, I was off.

7

The Tour

8

The Spartan trailer, Buick Roadmaster,
Shirley, Linda and me, summer of 1955.

Portland, Oregon
June 23, 1955

We kept the ocean on our left and the country on our right as we departed Chula Vista and headed up the coast. There was no brass band, no bon voyage party, no headlines in the newspaper announcing the Caspers were setting out to join the professional golf Tour. It was just the four of us: me, Shirley, ten-month-old Linda, who sat in the back in a pre-car seat contraption called a porta-crib, and Pipper, our little black-and-white mutt dog. We didn't wear seat belts. We didn't have seat belts. This was 1955.

Shirley had spent weeks provisioning the expedition. There was food and bedding in the trailer cupboards, all our clothes, a toolbox, a flashlight, a road atlas of the United States, my golf clubs, everything we owned and everything we thought we would need to survive on the road. We left nothing behind. In 1955 there was no such thing as a storage unit, either.

The first time we stopped we realized what we didn't have: something to keep the cupboards secured. Most trailers in those days were parked, not towed around the country. Pots and pans and sugar and flour and all sorts of other stuff had spilled everywhere. We jerry-rigged some latches for the cabinets and kept on going.

Our new home was twenty-eight feet, six inches long, and made by the Spartan Aircraft Company of Tulsa, Oklahoma. Their motto: "You may not find a house in every place you roam—but when you own a Spartan you always have a home." Our traveling Spartan home had air conditioning, a fully operational kitchen—the appliances ran on propane—and a bedroom so small it was best to back into it. At that it was an upgrade. Our house on wheels was larger than the trailer we left behind in Imperial Beach. And this one also had an indoor bathroom.

WE SPENT THE FIRST NIGHT at a trailer park somewhere in central California. The next day we drove into San Francisco, where the U.S. Open was being played at The Olympic Club. We didn't stop, or even slow down. Earlier in the spring I had tried to make it into the Open field at a sectional qualifying tournament in Los Angeles, but missed by a stroke. Neither the Open nor The Olympic Club, which was hosting the National Championship for the first time, figured in our plans. Portland, Oregon, was our destination, site of the Western Open, the next scheduled stop on the PGA Tour.

Except for the U.S. Open, the Western Open is America's oldest golf tournament. It dates back to 1899, when a Scotsman, Willie Smith, won the first one in a place named, appropriately, Golf, Illinois. Smith also won the U.S. Open that year, the fifth person to hoist the trophy since the National Championship began in 1895. Like the U.S. Open, the Western moved around to a different course each year, mostly in Illinois, Ohio, Michigan and Wisconsin—back when the Midwest was considered the West. After 1940 the tournament branched out to the real West until it made it to the Portland Golf Club in 1955 for the one and only time it was ever played in Oregon. (In 1962 the Western Open returned to the Chicago area, where it remains to this day.) In its early years the Western was regarded as a "major" championship, one of a relatively few annual summer events and always a big draw for spectators and players. Into the 1950s it still loosely carried that distinction and always attracted a strong field. I wasn't starting off easy.

WE PULLED INTO A TRAILER park near downtown Portland on Sunday, about the same time Jack Fleck was defeating Ben Hogan in their eighteen-hole playoff to decide the U.S. Open in San Francisco.

Fleck and Hogan didn't come along to Portland, but almost everyone else who played in the Open did, including Sam Snead, Tommy Bolt and Julius Boros, the three players who finished behind Fleck and Hogan. Gene Littler and Bud Holscher, my friends from junior golf, had also played in the Open, where they distinguished themselves by placing in the top twenty. Holscher finished seventh and Littler fifteenth. They pulled their trailers into Portland on Monday and joined Shirley and me in the trailer park.

By that time I'd already played my first practice round at Portland Golf Club. Early Monday morning I got to the course and started preparing for my first official tournament as a member of the PGA Tour. (In January, while I was still in the Navy, I began my six-month "income-prohibited" probationary period when I played in the Brawley Open in Brawley, California, a secondary PGA Tour event that attracted pros who weren't invited to the Thunderbird Invitational in nearby Palm Springs. I shot 279 and placed twenty-fourth, a couple of shots behind another Tour rookie serving out his probation named Arnold Daniel Palmer. Neither of us left with a penny.)

The PGA Tour wasn't new in 1955, or even particularly young, but in many ways it was just starting to grow up. The PGA had been around since 1916, when the Professional Golfers' Association of America was organized back when being called a "professional" golfer wasn't much of a compliment and amateurs who played for cups and trophies, not for filthy lucre, enjoyed a much higher status. The PGA was formed in an attempt to bring dignity and unity to the profession as well as to better organize the tournaments where the pros competed for money. Almost all of these tournaments were held in the South in the wintertime when the pros could get away from their club jobs.

In the 1920s a "tour" of these winter tournaments began to take shape and by the 1930s a handful of summer events, beyond the U.S. Open, PGA Championship and Western Open, started to also be added to the calendar. Purses were small. The first professional stars, Walter Hagen and Gene Sarazen, used the recurring annual events as a springboard into exhibitions, where the real money was. One year, Hagen didn't bother to play in the PGA Championship at all because he had a better offer from an exhibition—and he was the PGA's four-time defending champion. The situation had changed, but not much, by the time Sam Snead, Byron Nelson and Ben Hogan came along to headline the Tour in the 1930s and 1940s. They used the regular tournaments to make a name for themselves and to wrangle representation deals with top country clubs, but still made most of their money from exhibitions.

After World War II a schedule resembling the modern PGA Tour emerged. By the early 1950s, the Tour had what might be considered a full calendar, winter and summer, although many top pros still returned to their club jobs in the summer.

Prize money increased as promoters like Illinois businessman George May came along. May was the first to capitalize on that new sensation sweeping the nation—television. At his "World Championship" at the Tam O'Shanter course outside Chicago, he was the first to offer $50,000 for first prize, and in 1953 he *paid* to have the event televised nationally. The following year, the U.S. Open was on national television for the first time, no fee required.

LARGELY OBLIVIOUS TO MOST OF it, I merged into all this history on June 23, 1955, opening day of the Western Open and a day before my twenty-fourth birthday.

Players from the days when the tour started to become a Tour were still around, guys like Sam Snead, Jimmy Demaret, Lloyd Mangrum, Henry Picard, George Fazio, Johnny Revolta, Johnny Palmer, Lew Worsham, and, occasionally, Hogan himself. Even Walter Hagen, who was sixty-two years old in 1955, and Gene Sarazen, fifty-three, could still be seen from time to time making a guest appearance.

But there was also a wave of new young players like Littler, Holscher, Bob Rosburg and myself. None of us had a club pro job to go back to even if we wanted. We were professional golfers, as opposed to golf professionals; people who played tournament golf for a living or bust. More and more players in their twenties were leaving amateur golf behind and turning pro. At Portland, three of the last four U.S. Amateur champions were in the field as new professionals: Billy Maxwell, Littler and Arnold Palmer.

I SHOULD HAVE BEEN PETRIFIED. I was green, young, a new father, a thousand miles from home, spending somebody else's money, driving a two-thousand-dollar car, pulling a four-thousand-dollar trailer, neither of which I had paid for, and the only chance I had of making it was by consistently outplaying very talented, very competitive people trying to do the same thing.

But for some reason I wasn't petrified. Shirley and I have often reflected on why we were so sure we were going to make it when there were so many reasons to think we wouldn't. Part of it was because we were young and naïve, but also we were used to making it on our own and we both knew there was no room for negative thinking. The trailer was too small. Our future had no room for it.

Nonetheless, I was a rookie, the new guy, totally unproven and unknown. If I doubted where I stood it soon became obvious when I went to the tournament desk to register and was assigned my caddy, a twelve-year-old kid named Eddie Ellis. Eddie's dad was Elan Ellis, one of Portland's biggest golf supporters who I would get to know later on as part of a group of businessmen promoting the Portland Open that called themselves the "Trembling Twenty." As I would discover, one of the great benefits of the Tour was the people you were able to meet and form lifelong friendships with. Decades later, in 2007, when the Portland Golf Club commemorated the sixtieth anniversary of the playing of the Ryder Cup there in 1947, none other than Eddie Ellis, my first caddy, called and asked if I would speak at the event.

But in 1955, our future was all in front of us, as they say, and we had a few kinks to work out.

Eddie, like most twelve-year-olds, was fascinated by the water, and all he was interested in doing was getting down around the stream that ran through the course. I can remember what happened next as though it were yesterday. "Eddie," I warned him, "don't take the bag down with you or everything's going in." Sure enough, on the eighth hole, a par three, he got too close to the edge and everything did go in—Eddie, the bag, the clubs, all of it. We had to pull him out and dry him and the clubs off with a towel as best we could. In the first round of my first tournament my caddy fell in the creek.

Maybe the distraction was just what I needed. I opened with an even par 72. On the second day I went under par with a 71. It wasn't the best round of the day or even close to it—Arnold Palmer shot 66 after opening with 76—but it was steady enough for sixteenth place among a starting field of 156 players. The cut line was 149, five over par, and I qualified along with sixty-eight others to stick around and play the weekend.

I followed with another 72 on Saturday in a group with Carl Johnson and Celestino "Tino" Tugot, the national champion of the Philippines. For the final round I was paired with two Als: Al Mengert, runnerup in the 1952 U.S. Amateur and sixteenth at the U.S. Open the previous week, and Al Besselink, a veteran who'd won twice on Tour. I closed with 72 while Besselink shot 76 and Mengert 75.

Outscoring players with the credentials of the two Als and holding up under the Sunday pressure did wonders for my confidence. I didn't win the tournament. Cary Middlecoff, the Masters champion that year, shot 63 in the final round, tying the course record set by Ben Hogan in the 1947 Ryder Cup, and won by two strokes over Mike Souchak. I finished tied for thirtieth, last place money (back then you could make it to the weekend and still wind up playing for nothing; it wouldn't be until the late 1960s that it became standard that everyone who made the cut made a check). Three of us—Tommy Bolt, Lawson Little and me—split $100. I won $33.33. Ray O'Brien, the PGA Tour's tournament director, handed me my check about a week later.

I would have higher finishes and bigger paydays in my career. I later won three Portland Opens and the 1969 Alcan in Portland, and I would win the Western Open four times in and around Chicago. But none were any more psychologically important than that first one. I came away from Portland knowing I could play with these guys. They just knew a little bit more about how to score than I did. And that was something I was sure I could learn.

Back in town, we hooked up the trailers. Shirley, Linda and I joined a caravan that included Gene and Shirley Littler and Bud and Bonnie Holscher. We all left Portland money ahead. Gene won $1,300 for finishing third and Bud tied Sam Snead for thirteenth place and collected $341.66.

The next tournament was across the border in Canada, the British Columbia Open in Vancouver. After that we were scheduled to play in St. Paul, Minnesota. We drove east to Spokane, Washington, left our wives and trailers there, and caught a plane to Vancouver. I tied for sixteenth place and flew back with $220. Then we drove 1,200 miles to St. Paul, arriving just in time for the start of the tournament. By Sunday afternoon I had tied for thirtieth place, last place money again. There were four of us this time so when the hundred dollars was divided up I got $25. I wasn't getting rich by any means, but I hadn't missed a cut or a check, and I could say I was making a living.

WE SAW A LOT OF America that year, almost all of it on two-lane roads. In 1955, the interstate highway system was just being organized. Freeways and seventy-mile-an-hour speed limits were still around the corner. Something else that we now take for granted but was yet to catch on, Shirley would be the first to tell you, was disposable diapers.

Gas was twenty-nine cents a gallon and that V8 Buick drank plenty of it. Going downhill was great but going uphill we'd slow down to twenty-five or thirty miles an hour. Overall, we didn't average more than five miles to the gallon.

Still, it was the way to go on the PGA Tour in 1955, particularly for married players. Arnold and Winnie Palmer were newly married and they towed a trailer that year, as did veterans like Doug Ford and Tommy Bolt and their wives. We often stayed at the same trailer park when we got to the tournament site. Along the way Shirley and I stopped mostly at truck stops, because they didn't cost anything. We'd pull in and park right next to the truckers. Such was the glamorous life of a touring golf pro in 1955.

WE MANAGED TO AVOID ANY serious injury and mechanical problems that first year, although on our way to the Canadian Open it rained so hard I failed to notice an abrupt dip in the road and bounced the trailer so hard it severed the bolt off the hitch. When we got to Toronto there was no way to unhitch the trailer from the car. The people running the tournament let us park on the grass next to the clubhouse, but it was three days before we could get a welder to come out to the course and replace the bolt. Shirley had to hitch a ride or borrow someone's car when she needed something from town.

Arnold Palmer heated up that week and went twenty-three strokes under par to win by four shots—the first victory of his PGA Tour career (and the lowest he would ever go under par). I finished at eleven-under, a distant twelve shots behind. But I had a breakthrough of my own, making it into the top ten for the first time. My tenth place finish was worth $327.15—enough to pay the welder and make it to Quebec the following week for the Labatt Open, where I placed sixth, my highest finish of the season, good for $1,100. Gene Littler won the tournament, his fourth title of the year.

Then, before we knew it, it was over. That half-a-season seemed to fly by. The Tour's last stop was at the Eastern Open in Baltimore. Frank Stranahan won. I tied for twenty-sixth place and received a final check for $120.00—just enough to get the Buick back to San Diego.

It was early November by now. Shirley's mother called with news that the Navy had assigned Shirley's stepfather to the Philippines, so Shirley got on a plane with Linda and flew to San Francisco to see her mother and send them off. That left Pipper and me on the East Coast. We piled into the car, pointed it west, and drove across America. I knew how tall that trailer was because in Alabama I drove under a highway overpass that said twelve feet six inches and I just scraped the top of the ventilation unit. It might have been twelve-six and a half inches going in, but it was twelve-six coming out.

There's no rushing it when you're pulling a twenty-eight foot trailer and freeways haven't yet been invented. I must have hit a thousand stop-lights on my way back home. As the days passed I had plenty of time to reflect on all that I'd experienced in four and a half months. I'd played in fourteen straight events on the PGA Tour, made every cut, won money in thirteen of them, and circumnavigated the country. I finished with exactly $3,243.82 in winnings, fifty-eighth on the money list. (Julius Boros won the money title at $63,121.55, most of that a result of the $50,000 he won at George May's World Championship.)

With their thirty percent cut, my sponsors got $976.20—and I still owed them $14,000 for the car, the trailer and the monthly expenses I'd been advanced. I hadn't come close to breaking even. I was still deeply in debt. But I felt like I'd already won the lottery. I'd been able to play tournament golf from one side of the continent to the other, competing against the best players in the game at the top golf courses of the day. I couldn't think of anything I'd rather be doing.

Near the end of the trip I drove through the southern part of New Mexico, just below Silver City, where I first hit a golf ball in my grandfather's pasture when I was four years old. Twenty years had passed since then. My grandfather was no longer there. He died when I was still a teenager from a number of weight-related health issues. My grandmother had moved to Albuquerque. There was no reason to take a detour and go back; not a soul remained at the old homestead. The three golf holes my dad carved out of the farmland had to be long gone by now, reclaimed by the red ants. But here I was, still chasing the little white ball; chasing it over the finest fairways in North America, and wanting nothing more out of life than to keep chasing it. I thought about that as the Roadmaster strained to get the trailer over one more hill. I thought about it all the way to San Diego.

8

Breakthrough

Clutching the hardware that came with my first PGA Tour
win at the 1956 Labatt Open in Quebec.

Quebec, Canada
July 16, 1956

On the same day I received the best golf tip of my life I also won for the first time on the PGA Tour. It was no coincidence.

The tip was five words long: *Better hit your straight club.*

I was standing on the twelfth tee of the Royal Quebec Golf Club in Boischatel, Quebec, Canada, playing in the Labatt Open, a tournament sponsored by a Canadian brewery that for some reason was especially generous to golfers from southern California. Bud Holscher and Gene Littler were the past two champions. Now, after opening with rounds of 68-68-67, I had a comfortable lead with seven holes remaining.

My playing partners in the final round were Al Besselink and Ted Kroll, two Tour veterans.

It was Kroll who made the comment about the straight club after I hooked my drive into the rough off the twelfth fairway.

I looked over at Ted as I picked up my tee.

"Billy, it looks like you can win this tournament," he said, "but on the last few holes the fairways are very narrow and more than anything you need to keep the ball in play. Better hit your straight club."

There was no elaboration. Ted Kroll, who would finish the 1956 season as the Tour's leading money winner, was twelve years older than I was, a no-nonsense stocky former Army sergeant who had been awarded three purple hearts in World War II. He was not the nurturing type.

Three holes later I stood on the fifteenth tee, took out my driver, got my hips too far forward and blocked the shot way to the right. The ball rattled around in the pine trees until it disappeared from sight. Ted didn't say anything, just shot me a look. I got the point. On the last three holes I left the driver in the bag and teed off with my 2-iron. That was my straight club. I hit the last three fairways dead center, made three pars, shot one-under 71 and collected my first victory on Tour by two strokes over Jimmy Demaret. To this day I'm not sure if Ted was trying to help me or if he was giving me the needle, but if he was I was too young to know it.

I know I'll never forget what he said. His advice allowed me to break through the invisible barrier that separates playing from winning.

IT HAD TAKEN A FULL year to get there. The Labatt Open win came halfway through the 1956 season, just days after Shirley and I marked our first anniversary on Tour. The quest had been almost nonstop and involved no end of trial and error. I learned firsthand what it means to pay your dues, and the importance of laying a foundation. The first tournament win was set up by all the tournaments that preceded it that I didn't win.

We had been able to take most of November and December off, basically just Thanksgiving and Christmas, once we returned home in 1955. We continued to live in the trailer but gave it a well-deserved rest by putting it in a mobile home park in National City, just north of Chula Vista. George Bigham, another touring pro, and his wife Bonnie pulled their trailer near ours. Gene and Shirley Littler and Don and Monica Whitt—Don was a friend from the Navy also giving the Tour a try—parked their trailers in mobile parks elsewhere in the county. The golf pros were home to roost.

While we were out on Tour, I'd told George about a girl I knew back home who could out-drive any of us if we weren't careful. He didn't believe me that a woman could hit as far off the tee as a male Tour professional, so when we got back to San Diego I arranged a game with her at San Diego Country Club.

On the first tee I introduced George to Mickey Wright.

I'd first met Mickey as a teenager when we were both involved in junior golf. She was four years younger than I was and could already hit the ball a mile. It was really unbelievable, watching a girl hit it as far as she did. And the rest of her game was just as strong.

She turned pro and joined the Ladies Tour in 1955, the same year I got started, and came back to San Diego to spend the winter. Mickey and I teamed up for several matches that December against Don Whitt and George Bigham, and we won more than our share. George became a quick believer. If he didn't get all of it—if any of us didn't get all of it—she would out-drive us every time.

She also went on to get her first Tour win in 1956—the first of her eighty-two LPGA victories, a list that included thirteen majors.

CHRISTMAS CAME EARLY WHEN Wilson Sporting Goods called in December with a sponsorship offer.

In exchange for agreeing to exclusively use their equipment, they offered $4,400, a set of Wilson Staff clubs, and all the Wilson Staff golf balls I needed. I must have thought it over for a good three seconds before agreeing. I made more money just by signing my name than I did by playing half of the season in 1955.

WITH THAT WE WERE OFF again, pulling the trailer up the coast for the winter Tour's first stop at the Los Angeles Open in early January.

Because of all the club pros taking their cold-weather breaks and coming out West to compete, I found that the winter Tour was considerably more crowded than the summer Tour. Even as a fully registered member of the PGA Tour you had to qualify in a Monday qualifier. But the odds were good. There were usually twenty to forty spots for maybe three times that many players. And you could avoid Monday qualifying completely by making the cut in the tournament, which automatically qualified you for the next Tour stop. Keep making cuts and you never had to play on Monday again. I realized very quickly that life on Tour got a lot easier if you didn't have to qualify every week. Even in the days when playing on Saturday and Sunday didn't guarantee a check, it was a great incentive to make the cut.

I shot 74 in the Monday qualifier at Wilshire Country Club, made the tournament field, then made the cut, and after that kept making cuts until it was summer and there were no more Monday qualifiers to worry about.

But if I had figured out how to survive on Tour, figuring out how to finish first in a tournament was a different matter entirely. As anyone who has played even a little bit of competitive golf knows, winning a golf tournament, any golf tournament, is one of the hardest things to do in sports. In any given tournament on Tour, 150 or more golfers, all of them perfectly capable of shooting par or better, start out with the exact same goal in their mind that you have in yours, and that's to win. And there is always only one first place. Every tournament is guaranteed to have one winner and by definition a hundred and something losers.

Each week I thought about getting that first win. When would it happen? Where would it happen? Would it ever happen?

THE FIRST TIME I HAD a legitimate chance to win on the PGA Tour was at the Carling Open in St. Louis early in the 1956 season. I had the lead going into the fifteenth hole at Sunrise Golf Club and got so excited I kept knocking the ball over the green. I shot two over on the last four holes and Dow Finsterwald passed me for the win. The $2,160 I received for second was the biggest check of my life, but I was disappointed with myself. The tournament had been mine for the taking, and I didn't take it.

I discovered that there's a different atmosphere when you're in contention in the final round. Everything slows down and speeds up at the same time, and the adrenaline you get from all that excitement can be both a blessing and a curse. You have to learn how to control the increased energy along with your emotions so you can embrace the pressure and play your normal game. In short, I realized that you have to prepare yourself to win.

Part of the problem was my driver. I'd always had a fast swing and as a result I tended to hit dive hooks off the tee if I wasn't careful, especially when the pressure was on and I got too quick. I was constantly forced to rely on my ability to chip and putt my way out of trouble. The short game was my long suit, but I was counting on it way too much.

Not long after St. Louis, I hit one too many wayward drives in a tournament in Chicago and paid for it by missing the cut. That turned out to be a blessing in disguise. With time on my hands, I called my friend Bill Ogden, the pro at the North Shore course across town, and asked him if I could come over and use his range. He said it was mine as long as I wanted.

I hit more practice balls that week than I'd hit the entire time I'd been on Tour.

I didn't take a lesson from anyone. I just went back to the fundamentals and worked on changing from a hook to a fade with my driver. That was my total goal. I can tell you I gave my Wilson Strata-bloc driver a real workout that week.

I kept my same grip but opened my stance and worked on a higher, more pronounced follow-through. It took a lot of time. I'd been swinging the old way for years and it's not easy training your muscles and your brain to do something even incrementally different.

But by the end of the week I could fade my drives.

I'd always hit my irons fairly straight, with just a slight draw, so that didn't change, and if I needed to hook a ball off the tee I used my 3-wood, but from then on I faded my driver. I'd aim at the left side of the fairway, hit it low and for some reason it would roll like mad once it hit the ground. I got more roll out of my fade than I ever got out of my hook. Bo Wininger called it a gorilla drive and the name caught on. Later on, *Golf Digest* did an article on my drives and dressed me up in a gorilla suit. I used that same fading drive, and that same Wilson Strata-bloc driver, for the next twelve years, until the shaft broke during a tournament in the Philippines (probably from the humidity.) I never found another driver I liked as well, or that could fade the ball like that one.

In June, my newly controlled fade off the tee helped me to a fourteenth place finish in my first U.S. Open, held that year at Oak Hill in Rochester, New York. That win qualified me for the Masters the next year.

A month after that I got the break-out win at the Labatt Open, when Ted Kroll taught me that sometimes it's better to leave the driver in the bag no matter which direction you hit it.

The win paid $5,000 and a month later I finished fourth in the Miller High Life Open—ironically, for a guy who didn't drink, the breweries were good to me that season—and a $2,200 payday. The money was finally rolling in almost as fast as it was going out.

By year's end I had competed in twenty-nine events, won my first tournament, finished in the top twenty-five twenty-six times, and collected $18,733.41 in official winnings for twelfth place on the PGA Tour money list. When Shirley and I packed up on the East Coast and towed the Spartan back home to San Diego we weren't out of debt yet, but we were getting there.

WE BACKED THE TRAILER INTO its familiar spot in the National City mobile park, but its days were numbered. On November 2, 1956, just after we returned, our son Billy was born. I was playing in an unofficial offseason event in Ontario, outside Los Angeles, when I got the news. I would have preferred to be there, of course, but the birth came without much warning. A neighbor in the trailer court rushed Shirley to the hospital and little Billy came close to being born on the hospital lawn. Elated when I got the news, I finished with two birdies on the last two holes of the tournament, then birdied the first hole to win in a sudden-death playoff over Charlie Sifford, who never knew what hit him.

We used the winnings to move our newly expanded family into a furnished apartment in Chula Vista. We turned in the trailer. Its days were done. We replaced it with a new tan Cadillac. For the Caspers, the motel era on the PGA Tour was about to begin.

IN 1957 I DOUBLED MY 1956 output and won twice on Tour, once because of putting and once in spite of it.

The first win came in February at the Phoenix Open. I was playing the final round with Lloyd Mangrum and Cary Middlecoff, two seasoned pros with three U.S. Opens and a Masters between them. On the first hole I rolled in a long putt for birdie. On the second hole I did it again. Mangrum turned to Middlecoff and said, "Well, let's go in, no one's going to win the tournament today other than Casper," and Middlecoff agreed with him. Those veterans had no idea what a comment like that from players of their caliber did for my confidence. The putter stayed hot all day and I ended up winning by three shots over Middlecoff and Mike Souchak.

Win number two came in April at the Kentucky Derby Open in Louisville when I three-putted the last two greens for consecutive bogeys. I had a big enough lead that I got away with it and won by one stroke over Peter Thomson, although I did my best to blow it.

But the most memorable moments of my second full year on Tour weren't my second and third career wins. I had two experiences in 1957 I'll never forget.

The first was playing in the Masters in Augusta, Georgia.

It's hard for me to believe now, but in April of 1957 I was totally unprepared for the impact the drive down Magnolia Lane would have on me. I knew about the Masters, of course, but until I experienced it firsthand I couldn't appreciate that this really was the cathedral of golf, run by the game's royalty.

Looking back, it's like a scene out of a movie. I turned off Washington Road, drove past the iconic magnolia trees to the Augusta National clubhouse, where I stepped out and was welcomed by the tournament founders, Bobby Jones and Clifford Roberts.

The Masters exceeded my every expectation. I'd never seen anything like it. The magnificent golf course. The way they treated the players. The way they ran the tournament. Even the fans—the Masters insists on calling them patrons—seemed somehow different. When I came on Tour I had three very distinct goals. The first was to win money, the second was to win a tournament, the third was to win the U.S. Open. Now, after experiencing the special aura that is Augusta, I had a fourth. Before I was through I wanted to win the Masters.

In my first attempt I finished twelve shots behind the winner, Doug Ford, but I placed sixteenth overall, earning entry into the next year's tournament by finishing in the top twenty-four.

THE SECOND UNFORGETTABLE EVENT CAME in late July in upstate New York where I played for the first time with Ben Hogan.

He was a bit past his prime by then. I was twenty-six years old, he was forty-five. But he was still Ben Hogan and still a giant. We were paired in a foursome in the Palm Beach Round Robin, an invitational for sixteen players. Every day for four days you played with a different foursome. For the first round I was paired with Fred Hawkins, Dow Finsterwald and Hogan. It was pure pleasure, watching Hogan negotiate his way around a golf course. He was cordial but not talkative, completely focused and all business, exactly as I expected and hoped. Hawkins and I both had the putter going that day; we ran in putts from everywhere. Fred wound up shooting 67, I shot 68, Hogan shot 70 and Finsterwald 71. As we were walking back to the clubhouse after the round, Hogan looked at Fred and me and, with that trademark icy glare, said, "If you guys couldn't putt I'd be buying hotdogs from you on the tenth tee."

The next morning, there was Mr. Hogan in the locker room, changing his shoes. I'd assumed (hoped) that his comment the day before had been a compliment. That assumption proved correct when he offered a cordial, "Good morning, how are you?" I answered, "Fine," after which he said, "Billy, come here please."

So I went over and sat down by my role model, the man I patterned my game after, the reason behind pretty much everything I did on the golf course.

He said, "Billy, how do you putt?"

"What?" I replied.

"Show me how you putt."

So I gave my idol a putting lesson.

It was almost unheard of, Hogan befriending a young guy on Tour, but he selected me to be one of his friends that day. Maybe it was because he saw something of himself in how I tried to play the game. But it was the beginning of a special relationship. From that day forward, he always had a kind word or encouraging comment when we met. I later played for him when he was captain of the Ryder Cup in 1967, another choice experience. He always said, "If you're coming through Fort Worth give me a call and we'll get together and have lunch." I never took him up on that. I wish I had.

IN MY THIRD FULL YEAR on the PGA Tour I won four times, had one of the wins later discredited because of Fidel Castro (or so I suspect), and discovered a new secret weapon.

Fishing.

The three wins that "counted" came in January at the Bing Crosby National Pro-Am, in March at the Greater New Orleans Open, and in June at the Buick Open in Michigan.

There was a common thread to the three: All were preceded by time off when I went fishing.

As far back as I could remember, I'd always enjoyed fishing. I'd fished by myself in the San Diego river bottoms with nothing but a string and a hook, then later with my dad in any number of rivers, lakes and streams. I'd found it to be the perfect getaway from just about everything. It took me three years to realize it was also the perfect getaway from the stresses of tournament golf.

In my first years on Tour I didn't take any breaks. When we were living in the trailer we couldn't very easily take off for home so I worked every week. (The twenty-nine tournaments I entered in my second year would be the most my entire career.) But by 1958 things were looking promising enough financially that I decided I could afford to take some time off now and then. The natural diversion for me was fishing.

I started going out on sportfishing charters from the harbor in San Diego. We'd leave at 2:30 in the morning and fish the waters off the Coronado Islands in the Pacific Ocean near the coast of Mexico for bluefin tuna, yellowfin tuna, yellowtail, albacore and marlin. Sometimes

I'd go out just for the day, but more often than not I'd be gone for anywhere from four days to a week. It proved to be terrific therapy. Fishing
requires all your attention; you can't think about golf or anything else.
I found that after a few days fishing my mind was cleared and ready for
golf again. Throughout my career I studiously avoided physical activity
that might interfere with my golf swing or cause injury. I was pretty
fanatical about it. I didn't ski, I didn't play contact sports, I didn't ride
motorcycles, I didn't do heavy manual labor. But I did fish. It became
my refuge of choice and over time I developed a routine. I would leave
the Tour when I was mentally worn out, come home, get on a fishing
boat, and come back refreshed.

I STARTED THE SEASON BY winning the Crosby by four strokes over my
good friend Dave Marr. I recall that afterward Jay Hebert remarked how
the Crosby should be considered a major, and I thought he made a good
point. The tournament attracted all the top players and was played on three
of the best courses we'd see all year—Pebble Beach, Monterey Peninsula
Country Club, and one of my personal all time favorites, Cypress Point.

For my second win, at New Orleans, I did something that probably
ought to be in the modern PGA record books. I won the tournament
on Wednesday.

Gene Littler, Bud Holscher and I were staying at a motel in downtown New Orleans. On Thursday and Friday Gene and Bud had early
tee times and both days they were back before I left the room, the days'
play rained out. On Saturday I went to the course in the morning and
came back to tell them the day was a washout. All scores were cancelled,
which is how it worked back then. A rainout wiped out everything, even
if some golfers finished a full eighteen.

The tournament finally began on Sunday, the day it was slated to
end. We got in eighteen that day, another eighteen on Monday and on
Tuesday we played thirty-six holes. Ken Venturi and I were tied for the
lead at the end of regulation and an eighteen-hole playoff was scheduled
for the next day. But when we got to the course it was pouring rain

again. They decided we'd play nine holes instead of eighteen. But it kept pouring. Finally there was a slight break and they said we'd play sudden death. We both parred the first playoff hole and on the second hole, a dogleg par five, Ken was about thirty yards short of the green in two and I was on the green, twenty-two feet from the hole. He pitched to twelve feet and I holed my putt for an eagle, finally putting an end to the tournament on Wednesday, nearly a week after it began. As soon as I got back to the motel, I got in the car and made it to Pensacola, Florida, just in time for the start of the next tournament.

EVEN THOUGH THE BUICK OPEN in Flint, Michigan, was a new event on Tour in 1958, everyone wanted in. The reason: the $9,000 first prize. That was a thousand dollars more than the winner's share in that year's U.S. Open. Plus the winner got a new car.

Tommy Bolt, coming off a four-stroke victory in the U.S. Open in Tulsa, was the leader after each of the first two rounds. I was two strokes out of the lead and followed Tommy into the press conference, where I heard him chewing out a writer from the *Detroit Free Press* about an article in that morning's paper. Tommy said, "I'm thirty-nine, not forty-nine like you had in the paper this morning." The writer said, "Sorry, Tommy, that was a typographical error." "Typographical error!" said Tommy, "that was a perfect four and a perfect nine."

I played in the final group on Sunday with Bolt and Ted Kroll. I was behind both of them when the day began. But by the time I got to the eighteenth tee I had a one-shot lead over Kroll and a charging Arnold Palmer, who had already finished his round. I needed a par to avoid a playoff. My approach shot landed well short of the pin but I managed to two-putt from forty feet for the win, the biggest payday of my life, and a brand new Buick.

I played in the PGA Championship for the first time in 1958. Under rules then in effect, new pros had to wait out a probationary period before being allowed in the field. It was the first year the tournament switched from match play to medal play, to accommodate television coverage. I was just one stroke behind Sam Snead going into the final round at the Llanerch Country Club in Havertown, Pennsylvania, and shot even par 70 to Snead's 73. But while I was passing Snead, Dow Finsterwald shot a 67 to pass us both. It would be my first of three runnerup finishes in the fourth major.

I accepted an invitation to play in the Brazil Open in September in Sao Paulo. I won by nine strokes over Leonardo Ruis, an Argentine pro, and collected 150,000 cruzeiros—$931 in American money.

Then, in mid-November, I played in Cuba in what would turn out to be the last Havana Invitational. The tournament, a regular PGA Tour stop during the 1950s, was held at the Havana Country Club, which would itself soon cease to exist.

Revolution was in the air. Fidel Castro and his guerillas were in the hills, plotting to overthrow the government of Fulgencio Batista. All year there had been plenty of locker room talk about whether Cuba was a safe place to be playing golf in the fall of 1958. The week before, when we were in Atlanta, I was riding back to the hotel in the shuttle car with Fred Hawkins, who was chairman of the players' committee, and Frank Stranahan, who came from a wealthy family. Hawkins laid the needle to Stranahan. "You know, you should play in the early morning in Cuba," he said, "In the afternoon the rebels come down with a net and they'll hold you for ransom." Then he added, "Stranny, I just got the pairings from Havana. Your partners in the pro-am are Batista and Castro." Stranahan didn't go to Cuba.

But I did. I figured if I did get held for ransom, Dick Haas and Russ Corey would bail me out.

I played in the pro-am with a very friendly but very nervous Cuban attorney named Jose Mestre. He invited Shirley and me to his home and was extremely kind to us but at the same time you could tell he was anxious about what was going on in the hills. And for good reason. Just weeks after the tournament, we read about Castro taking over. One of the first things he did was bulldoze the country club, and golf all but disappeared in Cuba. The $2,400 I collected for first place was one of the island's last acts of capitalism. Later, the PGA Tour erased the Havana Invitational from the record book. I assume this was in response to Castro's politics, although no one ever told me the reason. All I know for sure is that to this day I remain the defending champion of the Havana Open.

For years I wondered what happened to my friend the Cuban attorney. Did he make it out? Did he become part of Castro's regime? Did he wind up in jail? Fourteen years later, when I flew to Sardinia, Italy, to play in the 1972 Is Molas tournament, I got my answer. I was waiting for my golf bag at the airport when a man came up to claim his own golf bag. It was Jose. We embraced and I asked him what happened. He said he got out of Cuba just in time and found sanctuary in Europe. He'd been living in Switzerland ever since.

NINETEEN FIFTY-EIGHT WAS A YEAR of firsts for golf. It was the first time the Masters, U.S. Open and PGA Championship were all televised live. It was the first time Arnold Palmer won the Masters (he made an eagle three on the thirteenth hole, just in time for the TV coverage). It was the first million-dollar purse for the Tour. It was the first time a major corporation like Buick sponsored a tournament, opening the door for many more large corporate sponsorships down the road. It was the first time a twenty-two-year-old South African named Gary Player won on Tour—at the Kentucky Derby Open. And it was the first time my bank account went in the black.

I played in twenty-four events in 1958, two less than the previous year, but won twice as many tournaments (if you count Cuba) and almost twice as much money. My $41,323.75 in official earnings was good for second place on the money list. Arnold Palmer made $42,608 in thirty-two events and beat me by just over a thousand dollars. In one season I had made nearly as much money as in my first two and a half seasons combined. After three and a half years on tour, I'd collected $84,119 in ninety-two tournaments, an average of $914.33 per event.

Back home in San Diego, I was able to pay off my backers on time and in full. I promptly ripped up the contract. I didn't need another one. In the end, Dick Haas and Russ Corey made more than $25,000 as a percentage of my winnings, plus they got their original investment back. But in the end it was a bargain for both sides. Without their backing, I'd have never been able to set foot on the Tour in the first place.

With what was left, Shirley and I bought a 1,000 square-foot house from Russ Corey that backed onto the seventeenth green at San Diego Country Club. It was next door to Don and Verla Collett. We parked our Buick in the driveway and had $5,000 left in the bank.

I had won seven tournaments so far on Tour, in Canada, Cuba and the U.S.A., plus another tournament in Brazil. When I came home the San Diego Country Club, the club I'd never officially belonged to, gave me an honorary membership with no expiration date. I seriously wondered how life could get any better than this.

9

Winged Foot

Holding the Golfcraft "Caliente" putter that stayed hot
throughout the 1959 U.S. Open at Winged Foot.

Mamaroneck, New York
June 13, 1959

Despite my successful 1958 season, there were plenty of reasons why I wasn't considered among the favorites to win the United States Open in 1959.

I hadn't won a tournament all year. I'd hurt my back early in the season. I also missed seven straight events leading up to the Open when a cold turned into pneumonia. My record in four previous U.S. Opens was good but hardly great—in 1955 I didn't make it out of sectional qualifying, in 1956 I finished fourteenth, in 1957 I missed the cut and in 1958 I finished thirteenth. At the Masters, the first major of the season, I shot 76-76 and failed to make the cut.

The odds-makers lumped me in with the 16-to-1 long shots.

Fortunately, it was not my nature to dwell on either the negative or the past—or the odds. Also fortunately, the first time I laid eyes on the West Course at Winged Foot Golf Club I felt right at home. It reminded me of the golf course I grew up on, the San Diego Country Club, with similar mounds and numerous traps guarding the greens—the kind of place where, when I wasn't playing my best, I knew how to invent shots and scramble and still make pars. Even with the usual USGA finishing touches of narrowed fairways, lengthened rough and slicker greens, from the very beginning I felt comfortable at Winged Foot.

After my first practice round on Thursday, a week before the tournament was to begin, I told Joe Bloom that if I were to ever win an Open, it would be this one.

Joe was a friend from the Navy, an oral surgeon, who lived in nearby Elizabeth, New Jersey. He invited Don Collett, who had made it through the Open's sectional qualifying, and me to stay at his home. (Once the Open started, Shirley and I stayed nearer the course in Mamaroneck at the home of Tom Nieporte's sister-in-law.) It was the first, and only, time I arrived early for a major championship. I was just getting my strength back after the pneumonia and wanted to make sure I was ready for the grind. Unlike regular Tour events, with eighteen holes a day Thursday through Sunday, the U.S. Open had a tradition that dated to its beginnings of finishing with thirty-six holes on Saturday. "Open Saturday" was billed as the toughest day in golf, and beware the pro who didn't prepare for the ordeal.

I brought with me a putter I'd recently received from the Golfcraft Company. It was a "Caliente" model—Spanish for hot. I used it in three tournaments leading up to the Open and I liked the way the ball came off the head and thought maybe it was just the right blade for Winged Foot's quick greens.

WINGED FOOT WAS FULL OF history. It was here, in 1929, that Bobby Jones won the third of his four U.S. Opens and solidified his reputation as the ultimate competitor when he made a curling four-foot putt on the final hole of regulation that tied him with Al Espinosa, forcing a thirty-six-hole playoff the next day. Jones had played an awful final eighteen and everyone had written him off when he rallied on the last hole and ran in the putt for a 79. The next day he shot 141 to Espinosa's 164 to win by twenty-three shots! Winged Foot also hosted the U.S. Amateur in 1940 and the U.S. Women's Open on the East Course in 1957.

It was immediately evident to me that the course was too difficult and too lengthy to overpower. The first obvious trouble spot was the third hole, a 217-yard uphill par three called "Pinnacle" with a large sand trap fronting the green on the left and an enormous grass bunker guarding the right. The green, surrounded by spruce, fir and oak trees, sloped heavily from back to front, with a succession of terraces.

After getting acquainted with all of the potential problems in my practice rounds, I decided I wouldn't go for the green on the third hole in the tournament. I would hit a 5- or 6-iron to a level area short and left of the green and pitch up to the putting surface from there. My game plan was to lay up—on a par three. In the week I had to prepare for the tournament, I spent a tremendous amount of time practicing my chipping and putting.

ON WEDNESDAY, THE FINAL PRACTICE day, I wanted to play the complete course from start to finish. Don and I arrived early and were warming up on the putting green when Phil Rodgers walked over and challenged us to a match. Phil was a friend from San Diego, a young amateur who had won the NCAA college golf championship the previous summer while playing for the University of Houston. He had just turned twenty-one and hadn't yet turned pro. He told us he had a friend waiting on the tee who would be his partner.

"Come on," he said, "it will be amateurs versus pros."

Don asked, "Who's your friend?"

"You'll see," he said.

We walked to the first tee where a kid even younger than Phil stuck out his hand and introduced himself.

"Hi," he said, "I'm Jack Nicklaus."

Jack Nicklaus was big and strong and nineteen years old and, as Don Collett likes to say when he retells the story, his drives were still rising when they passed where ours had landed. He shot 67 that day, Rodgers shot 76, Collett 78 and I managed a 79, nine strokes over par. Collett and I lost eight bucks each to the kids.

Maybe it wasn't the best way to warm up for the U.S. Open, but, as I've already said, I was never one to dwell on the negative or the past.

The next two days Jack shot 77-77 and missed the cut, as did Phil and Don. I opened with a 71 and followed that with a 68. I was one under par through thirty-six holes and had the outright lead in the U.S. Open.

It was definitely an adventure getting there. Thursday's 71 could have easily been another 79. I missed fairways right and left, but I scrambled well and needed only one putt on eight greens. On day two I was straighter—my 68 was the low round of the tournament. I also continued to take advantage of the Caliente with five more one-putts.

As I left the course Friday night I ran into Jack Murphy, sports editor and columnist for the *San Diego Union*, who was there to cover the tournament.

"Well, I can always say I led the U.S. Open after thirty-six holes," I said. I remember Jack, not wanting to jinx anything, quickly changing the subject.

THE WEATHER HAD MADE AN abrupt about-face when the tournament began. All my practice rounds were played in hot and sultry conditions, but on Thursday it turned cold and windy. A front straight out of Canada blew in on gusts as high as twenty-five miles an hour. The rains and lightning came on Saturday, causing a delay of more than an hour in the morning and nearly a two-hour stoppage in the afternoon.

As the day wore on it became obvious to the USGA that the sixty-one players who had survived the cut line of 150 (10 over par) would not all be able to complete thirty-six holes before dark. The decision was made that for the first time in history, after everyone got in eighteen holes, the U.S. Open would conclude on Sunday.

I kept the ball under the wind as best I could and shot 69 on Saturday, thanks again to a lot of good work around the greens. This time I had nine one-putt greens, including the last four holes, where I closed with putts of ten feet, eight feet, eleven feet and four feet. To this point in the Open, I had twenty-two one-putt greens in fifty-four holes for a total of 86 putts—and the best was yet to come.

I ran into Jack Murphy after the round and again said, "Well, I can always say I led the U.S. Open after fifty-four holes." Again he quickly changed the subject.

MY LEAD GOING INTO THE final round was three shots, just comfortable enough to be uncomfortable. Behind me was a leaderboard for the ages. Ben Hogan was three back, Sam Snead was four back and Claude Harmon, Winged Foot's head pro and the last club professional to win a major when he won the 1948 Masters, was five back. They were all men in their mid to late forties who could remember when the Open's first prize was less than a thousand dollars. (In 1959 the winner's share was $12,000, a third higher than the year before.) Mixed in among these

This is me at sixteen, sitting on the hood of a jalopy in Chula Vista with pals Don Chase, left, and Jack Peacock.

22

On graduation day at Chula Vista High School, Shirley stood beside me.

23

I won this trophy while
in the service of the
United States Navy.

24

25

The Skyraiders Golf Team stationed at North Island in 1955.
We never lost a match. Front row: Bob Goetz, left, Leo Marchall,
Bill Blanton, Charlie Bartlett. Standing: Glen Pritchett, left,
Billy Casper, Bill Bisdorff, Don Collett.

At the 1959 U.S. Open at Winged Foot, playing partner Mike Souchak looks on as I perform an early rendition of the Tiger pump.

An official with the USGA offers his congratulations as I walk off the final green with Lionel Hebert at Winged Foot in 1959. I had the lead in the U.S. Open, but after this handshake I had to wait an hour for the rest of the field to finish and make it official.

28

The calm after the storm: After winning my first U.S. Open at Winged Foot,
Shirley and I pause to embrace the moment.

We were all smiles after a tournament at the Coronado Golf Course in 1959. John Alessio, owner of the Hotel del Coronado, is presenting the awards. That's Don Collett next to me. Gene Littler, on the far left, is about to receive the first-place check.

At a Wilson Sporting Goods get-together in 1961, Arnold and I tried to get close enough to Walter Hagen so some of the greatness would rub off. Julius Boros is on the far right, Dr. Cary Middlecoff on the left.

After Arnold Palmer birdied the last two holes at the 1960 Masters to charge
to the win, I was the first person to shake his hand.

I made my first Ryder Cup team in 1961 and traveled to England, where the entire squad made a visit to Harry Vardon's grave. From left to right, that's Doug Ford, Gene Littler, Art Wall, Arnold Palmer, Dow Finsterwald, Jerry Barber (our captain), Jay Hebert, Bill Collins, me, and half of Mike Souchak.

At Royal Lytham & St. Annes, Arnold Palmer and I made our Ryder Cup debut in a foursomes match against Ken Bousfield (far left) and Dai Rees in 1961. We prevailed, 2 and 1.

I had an ace in the hole in this clubhouse card game
with Doug Ford and Mike Souchak.

Here I'm enjoying a moment
in the locker room with
Roberto De Vicenzo,
the great and gracious
Argentine champion.

Hauling in albacore proved to be highly effective golf therapy. Fishing buddy John Scott is as happy as I am.

This big one didn't get away.

That's pure admiration on my face. I used this trusty Wilson Strata-bloc driver for over thirteen seasons, until the shaft snapped in the Philippines. I never found another driver that could fade the ball nearly as well.

No one was more fit than the man in black, Gary Player. Here, we're in Las Vegas posing with Allard Roen, owner of the Desert Inn, and Bo Wininger.

My caddy and good friend Del Taylor: we just happened to hook up at Pebble Beach in 1963. He carried my bag for the next thirteen seasons.

When I first attended Bing
Crosby's annual tournament
as a boy with my father in
San Diego, I never dreamed
I would ever get this
close to the tournament's
namesake. Arnold Palmer
rounds out the trio.

41

42

That's President Eisenhower congratulating me after I made a three-foot
putt to win the Bob Hope Desert Classic in 1965. Ike called the putt a "knee-knocker."

43

Dave Marr was such a popular pro on the Tour, even Jack Nicklaus and I were happy when he won the 1965 PGA Championship—and we tied for second.

To the victor go the spoils: Here I'm getting a victory kiss after winning the 1965 Sahara Invitational. That's my wife, Shirley, by the way.

45

At the 1965 Ryder Cup, Gene Littler and I were all ears when our
captain, the incomparable Byron Nelson, offered advice.

46

We were a happy bunch after winning the 1965 Ryder Cup at Royal Birkdale. In a clockwise direction from our captain, Byron Nelson, holding the cup, that's Gene Littler, Tommy Jacobs, Johnny Pott, Ken Venturi, me, Julius Boros, Arnold Palmer, Don January, Tony Lema and Dave Marr.

47

The women behind the men at the 1965 Ryder Cup: Standing, left to right, Connie Venturi, Shirley Littler, Betty Lema, Mary Rose Pott, Winnie Palmer, Pat January, Louise Nelson, Shirley Casper; seated, left to right, Arman Boros, Susan Marr, Sally Jacobs.

I never made it past the rank of Seaman, but on my visit to the troops in Vietnam the officers did pay attention. Hack Miller is kneeling to my right.

Giving a clinic inside an aircraft carrier meant you really had to watch your backswing.

veterans were Arnold Palmer and Bob Rosburg, both four behind, and Mike Souchak, five back. All of them were younger than thirty-two, and lurking just behind them was twenty-three-year-old Gary Player.

At twenty-seven, I was bidding to become the youngest U.S. Open champion since Byron Nelson won at the same age in 1939.

The rain stopped on Sunday but the wind picked up, with gusts as high as forty miles per hour, creating a wind chill in the 50s. Mike Souchak, once a star end and kicker on the Duke University football team, took one look at the gridiron-like weather and said, "If I win the coin flip I'm going to receive and take the wind at my back."

Because of New York's "Blue Laws"—rules that prohibited or restricted the playing of sporting events on the Sabbath Day—the tournament couldn't start until two o'clock in the afternoon. If this had been a normal Tour event, I would have been paired with Ben Hogan in the final twosome of the final round. But this was not a normal Tour event, or even a normal U.S. Open. TV staggered the leaders for the final round and instead of going out with Hogan, the closest contender, I was paired with Lionel Hebert, who was five strokes behind going into the last eighteen. We teed off several groups ahead of the final twosome. Hogan started four twosomes ahead of me, Rosburg and Souchak were in separate twosomes well behind me. It gave them the advantage, or disadvantage, of still being out there when I finished and knowing what they had to beat.

DESPITE THE COLD WIND BLOWING out of Canada—it was directly in our faces for the first four holes—the Caliente stayed hot. On the first hole, a 442-yard par four, I came up short with my approach, chipped to four feet and made the putt. On the second hole, a 415-yard par four, I drove into a fairway bunker, blasted out short of the green, chipped to eight feet, and holed that. On the par-three third I stuck to my game plan, hit a 5-iron in front of the green, chipped to nine feet and sank the putt. On the 435-yard fourth hole, another par four, I landed my approach shot in the bunker right of the green, and blasted out to seven feet. I did this after a bee somehow got between my black alpaca sweater and my stomach—not an easy proposition for the bee in what might be called my hefty era—and stung me just at the bottom of my diaphragm as I was walking out of the sand trap. It hurt like crazy and took my breath away for a moment, but I couldn't call timeout. I paused at the side of the green long enough to catch my breath and fiddle with my sweater until the bee dropped out. Then I made the seven-foot putt.

At this point I stopped to talk to fellow pro Frank Stranahan, who had missed the thirty-six hole cut but stayed around for the finish. He told me he was on his way to watch Hogan; he figured that's who was going to win. But he'd started following me instead and stuck around after watching me make all those putts. He never did leave.

On the long par-five fifth, going with the wind, I hit a short wedge shot onto the green in three and made an eighteen-footer for birdie. Going back to the last four holes of round three, I now had nine one-putts in a row. I was one under par for the day, three under for the tournament, and six shots clear of the field.

But no streaks last forever and winning a U.S. Open is never easy. After missing yet another green on the sixth hole, I chipped to twelve feet—and missed the putt and made bogey. For the next six holes I continued my retreat, again and again employing the disastrous formula of missing greens and two-putting for bogey. On the tenth green, for the first time all week, I three-putted. With six holes to play I was three over par for the round and one over for the tournament.

The brutal conditions were equal for everyone in the field, and no one escaped. Ben Hogan, searching for his fifth U.S. Open title, scored 76 that day, and Sam Snead, searching for his first, scored 75. Hogan was two over after the first four holes; Snead made double-bogey five on that unforgiving par-three third. He and Hogan wound up tying for eighth place at 287. Arnold Palmer shot 74 for 286 and a tie for sixth place. Gary Player scored 76 and finished sixteenth at 292. Every single round played at Winged Foot that Sunday was over par. The average score was 76.

I finally stopped my back-slide on the fourteenth green by making a curling twelve-foot putt for birdie, just enough to withstand more bogeys at fifteen and seventeen. A par on eighteen gave me a score of 74 for the day, 282 for the tournament. Immediately I started receiving slaps on the back for winning the Open. But there was a slight problem. Rosburg and Souchak were still on the course with a chance to tie or win. Both were now only one stroke behind.

From the warmth of the clubhouse grill I watched Souchak miss the green and fail to chip in for the birdie at eighteen he needed for a tie.

That left only Rosburg. He had a terrific round going until he double-bogeyed thirteen to go one over par for the day and three over for the tournament, one more than my final score. He needed a birdie coming home. He almost got it on the sixteenth green but his putt lipped out. At seventeen his birdie putt came up eight inches short and on eighteen he needed to make a thirty-footer that ended up two feet short. I was being hooked up for a television interview, receiving congratulations for my victory, when I heard the collective oohs and aahs from the crowd around the eighteenth green. That's when I knew I won the Open. If I'd heard cheers then Rosburg would have "Done a Bobby Jones" on the eighteenth green at Winged Foot and we'd have been in a playoff. Rosburg finished one stroke behind at 283, Souchak and Claude Harmon tied for third at 284. All three shot 71 on Sunday, one over par and the three best rounds of the day.

Putting is what saved me. I had a total of 114 putts for seventy-two holes—28 on Thursday, 31 on Friday (my best round, tee to green), 27 on Saturday and 28 on Sunday. I had one three-putt for the tournament and thirty-one one-putts, including one every day at the par-three third for four consecutive pars. Until the day he died my good friend Bob Rosburg was mad at me for laying up on that third hole every round. He's in the hereafter now and I'm sure he's still mad at me.

After the tournament, the people at Golf House asked for my putter and I gave it to them. I said I'd done enough with that putter, it needed to rest. Never has a putter gotten more praise for less work—or been more aptly named. The Caliente is still in the USGA museum, as far as I know. People have conjectured how many more tournaments I might have won with it. I like to think it's the Indian, not the arrow, but you never know.

IT WAS THE '59 OPEN that cemented my reputation as a putter. Herbert Warren Wind, the great golf writer, covered the tournament for *Sports Illustrated*. Under the headline "The Man With The Devastating Putter," he wrote: "There has probably never been such a devastating putting performance in the history of the National Open." In describing the five consecutive one-putts to start the final round, Wind wrote, "Incidentally, each of these five putts would have gone in if the cup had not been four and a quarter inches but only two and a quarter inches."

Herbert Warren Wind had a way with words that made them stick. At the Masters the year before, when Arnold Palmer charged to the title with his eagle on thirteen, Wind coined the term "Amen Corner" to describe the decisive nature of the eleventh, twelfth and thirteenth holes at Augusta National. The phrase instantly became part of golf's lexicon. His description of my putting at Winged Foot had the same effect. After the '59 Open I was the man with the devastating putter.

Making putts was never a surprise to me. From as early as I could remember, I could get the ball in the hole. I had a natural feel for putting, and I always maintained that practicing in the dark back during my caddy days was a big factor in developing that talent. They didn't all drop, however, and throughout my career I went through those periods when I thought nothing would drop. But putting is as much a matter of feel as anything else. At Winged Foot I got in sync with the greens early on and it never left.

I always spent more time practicing my putting than any other part of the game. Over time, I developed my own unique style. I used more wrist, especially on short putts, than most players, and that any of the Tour players use on today's perfectly manicured greens. Most of the greens we putted on in the 1950s and 1960s were more like the fringe of today's putting surfaces—longer and shaggier and not as consistent. I concentrated on the basics—keeping the blade square, head still, and following through. Whatever the back of the left hand was doing, that's what the clubface was doing. I liked to anchor the top of the putter against my left thigh for stability. The long putter wouldn't come along until years later, but I've always thought if it had been a possibility when I was playing the Tour, I'd have used it. Anchoring the club into your chest creates a solid pendulum and eliminates a moving part of the putting motion, and that can't be a bad thing.

Then and now, the most important fundamental hasn't changed: the need to be able to read the greens. It's essential to know which way the grain is running, to identify the high point of the surrounding terrain and the natural flow of gravity and to recognize what type of grass you're putting on. There are so many nuances you need to be aware of. Every green is its own book.

A MONTH AFTER THE OPEN at Winged Foot, Bob Rosburg got a measure of revenge at the Utah Open outside Salt Lake City, where he won and I placed third. The tournament had been on the PGA calendar the year before, but was not an official event in 1959. Many tournaments went on and off the schedule back then, depending on whether the organizers could raise a large enough purse. Because it conflicted with the regular Tour stop in Hartford, the commissioner fined me $100 for my visit to Utah. I would later call it the best hundred dollars I ever spent.

AFTER WINGED FOOT, I DIDN'T win another Tour event for four months. In the papers they wrote that I had fallen victim to the dreaded "U.S. Open jinx." But I had the perfect antidote—a return to Portland. Playing at the Portland Golf Club, site of my first Tour event and first paycheck, I won the Portland Open comfortably by three strokes over Bob Duden and Dave Ragan. For the first time, I won with all four scores in the 60s—69-64-67-69—to record the lowest seventy-two-hole score to that point of my career, 19-under-par 269.

After that I placed sixth at the Hesperia Open in California and then as the Tour swung to the South, won twice more, first at the Lafayette Open in Louisiana and then at the Mobile Open in Alabama. I placed fourth on the 1959 money list with $33,899, down from the year before, but I'd taken more time off because of health problems, and this total included a U.S. Open—the gift that keeps giving.

From the day I won at Winged Foot, my phone started ringing with offers for endorsements, sponsorships and exhibitions. One of the calls was from a man named Mark McCormack, a Cleveland attorney about my age who had played golf in college and understood the game and its culture. He introduced himself as a sports agent and said he was starting a company called National Sports Management and was interested in representing me. He had already signed Arnold Palmer, the 1958 Masters winner, and had signed or was in the process of signing Dow Finsterwald, the 1958 PGA Champion; Art Wall, who won the 1959 Masters; and Gary Player, the 1959 British Open winner. He wanted to know if he could add the 1959 U.S. Open winner to his client list. I said, "Yes, absolutely, sign me up."

10

Prosperity

11

Traveling in style in the early 1960s with
Shirley, Linda, Billy and Bobby.

PGA Tour
1960

I have often been asked, and have often wondered myself, why I didn't place more emphasis on major championships during my career, particularly after I won my first one.

I guess the simple answer is I was too busy trying to win golf tournaments.

For all the times I won, I never strayed far from the thought that I was one step away from working the assembly line at the rivet factory.

I was interested in winning, period, and winning *now*. I focused on the present, in my golf game and my golf career. I knew intuitively that winning checks was how I would stay on Tour and provide for my family, and those were always far and away my top priorities. Where and when I won didn't matter as much as that I kept winning. The tournament of the moment was the one that counted. I kept my eye on the little picture and let the big picture take care of itself.

Growing up the way I did, watching my parents constantly trying to make ends meet, had a big impact on me. I was given this talent to swing a golf club and I realized early on that it was my ticket out of that life. Like a lot of people who grew up during the Depression, I was pretty conservative because of it. I wasn't one to get ahead of myself. To paraphrase what the football coaches say, I liked to play them one tournament at a time.

It was my dream to win the National Open, as it was for every golfer I knew. Early on in my career I added winning the Masters to that dream. But as important as they were to me, I wasn't willing to let those tournaments get in the way of making a living. What winning the majors would mean for my legacy did not enter my mind. I wasn't one to look very far into the past, either. When I came on Tour I couldn't have told you who had the record for the most wins at the U.S. Open or the Masters, or who had won the most majors. The record book to me was an unread book, and throughout my career it remained that way. I did not keep track of where I stood in relation to others, past or present.

In 1960, when Arnold Palmer put the British Open back on the map, so to speak, and invented the notion of the professional Grand Slam, I wasn't about to rearrange my schedule to include a trip every summer to the U.K. for the basic economic reason that I figured it would cost me two weeks' pay. I could make much more by staying home. I skipped the British Open the first thirteen years of my career and played in the tournament only five times total. Looking back, it's one of my biggest regrets, but at the time it seemed like the prudent thing to do, and at least for the short term, it was.

BESIDES IGNORING THE BRITISH OPEN, I made another *What was I thinking?* decision in the early sixties.

I left Mark McCormack.

McCormack's sports agency was thriving. Sometime not long after I signed on, he'd given National Sports Management a new name, International Management Group, and IMG was well on its way to becoming the premier agency for elite athletes all over the world. In time it would rival the PGA Tour itself for power and clout. But Mark's approach to business was decidedly aggressive, not something I was used to. At times I was uncomfortable when he would use his clients as leverage to get deals for other clients. If a corporate outing or a sponsor wanted Billy Casper they also had to take, say, a Bayer or a Finsterwald. I didn't like being used as a wedge in that way, or to feel that others were being used as wedges to get me a deal. I felt I'd be better off with more individualized representation, and when Mark's partner, Dick Taylor, decided to break off from IMG to start his own agency, I decided to go with him.

Dick had big goals. He started the Carling World Championships, a series of international tournaments that he planned to evolve into a world golf tour. It was a grand scheme but it took the lion's share of his time, and in the end wasn't successful. Within a few years he was out of the sports agency business entirely and I was back on my own. In the meantime, Mark had signed Jack Nicklaus when Jack turned pro in 1962 and turned Nicklaus, Palmer and Player into The Big Three. The Big Three *did* put an emphasis on major championships, and they won them at a prolific rate. At the Masters alone, between the three of them they collected eight of the nine green jackets from 1958 through 1966. And Mark McCormack marketed those wins like no one ever had before.

As always, arnold palmer took the lead. In 1960, he used comeback wins in the year's first two majors, the Masters and the U.S. Open, to both establish his reputation for charging from behind and place a modern emphasis on winning major tournaments.

At the Masters, where I placed fourth, he birdied the last two holes for the victory and at the Open at Cherry Hills Country Club in Denver he passed me in the final round to get the win.

Me and thirteen others.

After shooting 73 in the morning, I was tied for eleventh place at 214 going into the final eighteen holes on Open Saturday, six shots behind the leader, Mike Souchak. My odds of defending the title I'd won at Winged Foot the year before did not look particularly good, but at that they looked better than Palmer's. He stood in fifteenth place at 215, seven shots back of Souchak. Besides me, among the fourteen players ahead of him were Sam Snead, Ben Hogan, Julius Boros, Gary Player and Jack Nicklaus.

Then Palmer drove the green on the 364-yard par-four first hole, made birdie, went on to shoot 65, pass all the legends, and win by two over Nicklaus. Souchak shot 75 and faded to a tie for third place. I managed a one-over-par 72 and finished twelfth.

The momentum from Palmer's victories at the Masters and the U.S. Open is hard to overstate. He went on to win eight times in 1960 and his trip that summer to St. Andrews for the British Open single-handedly made it fashionable for American pros to play in that tournament. It was on the way to Britain that Palmer came up with the notion of the modern Grand Slam. Up till then, golf's Grand Slam consisted of two amateur tournaments, the U.S. Amateur and British Amateur, and two professional tournaments, the U.S. Open and British Open. When Bobby Jones won all four of these events in 1930, he became the first, and so far only, person to win the Grand Slam in a single season.

But by 1960, the Grand Slam Bobby Jones made famous was mostly a relic, a trophy few were pursuing. The vast majority of golf's top players relinquished their amateur status as quickly as possible and turned professional, disqualifying themselves from even playing in two of the four original Grand Slam events. After he won the Masters and U.S. Open that year, Palmer mused about a new Grand Slam, this one consisting of four professional tournaments—the Masters, U.S. Open, British Open and PGA Championship. His sportswriter friend, Bob Drum of the *Pittsburgh Press*, carried the idea to his newspaper column and in no time golf's Grand Slam had a new definition.

Arnie was the first to chase the modern slam and almost got the "third leg" when he finished second at St. Andrews in 1960 after charging from behind with a 68 on the final day that came within a shot of catching the winner, Kel Nagle.

Between 1960 and 1962, Arnold won twenty-two tournaments, a total that included five majors. He collected $220,000 in winnings in that span, bought his own airplane and flew it from Tour stop to Tour stop, often piloting it himself. More than anything else, I believe the interest generated by what Arnold Palmer accomplished in those three seasons, and the flair with which he did it, ushered in the golden age of golf in the sixties and revolutionized the game. The rest of the golf world basically slid into his slipstream.

MEANWHILE, MY CAREER CONTINUED STEADILY upward, but with no private plane. The big news for the Caspers was another addition to the clan. Shortly after I played in the U.S. Open, our son Robert Reynolds

Casper—we called him Bobby from the start—was born in July. He was named after my good friend, Robert Reynolds, the president of the Los Angeles Angels baseball team.

As great as Arnold Palmer's 1960 season was, he didn't win all the prizes. I slipped past him to capture the first Vardon Trophy of my career. It was the first year I was eligible for the award, named for English golf legend Harry Vardon and presented annually to the player on the PGA Tour with the lowest per-round scoring average for the season. The PGA mandated a five-year waiting period back then before you could qualify for the Vardon Trophy. As it was with Palmer, 1960 was the first year I could win it.

I played consistent golf all season, with very few rounds over par, but by the end of September I still didn't have a victory. Then I went on a tear of my own and won three tournaments in a row. As had happened the previous year, the streak started with the Portland Open, followed by wins at the Hesperia Open and the Orange County Open, both in California. I averaged 68 strokes per round during that stretch and vaulted to an all-but-uncatchable lead in the race for the Vardon Trophy.

But there was a hitch. I hadn't yet played the minimum number of rounds to qualify. So instead of going home to San Diego and getting on a fishing boat, I made my way to the South for the Tour's final three events. I tied for fourth in Louisiana at the Cajun Classic Invitational— the former Lafayette Open that I'd won the year before—and then tied for fifth in Mobile, Alabama. After that, all I needed to do was show up for the year's final event in West Palm Beach, Florida. I could just go through the motions, which is more or less what I did. I shot 75 in the opening round, then 76 to barely make the cut, then 77. If I wasn't in last place, I was next to it. In the final round I was paired with the ever-colorful Tommy Bolt. I remember Tommy looking over at me on the first tee, setting his jaw, and saying, "How can you win the Vardon Trophy playing like that?" But I could and I did. In twenty-four events and ninety-seven competitive rounds that year I averaged 69.95 strokes per eighteen holes.

PALMER AND I ALSO BECAME eligible to begin accumulating Ryder Cup points in 1960, after the requisite five-year probation period mandated at the time by the PGA.

Players qualified for the Cup strictly on a points basis according to weekly finishes in tournaments. There were no at-large captain's choices at the time. The ten players with the most points made the team, period. (Teams were expanded to twelve players in 1969.) In 1960–61 I qualified for the team along with Arnold Palmer, Mike Souchak, Dow Finsterwald, Jay Hebert, Gene Littler, Bill Collins, Art Wall, Doug Ford and Jerry Barber, who was our playing captain. We competed in the 1961 Ryder Cup matches against the team from Great Britain at the Royal Lytham & St. Annes Golf Club in England.

The Ryder Cup gets its name from a wealthy English seed merchant named Samuel Ryder, who watched a team of Americans play a team from Great Britain at Wentworth Club in Surrey, England, in 1926. The Brits won in a landslide, 13½ to 1½, and the euphoria he felt from that victory caused Ryder, a keen golf enthusiast, to suggest that the matches become a regular event. He offered to donate a gold cup as a traveling trophy to get things started. The golf federations from the two countries accepted the offer, settled on a biennial schedule, and Ryder's Cup became the most sought-after trophy in golf. Every two years, the country that wins the competition gets to take the Cup home.

That's it, too. Just the Cup. There is no prize money. But I've yet to meet the professional golfer who doesn't list playing in the Ryder Cup as one of his highest goals.

Everything about the competition is appealing. It's a chance to represent your country in international competition. You get the opportunity to play for a team instead of just for yourself. The match play format is entirely different from medal play, bringing a welcome change of pace. And there is no pressure quite like Ryder Cup pressure. In all the places and conditions I've competed in as a golfer, I've never been as nervous as teeing off in the Ryder Cup.

IMAGES FROM MY FIRST CUP experience in 1961 are etched indelibly in my mind. We gathered as a team in Washington, D.C., and flew together to England, where we were met by the Lord Mayor of London in an elaborate welcoming ceremony. It was more pomp and circumstance than I'd ever seen. The British made it feel like a really big deal and the tone was set. The Ryder Cup never stopped being special for me after that.

The next morning we boarded the train in London. As captain, Jerry Barber was carrying the Ryder Cup with him, since America had won it in 1959. When he boarded the train he stowed the Cup in an overhead bin, then he and Palmer got in a gin game and forgot all about it. When we got off the train in Lytham & St. Annes the president of the PGA was there to meet us.

He looked around and asked Jerry, "Where's the Ryder Cup?"

"Oh it's in the overhead," Jerry answered, only then realizing we weren't still on the train, and the Ryder Cup still was.

The bobbies met the train in Blackpool, retrieved the Cup and sent it back to us. But the British had the Ryder Cup there for a few hours. We managed to lose it before the matches even began.

Our stay in England took us back to golf's roots, which we immersed ourselves in. On one of the practice days we took time away from the course for a visit to Harry Vardon's grave. A number of golf fans were along on the trip. I remember in particular two Catholic priests who traveled with us. They were chaplains in the Air Force and every two years they liked to follow the Ryder Cup wherever it was being played. We were all staying in the same hotel and the priests set up a kind of hospitality suite in their room with all the fermented fruit juice you could imagine. I remember Jerry Barber telling some of the players, "You're off limits to the chaplains this week."

That was the Cup where Jerry Barber decided to pair Palmer and me, his rookies, in the opening foursomes (alternate-shot) matches. We beat Ken Bousfield and Dai Rees, who was captain of the British team, 2 and 1 in the morning and dispatched John Panton and Bernard Hunt in the afternoon, 5 and 4. In the Saturday singles matches, I was sent out against Bousfield in the morning and won 5 and 3. The U.S. retained possession of the Cup with a 14½-9½ victory. Of that total, Arnold won 3½ points—in his singles matches he had a win over Tom Haliburton and a tie with Peter Alliss—and I won three points in my three matches.

I HAD ONE VICTORY ON tour in 1961—at Portland, of course. It was my third straight win there, and for the third straight year I finished fourth on the money list.

In 1962 I won the inaugural Doral Open in Florida, the Greater Greensboro Open the week following the Masters, the 500 Festival Open in Indianapolis, where I went twenty under par and hit sixty-five of seventy-two greens, and the Bakersfield Open in California. And for the fourth consecutive year I finished fourth in money. The Tour was allowing me to provide for my family the way I always hoped it could, and to be honest, well beyond my expectations as purses continued to escalate. While the kids were still little we traveled together as a family to almost every tournament. We were motel gypsies now. We kept Howard Johnson and Alamo Plaza in business. We would fly to the Tour stop, either rent a car or use the courtesy cars more and more tournaments were starting to provide, and usually stay at the same motel as several other touring pros and their families. We carried these little portable barbecue grills with us and you could always spot the golf pros. They were the ones sitting outside the motel rooms grilling steaks and chicken together.

Shirley made every attempt to make life on the road as close to life at home as she could. She insisted that we sit down together for dinner whenever possible. One night we were in Grand Rapids, Michigan, staying at an Alamo Plaza and having dinner at the motel restaurant. Linda was just a little girl but she insisted she wanted to order a grownup dinner. Shirley tried to talk her out of it, telling her it was too much food, she should go for the chicken-in-a-basket, but Linda was adamant. So Shirley ordered her the full chicken dinner but only on the provision—and what parent can't relate to this?—that she finish the whole thing.

Sure enough, about a third of the way through her meal, Linda was full. But now it was her mother's turn to be insistent. Linda would sit there until she ate every bite. After an hour or so watching this, Billy Jr. and I were excused to go back to the room. I left Billy at the room and went around the corner to Julius Boros's room to join a card game that also included Bill Collins and Ted Kroll. By the time Shirley and a very full Linda got back to our room about an hour later, Billy had taken a pair of scissors and whacked a chunk out of the front of his hair. At this point Shirley was in no mood for such a thing. She grabbed Billy by the ear and said, "You're going to tell your dad about this!" The next thing I knew, I looked up from the card game and Shirley and Billy were standing in the door. She said, "Bill, look what your son just did!" I asked him why he did it and he said, "Dad, I just wanted to be a barber." At that, the three guys around the card table cracked up. Pretty soon everybody in the room was laughing, even Shirley, I think.

I STARTED STRONG IN 1963, placing ninth in the Los Angeles Open and third in the San Diego Open—still close but not quite in my hometown tournament—and then in the third event of the season broke through with a solid win at the Bing Crosby that came with an added bonus.

It was there that I met a man who would witness virtually every golf shot I would hit for the next thirteen years: Del Taylor, my first permanent caddy.

The PGA Tour's policy had recently changed regarding caddies. The old rule stipulated that you could only use a caddy for two weeks at a time in regular Tour events, and then you had to alternate with someone else. At major championships you were required to use caddies that were provided.

The situation at the majors wouldn't change for several more years, but beginning in the early sixties the two-week maximum was lifted for regular Tour events. It was now permissible to use a caddy indefinitely. The advantages of a regular man on your bag were obvious. Having a caddy who understood your game and personality and knew what was expected of him and, more importantly, what wasn't expected of him, could be invaluable. All over the Tour, players started sizing up caddies and signing them for long-term relationships.

Del had been caddying on the circuit for several years. He was a few years older than me, an African-American from the Los Angeles area, and, like me, he'd been in the Navy. He was on his way to his commission when he decided that, all things considered, he'd rather not go to war in Korea, so he dropped out and became a caddy. He had worked for a number of different players on Tour and established a good reputation. He came to the Crosby expecting to work for another player who, for some reason, failed to qualify. I happened to be shopping around for someone to carry my bag that week and hired him on the spot. That's how much long-range planning went into a relationship that would last the next thirteen years.

We made a good team. Del instinctively knew how to handle me and how to handle my golf game in a tournament. I didn't require a lot out of a caddy but I was adamant and precise about what I did require. If I asked a question I wanted an answer to that question, and nothing more. Del was as meticulous and conscientious as I was. He would measure his own yardages before every tournament and I would measure mine and when I'd ask him his opinion about a club selection during the competition, ninety-five percent of the time we selected the same club. He was a huge asset to my golf success. In the process we became very good friends. During the offseason or when I was taking a break from the Tour, he'd come down and visit me in San Diego and we'd play golf. He was a good player. I remember we enjoyed playing nine holes with one club. It could be whatever club you wanted, but you had to use it through the whole nine holes. Del and I both enjoyed that because neither one of us had to worry about clubbing me.

IN APRIL, I FINISHED ELEVENTH in the 1963 Masters, done in by a 79 in the opening round. I gained on the field the rest of the week but still wound up six shots behind the winner, Jack Nicklaus. He was only twenty-three years old and he'd already won two U.S. Amateurs and the 1962 U.S. Open, and now he had his first green jacket.

Nothing seemed to shake Jack's concentration. He was as focused as anyone I'd ever seen come on Tour. He wasn't standoffish, just incredibly disciplined at paying attention to the task at hand. I got to know his father, Charlie, when Jack started coming to the Masters as a teenager. Charlie Nicklaus was a terrific guy, easy to talk to, loved sports, and we had a similar physique. We hit it off from the start.

Jack was so long off the tee it could be intimidating if you weren't careful. Whenever I was paired with him I purposely tried not to look how far his drives carried. I remember one tournament early in his career when I was in a group with Jack and Arnold, who was nearly as long as Jack. I'd hit my drive and then wouldn't even watch them hit. I'd look around at the nice scenery or toward the last green. It wasn't going to do me any good to watch how far they hit the ball.

Following the Masters, I moved on to North Carolina for the Greater Greensboro Open, where I was defending champion.

Things were going along fine until the eighth hole of round three when my drive rolled into a deep divot. It was an uphill lie on a cold blustery day and I had to gouge the ball out. I hit 6-iron. It was a beautiful shot. The ball landed on the green close to the cup and I holed the putt for birdie. But it came with a steep price. The upward thrust of the 6-iron swing had dislodged one of the small bones in the back of my left hand. By the time I putted out my hand was throbbing. I ignored the pain as best I could, finished the round, completed the tournament the next day, and hoped rest would get me back to one hundred percent.

Two tournaments later I was at the Desert Inn course in Las Vegas for the Tournament of Champions. I was three shots behind the leader, Jack Nicklaus, when the final round began. I had made up two of those shots by the time I got to the ninth hole. I hit my drive in the fairway and then, never suspecting anything was about to go wrong, made my next swing and felt the muscle tear in my left hand. I literally could not wrap my hand around the club after that. I couldn't close my fingers. I hit my next shot about thirty yards. Joe Black, the PGA Tour official on the scene, said I had to play on. I said, "Joe, I can't play." There was nothing I could do but walk off the course and withdraw from the tournament.

I saw all sorts of orthopedic specialists, including Dr. Frank Jobe, who had a good reputation from working with big league baseball players. To a man, the doctors wanted to operate, but I was hesitant. My hands were my golf game. I didn't want to do anything that would risk changing them in any way. We had recently purchased a house in Bonita, next door to Chula Vista, and I settled down in our new home, hoping that rest and light exercise would be the cure. Since I only needed my right hand for casting, I went fishing to keep from going stir crazy.

But as the weeks passed, the hand did not improve. My patience was running out as fast as my anxiety was increasing.

As happened so often in my life, the answer to my problem came from a completely unexpected source.

A young man named Emory Allen was living with us at the time. We had plenty of room in the new house. When we could we liked to take in troubled young people with nowhere else to go and try to help them get back on their feet. Emory became like one of our own kids. One day he returned to the house after playing golf with a retired osteopath, Dr. Carl Stillman. Emory had explained my situation to the doctor, who said he wanted to take a look at my hand. He thought he might be able to help. This was seven o'clock at night. By eight o'clock Emory and I were at Dr. Stillman's door. That's how desperate I was.

The doctor immediately took my left hand in his and began to manipulate the bones. It was not a pleasant experience but as he continued to work the bones and the joints I felt a click. Just like that, he put the bone I'd dislodged in Greensboro back in place. My hand hurt like crazy but, despite the pain, it felt better. For the next week, Dr. Stillman continued to massage and manipulate my hand. By the end of seven days I felt good enough to grip a golf club again.

I HAD MISSED THE U.S. Open and the PGA Championship and been away from the Tour a total of fourteen weeks—the entire summer—when I registered for the Insurance City Open in Hartford, Connecticut, at the end of August.

All sorts of questions raced through my mind. Would my hand hold up? Would I be able to play seventy-two holes? Would I ever win again?

I shot 67-68-71-65—271 and won by a stroke over George Bayer.

I never won a tournament before or since that was any more gratifying than that one. My career wasn't over. My hand felt fine, as good as ever. I was back.

I played in eight more tournaments that season and capped the year at the Ryder Cup matches, which were held on American soil at the Atlanta Athletic Club. Arnold Palmer was our playing captain and that was the first time four-ball (best-ball) matches and a third day of play were added to the schedule. I teamed with Dave Ragan for a 1-up win over Peter Alliss and Christy O'Conner in the morning foursomes. In the afternoon Arnold and I beat Brian Huggett and George Will 5 and 4. We would both go on to make the next five American Ryder Cup teams, but it was the last time Palmer and Casper were paired together, so as a duo we retired undefeated.

On Saturday I teamed with Billy Maxwell for two wins in four-ball matches, and I halved my Sunday singles match against Neil Coles. I helped contribute 4½ points to the 23-9 U.S. win.

I finished eleventh on the money list that year. It was the first time I'd been out of the top five in six seasons, but the $32,746.19 I won was more than my total just three years previously when I played a full year and finished fourth in the money. I won my second Vardon Trophy in 1963, with a scoring average of 70.58, ending Arnold Palmer's two-year hold on the award. The year that began so promising, then looked so dark in the middle, ended on an even higher note than it started.

BUT FOR ALL THE RELIEF that came with the win at Hartford and the success at the Ryder Cup, I had a nagging worry about my health. My hand injury wasn't my only concern. For some time, I'd been feeling sluggish and lethargic, particularly in the mornings, and it was getting worse. My vision was sometimes blurry and my hands and face would swell. I had sinus troubles, muscle spasms, backaches, difficulty getting to sleep, and often found it hard to concentrate. Sometimes these symptoms would disappear entirely, but they always returned, and I never knew why.

It was exhausting. Some days I'd be playing in the fresh air and bright sunshine and just want to find a bench and lie down. It got so bad in Miami, in the old Eastern Open, that I withdrew in the third round when I was only two shots out of the lead. My fingers were so swollen I couldn't hit a wedge. One of the writers who regularly covered the Tour, Will Grimsley from *United Press International*, saw me the morning I withdrew and later told me that I looked like I'd been on an all-night binge. But he knew I didn't drink.

It was the kind of thing that *could* make a man drink. My sluggishness and illnesses affected my mood, on the course and off. Newspaper accounts that once referred to me as "congenial Billy Casper" now saw me as surly, withdrawn, touchy. Small things I wouldn't have noticed before irritated me. I had no idea what the problem was. My weight wasn't perfect, but there were plenty of overweight players doing just fine on the Tour. I was barely past thirty and felt like I was eighty.

In the spring of 1964 I reported to the Masters as usual. I tied for fifth place, my second best showing in eight tries, but again came up short for the green jacket. Arnold Palmer again won it—his fourth time. While I was there I talked about my health issues with Bill Kerr, a good friend. Bill was in investment banking in New York with Cliff Roberts, the man who started Augusta National with Bobby Jones. Every year Bill came to Augusta and helped Cliff by handling the media. He always instructed the TV commentators that he didn't want them talking while the players were hitting shots. "Let the golf tell the story," he'd say. Gene Littler and I liked to come in early and play practice rounds with Bill and Cliff before the Masters. Over the years we developed a close relationship—so close we all spent Thanksgiving together one year in San Diego. I felt comfortable confiding in Bill about my health problems. I didn't expect him to solve them; I just knew he would be a sympathetic listener.

But after he heard me describe what I'd been going through, the look on his face was more empathetic than sympathetic.

He said my symptoms sounded very much like what he'd also been experiencing, and recommended that I get in touch with a physician in Chicago who had helped him. His name was Dr. Theron G. Randolph.

Dr. Randolph's specialty, Bill Kerr said, was allergies.

11

Buffalo Billy

12

Posing for a publicity stunt prior to the
Tucson Open. I'm sizing the buffalo up
for lunch, and vice versa.

Chicago, Illinois
August, 1964

Like most every other male in America, there were two things I loathed to do—admit I was sick, and go to the doctor.

Despite Bill Kerr's resounding endorsement of Dr. Randolph's remedies, I kept putting off seeing him. But my problems only got worse. I was almost always dizzy in the mornings and constantly fighting some sort of muscle ache or swelling problem. I was going through aspirin like candy.

But the worst part by far was the mood swings. One minute I'd be fine, enjoying life, the next, for no reason at all, I didn't want to get off the couch. All my life I'd been a positive person. It was the key to my survival and it was absolutely essential to my golf game. I made a lot of putts because I *knew* I would make a lot of putts. Now I found myself having to fight through dark, negative thoughts. For the first time in my life I began to understand what people meant when they said they were mentally depressed. It never got to the point where I wanted to jump out a window, but if I had continued the way I was going, who's to say?

I could talk myself through golf tournaments. I could concentrate and focus when I had to, for short stretches, and I could still get good results. Prior to the '64 Masters I won again at Doral and in May I won the Colonial at Ft. Worth—Hogan's tournament—for the biggest check of my life, $14,000. At the U.S. Open in June at Congressional in Washington, D.C. I finished fourth. But it was all so much harder than it used to be.

In July the Tour arrived at the Western Open, which was now held permanently in Chicago, Dr. Randolph's town. His office wasn't far from the golf course. Shirley made an appointment and the whole family accompanied me to see him. It was one of those experiences where, once you've done it, you wonder why you were such a knucklehead not to do it earlier.

Simply put, Dr. Theron G. Randolph saved my career, if not my life.

The medical community considered him a maverick because of his unorthodox prognosis that a large variety of illnesses and reactions were the result of exposure to toxins in the everyday foods we eat, the air we breathe, the pesticides that are all around us, and the products we use or come in contact with. Only over time would he be vindicated. Much of what medical science has since learned about allergic reactions and their connection to food and the environment fits with what Dr. Randolph was saying when I went to see him in the summer of 1964 at his office on Michigan Avenue. But he was a chorus of one back then.

After a series of tests he informed me I was allergic to wheat, citrus, eggs, peas, beans, pork, chocolate and peanuts. That meant, for starters, that my regular breakfast of eggs, bacon, toast and orange juice was killing me. The rest of my diet was almost as bad.

Food was just the start. Dr. Randolph's tests also showed I was allergic to a number of chemicals and petroleum products. I was allergic to the natural gas we used to cook our food, for example, and to the foam rubber products in our bedding, and many of the fertilizers and pesticide sprays used at golf courses where I played. My workplace was making me sick.

Among other things, this diagnosis explained my "drunken state" at the Eastern Open. My swollen hands and face were the result of a chain reaction that began when my caddy dipped my bag towel into a lake on the course that had been treated with pesticide. He used the towel to clean my golf ball. When I touched the golf ball the pesticide caused my hand to swell and when I touched my hand to my face it caused my neck to swell.

The good news was that I now knew what was at the root of my problems. The bad news was that it encompassed my entire lifestyle.

It also turned out that allergies ran in the family. Shirley, who had been suffering from dizziness, migraine headaches and swelling of her feet from edema, and Billy, who'd been taking shots for anemia, were also carrying a variety of what Dr. Randolph called "environmental allergies."

The result was a drastic Casper family lifestyle overhaul. We began making changes immediately. We started staying in motels or with friends on the road where there were electric stoves instead of gas. We carried our own pillows or made sure the ones we slept on weren't made of foam rubber. We did our best to avoid areas with elevated levels of air and chemical pollution. I dropped out of some tournaments in Florida, where they do a lot of spraying for mosquitoes and other pests.

Our home in Bonita went through a major transformation. We changed drapes, carpet, bedding and mattresses. Shirley bought steel pans for cooking. We avoided preservatives in our foods. We ate "organic" before anyone knew what organic was. My diet changed almost entirely. I completely eliminated eggs, bacon, chocolate, breads, pastries, and anything that contained peanuts. Dr. Randolph prescribed not eating the same food more often than every third or fourth day, so we were constantly altering our dinner menu. One night Shirley would cook bear, the next elk, the next hippopotamus, the next buffalo. One time we tried elephant. Shirley kept records of what we ate and when, and if there was a question about some new food, she would take one for the team and eat it first—because I was the one who had to make a living playing golf.

We found a store in Chicago, Czimer's, that specialized in wild game. They'd pack it in dry ice and ship it to us wherever we were staying. I was eating three times as much food and still losing weight. Within two months I was down eighteen pounds.

The weight loss naturally attracted attention from members of the press, who asked what was going on. When I told them I was eating buffalo, the legend of Buffalo Billy was born. I got more publicity from my buffalo diet than anything I'd done in ten years on Tour, and that included winning the Open. The buffalo became the logo for Billy Casper Enterprises, the company I'd recently created. My agent arranged for a photo shoot with me and a herd of buffalo. I got right in there with them. The photographer kept telling me to get closer, they wouldn't attack, but I kept my distance. They were my dinner, I didn't want to be theirs.

The result? Relief. My sinuses began clearing up, my backaches and muscle spasms were gone, the swelling in my hands and face disappeared. I again slept through the night. Best of all the lethargy left and my depression lifted. My head was clear. I could focus again. I stopped being a grump. People would wonder how I could be so disciplined to stay on my new "diet." The answer was easy. Because it felt so good to feel good again. (Shirley's migraines, edema and dizziness also cleared up and eight-year-old Billy's anemia disappeared.)

MY SYMPTOMS DID NOT STOP overnight or entirely. I had relapses. I still encountered problems with chemicals in the air. At the Tour stop in Akron I realized why the city was called the Rubber Capital when my sinuses tightened, my head pounded and I struggled to get through the tournament because of all the pollutants from the rubber factories. In Jacksonville I passed out briefly on the third hole from a heart palpitation. At first it looked like a problem with my heart until I visited Dr. Randolph after the tournament and he diagnosed it as a reaction to lamb and apples, foods I hadn't previously had a problem with. Out they went. I had to continually experiment with my diet, eliminating some foods and adding others. Allergies are like ants at a picnic. As soon as you get rid of one, another one takes its place. But Dr. Randolph predicted that over time the allergic reactions would die down, along with the symptoms, and that proved to be true. After three or four years the "buffalo" phase of my life would be all but over.

At the rate I was going, without help I could have wound up with a lifetime of health problems, and no doubt a short lifespan that didn't include much more of a professional golf career. Obesity ran in the Casper genes. My grandfather Adolf weighed 290 pounds when he died in 1946, not yet sixty, and that was after months of wasting away. He had one health problem after another as an adult and became ornerier and gloomier every year—largely the result, I suspect, of allergies that went undetected. I could have met a similar fate. Fortunately, I played a game for a living that wouldn't allow me to sit at home and eat myself into oblivion and feel sorry for myself, and I found the kind of medical help that gave me a new lease on life.

Two months after my consultation with Dr. Randolph I went to Seattle, dined on bear and buffalo, and won the Greater Seattle Open when I shot 64 in the final round to erase a three-shot deficit. Three weeks later I closed out the season at the Almaden Open in San Jose, California, with a victory in the longest tournament of my career. It took ninety-three holes to finally outlast Pete Brown after we tied in regulation, scored matching 68s in an eighteen-hole playoff, and then each made a birdie and a par in sudden death before I ran in a six-foot birdie putt for the win. I hit every green, twenty-one in a row, in the playoff and didn't make a single bogey.

I returned to San Diego that offseason a thinner, healthier, and happier version of my former self. Amid all the ups and downs I finished third on the 1964 money list with $90,653.08—as much as I'd made the past two years combined. The money came in handy. Hippo and elephant steaks are not cheap.

Homecoming that year was particularly gratifying. The city of San Diego proclaimed Dec. 16, 1964 "Billy Casper Day" and held a program and ceremony in front of three hundred invited guests at the Palm Room in the U.S. Grant Hotel. Frank Curren, the mayor, read a proclamation and gave me a fishing rod and reel, a plaque and the key to the city. Charlie Heaney, the San Diego Country Club pro who almost twenty years earlier had given me my only formal golf lesson, was one of the speakers; my good friend Bob Reynolds, co-owner of the Los Angeles Angels, was another. There were about four hundred telegrams—the emails of the day. One was from Arnold Palmer, which was read publicly. "Billy can hit a shot sideways and it won't bother him a bit. He'll still come back and get his par," he wrote. To which I responded: "He should talk!" The highlight was when Dick Haas and Russ Corey, the businessmen who first sponsored me on Tour and more than tripled their investment, came on stage dressed in old tattered clothes, looking like a couple of bums. "I used to drive a Lincoln Continental before we staked Casper," said Haas. "What do you drive now?" asked Corey. "A couple of burros," answered Haas.

It was a humbling occasion for someone who had started out life dirt poor in San Diego, practically an orphan, and needed a loan just to get started on the Tour. The room was filled with people from my past—friends from the caddy shed, Navy officers and men I'd played with on the golf team; junior golf leaders, members I caddied for at San Diego Country Club, teachers and classmates from Chula Vista High School, fishing boat captains, the doctor who fixed my hand, and so many others. I always considered myself fiercely independent, a self-made man. I looked around the room at all the people who made sure I made it on my own.

BUT I STILL COULDN'T WIN my hometown PGA tournament. I started playing in the San Diego Open before I was old enough to vote and while I had come close the championship always eluded me. I thought 1965 might be the year. We played at the Stardust Country Club in Mission Valley and I kept improving with each round, scoring 70-68-65-64 for a 267 total, seventeen under par, a new tournament record. I was the leader in the clubhouse, but in the twosome behind me, both Wes Ellis and Johnny Pott could catch me with a birdie on the final hole. I was more worried about Pott when he hit his approach within fifteen feet of the pin. Ellis's approach was in the fringe, fifty feet away. But Ellis, who was one of the first players on Tour to use a cross-handed putting grip with his right hand on top, dropped his long putt. It hit the back of the cup hard, popped in the air and dropped straight down and disappeared—and Pott missed his. That sent Ellis and me into a sudden-death playoff. He birdied the first hole with a six-foot putt while I just missed an eighteen-foot putt for the tie.

MY FIRST WIN IN 1965 was memorable because it came in front of Dwight D. Eisenhower. The former President was in the gallery surrounding the eighteenth green at the Bob Hope Desert Classic at Bermuda Dunes. I was playing in the final group and watched as Arnold Palmer, in the group ahead, made birdie on the last hole, a five par, to move into a tie with me for the lead. I needed to make birdie to avoid a playoff. I hit a 4-wood onto the green that settled forty feet from the cup. I lagged to within three feet, in good position for the birdie I needed to win. As I walked toward my ball I noticed that seated on the front row of the gallery, directly in front of me, was Eisenhower. I walked up to the short putt, didn't take much time over it, and knocked it in.

President Eisenhower was one of the first to shake my hand.

"Congratulations," he said, "you sure made a knee-knocker there."

I later thought about what he'd said. To me that short putt wasn't a knee-knocker. I knew what I had to do and I did it. I had practiced for that situation so many times my response was automatic. I didn't allow myself to think about what it would mean if I *didn't* make the putt. What happens to a lot of players, especially younger players, is they start thinking how important it is, and then the knees start shaking. It becomes a knee-knocker. To be able to win you first have to learn to control your thinking and understand how to win. But it takes time and discipline. I could imagine if I watched Eisenhower make his decisions as President I would have described them as more than knee-knockers. But to him, after all his experience and training, I am sure he focused on the task at hand rather than the significance of what it all meant.

I MADE ANOTHER GOOD RUN at the PGA Championship that summer, finishing second for the second time. Jack Nicklaus and I were paired in the next-to-last twosome, in front of Dave Marr and Tommy Aaron. We were both one shot behind Dave coming to the eighteenth hole at Laurel Valley In Knoxville, Tennessee, a lengthy par four with a large pond in front of the green. Trying for birdie, I hit 4-wood into the trap left of the green and Jack went long on his approach. We both ended up bogeying. That gave Dave a two-shot advantage. He laid up well short of the pond and hit a 7-iron for his third shot that checked up two feet from the hole. Then he made the putt to win the major. Jack and I tied for second.

In June I returned to Chicago for the Western Open and in a tribute to Dr. Randolph, whose clinic was just down the road, shot 64 in the final round and won by two shots over Chi Chi Rodriguez and Jack McGowan. In July I won again in Hartford at the Insurance City Open Invitational, replicating the win I'd had there two seasons earlier after recovering from the hand injury. Johnny Pott and I tied at the end of seventy-two holes and went into a sudden-death playoff. Johnny made his par on the first playoff hole and I had a fourteen-foot putt for birdie that could end the tournament. I took my practice swing and got over the ball and was just about to start the putter blade back when a bell started ringing. It was the six o'clock horn at the fire station. I backed off, went through my putting routine again, and knocked it in.

IN EARLY OCTOBER I WAS able to play in my third Ryder Cup, qualifying for a U.S. squad captained by the great Byron Nelson. The matches were held at Royal Birkdale in Southport, England, and the highlight for me was playing four doubles matches with Gene Littler. The most memorable was a four-ball match that we halved against Peter Butler and Lionel Platts after trailing by four holes with four to play. On the fifteenth hole, a par four, both Gene and I missed the green on our approaches while Butler and Platts were on the green. We each pitched up close and one-putted and they both three-putted and we won the hole. Then we birdied sixteen, seventeen and eighteen, won all three holes, and salvaged the tie. It was an important half-point at the time, preserving a narrow 9-7 lead for the U.S. going into Saturday's singles, where the Americans took control and won the competition, 19½-12½.

TWO WEEKS AFTER THAT, THE year's final triumph came at the Sahara Invitational in Las Vegas. I'd never been lucky in Vegas. I'd finished second three times there in the Tournament of Champions, and had to withdraw with the hand injury when I was one shot behind Nicklaus in the final round in 1963.

It appeared my bad luck would continue. After opening with rounds of 66-66-68 at Paradise Valley I was leading the tournament when I came to the ninth hole of the final eighteen. I chipped to about two feet and without wasting any time tapped the short putt toward the hole. The ball started to go in, then spun around and hung on the back lip, balancing on the edge of the cup. I could see it was moving ever so slowly so I waited and it finally fell in. As I was leaving the green a rules official came up and cited Rule 35-1-H which states that a player must allow only "a few seconds" before determining the ball is at rest and hitting it again. I'd waited almost thirty seconds and the official said that was more than a few. I explained that I hadn't hit the ball because I could see it was moving and I didn't want to violate another rule of golf that states you can't hit a ball in motion. My playing partner, Tommy Aaron, backed me up all the way. He also saw that the ball was moving. Obviously there's a contradiction between those two rules.

But you can guess who won that debate. I left the hole with a two-shot penalty and a double-bogey six on my card. Luckily the ball dropped or it would have been a seven. It shook me up so badly that I birdied the next three holes, shot 69 and finally broke the Vegas jinx with a three-shot victory. I finished the season with four wins and $99,932 in winnings, third place on the money list. For the third time in six years I won the Vardon Trophy, averaging 70.85 strokes per round.

After the tournament, Shirley and I met Hack and Barbara Miller for dinner at the Flamingo Hotel. We had met the Millers several years earlier in Salt Lake City and become good friends. As we were passing through the hotel casino I stopped to watch a friend throwing dice at the craps table. Shirley and Barbara stood off to the side, where Barbara pulled out a book she wanted to give us as a present. The title: "Meet the Mormons."

12

Latter-day Saint

13

At a Mormon fireside in the 1960s.
For a guy who didn't pray until he was 34,
I did a lot of speaking from the pulpit.

San Diego, California
January 1, 1966

God works in mysterious ways. Barely two months after leaving that Las Vegas casino, I joined the Church of Jesus Christ of Latter-day Saints.

I didn't have much of what Mormons call a testimony—a personal witness that Jesus in fact restored His gospel in its fullness in the latter days through the modern-day prophet Joseph Smith. Shirley had a strong testimony from the beginning, but the attraction for me initially was the church's youth program that I could see taught good values and morals and offered the kind of wholesome activities that kept teenagers busy. Our three children were growing up. Linda was almost twelve. I thought it would be good for the family to join the church and that we should do it together.

After nearly half-a-century in the church I have to say my testimony has grown tremendously. I have seen the hand of the Lord in my own life and throughout the world and I have been privileged to know and feel the spirit of modern-day prophets. But in the beginning, my faith was as small as the mustard seed they write about in the Bible, a book I had never read.

Shirley was always the spiritual one.

She first met the Mormons when she was a young girl and went with her mother to Detroit to buy a new Dodge. Back then you could get a better deal if you went straight to the factory. They drove home to Washington through Salt Lake City, where they stayed with friends. Shirley remembers floating in the salt water in the Great Salt Lake and she listened to a broadcast of the Mormon Tabernacle Choir, an experience she never forgot.

The only Mormons either of us knew personally were Don Collett, my Navy pal, and his wife, Verla, our next-door neighbors when we lived behind the seventeenth green at San Diego Country Club. And they were what were called Jack Mormons—members who aren't active. Don and Verla didn't have anything against their religion, they just didn't go to church on Sunday and they drank the occasional crème de mint. Don was raised in Utah in a Latter-day Saint family but his parents weren't active in the church and consequently neither was he. We knew the Colletts as friendly, good-hearted people. If they were Mormons, whether they went to church or not, then Mormons were okay in our book. One Sunday morning when we were living in Bonita, Shirley was on her way to the Congregational Church, her usual place of worship. Instead, she felt impressed to attend the Mormon services simply because she knew the Colletts were members, even though she was sure they wouldn't be there.

Shirley was a churchgoer. She went every chance she got. She started going to church on Sundays, every Sunday, as a child and the habit continued. When we were on Tour she didn't attend services if there was a conflict with my golf schedule, but if she could fit them both in she would. When we were home in Chula Vista, Sunday meant church. She was raised Northern Baptist but attended the Congregational Church in Chula Vista and whatever church that was closest to the golf course on the road. The specific denomination didn't matter as much as the worship.

Our daughter Linda was like her mother. As soon as she understood what was going on she went to church with Shirley. When she was four years old and a family friend asked Linda if she knew what Sundays were for, she answered, "Sundays are for mommies and their little girls to go to church and daddies to play golf." It was one of those guile-less comments kids make, but when I heard what she said it had an impact on me. I remember making more of an effort after that when I was home and off the Tour to go to church with Shirley and the kids. But it was half-hearted. I had no habit of attending church whatsoever. My parents didn't practice any religion that I knew of. I believed in God in general. It was my opinion that the universe hadn't come about by mere chance, but I was content to leave the details to someone else.

In the summer of 1959 we had our first introduction to the Mormons and their culture when I played in the Utah Open in Salt Lake City. Seeing the headquarters of the LDS Church had nothing to do with my decision to go there. Fishing did. At the start of the year, Don Collett had recruited me to play in the tournament, even though the Utah Open wasn't on the Tour calendar that year. In 1958 the Utah Open had a $17,000 purse and was an official Tour event—Dow Finsterwald won and Arnold Palmer finished second; I took that week off and skipped the tournament. But in 1959 the purse dropped to $15,000 and that wasn't quite enough to qualify for the Tour, although the $1,500 first prize still managed to attract a number of Tour players.

Don had played in the Utah Open in 1957 and 1958 after he got out of the Navy. He almost won in 1957, when he placed second to Zell Eaton. He had a lot of friends in Utah from his days growing up there, and Steve Dunford, president of the Utah Golf Association, used Don as a pipeline to recruit players on the Tour, where he was competing occasionally. Back during the winter, when Don first asked me about playing in Utah, I turned him down. But then he started to talk about the great trout fishing in the mountains outside Salt Lake City and all the fun we'd have going after them. I was hooked when he threw in the fishing trip.

This negotiation took place early in the spring, months before Don and I traveled to New York and I won the U.S. Open at Winged Foot. After that he thought I would cancel the trip to Utah because the tournament was in the middle of July, the prime of the season and a month following the U.S. Open. I have to admit I thought about dropping out, especially when Ed Carter, a PGA Tour official, informed me I hadn't received permission to leave the Tour that week and it would cost me a hundred-dollar fine. But I had made a commitment to my friend, and if the trout were as big as he said they were, it would be worth the hundred bucks.

The week began, and nearly ended, the day I arrived in Utah when Don and I fished the Weber River thirty miles east of Salt Lake City. He had fished there as a kid and took me to his favorite spot, but as I stood at the edge of the river, casting out, the bank gave way and the next thing I knew I was in the water, washing downstream with the current. It was a good-sized river and moving fast. Luckily, Don was fishing below me. He ran along the bank and shouted for me to grab onto an overhanging tree branch, which I did. Then he reached out his pole and I grabbed onto it and he pulled me in. I was the only thing we caught all day.

At that point we realized we needed to leave right away to make our tee times in the pro-am at Oakridge Country Club. I was soaking wet so I took off my pants and held them out the passenger window to dry as Don drove west toward Salt Lake City, muttering about how he almost drowned the U.S. Open champion. In the pro-am, just glad to be in dry clothes and on dry ground, I shot eight-under-par 64 and set a new course record.

The next day, refusing to get skunked, we tried fishing again. This time Don brought along a local sportswriter, Hack Miller of the *Deseret News*, Salt Lake's evening newspaper. Hack took us to his favorite fishing spot on the East River, not far from where the Mormon Pioneers first entered the Salt Lake Valley in 1847. Hack—that was his nickname, his real first name was Harold—had written about Don when he was a sports star in the Navy and Don had contacted him in advance about fixing me up with a fishing trip. After I won the U.S. Open, Hack was more than happy to oblige. He had material for his column, and I finally caught my first fish (but far from my last) in Utah, a German Brown Trout.

The Utah tournament got a lot of attention. Not only was the U.S. Open champion entered, but so was Bob Rosburg, the Open runner-up. Rossie got a measure of revenge when he won the tournament. Porky Oliver finished second, one shot behind, and I was another stroke back in third place. I won $850—minus the $100 I owed the PGA Tour.

A pleasant Mormon woman named Oma Wagstaff was with the ladies golf association and served as Shirley's hostess for the week. She showed us the local sites. We saw "This is the Place" monument, walked around Temple Square, which was right next to Hotel Utah where we stayed, and sat in the hard oak benches in the tabernacle and heard the Mormon Tabernacle Choir's Thursday night practice. It so happened that Leonard Bernstein, the famous conductor and composer, was there that week, recording a Christmas album with the choir. The music was everything Shirley remembered and more. But what impressed us most about our stay in Salt Lake was the friendly, family-oriented atmosphere. Everywhere we went we saw families doing things together. It was that image we wouldn't forget.

We returned in 1960 for the Utah Open when it was again part of the PGA Tour. Billy Johnston, a Tour regular who had grown up in Utah, won that year at the Salt Lake Country Club, Art Wall finished second and Ken Venturi third. I tied with Don Collett for nineteenth place. But I caught a mess of trout on a fishing trip Hack Miller lined up before the tournament to the Gros Ventre River in Jackson, Wyoming— which may not have been the best way to prepare for the golf tournament. I played again in the Utah Open in 1963, finished fourth, and Hack and I went fishing again. We became fishing buddies. I'd see him at the Masters and other Tour events he covered for the *Deseret News*. He'd ask me about golf and I'd ask him about trout fishing.

Now and then Shirley would ask Hack what the Mormons believed. In February of 1965 the topic came up when we were all in the car driving back from a banquet sponsored by the San Diego Golf Association that honored junior golf. A number of players who had come up through the ranks were invited, Gene Littler and myself, Mickey Wright, Phil Rodgers, Chuck Courtney and others. Hack served in the National Guard and was coincidentally in San Diego on a military assignment at the amphibious base in Coronado that week, so we invited him to go with us to the program. On the car ride back, the entire family—Linda was ten, Billy eight and Bobby five—was a captive audience when Shirley asked Hack another of her Mormon questions. He took a big sigh, like a man entering a sand trap with a buried lie, knowing what he has to do but not sure at all how it's going to turn out, and laid out the whole Mormon story for us. He later said he'd been dancing around that speech for six years and finally decided to do his duty and give it.

For the next twenty minutes he was the only one to speak. He told the story of the Latter-day Saints from start to finish. He talked about Joseph Smith seeing a vision of the Father and the Son when he was a fourteen-year-old farm-boy in upstate New York; about how he was directed to gold plates buried in a nearby mountain that contained holy scripture from ancient remnants of the House of Israel who lived in the Americas; and about Joseph Smith translating those gold plates into the Book of Mormon. He told about God restoring the fullness of the gospel of Jesus Christ through Joseph Smith and of the succession of prophets who continued to lead the church.

Hack finished just as we pulled into the driveway. Billy and Bobby, seeing their escape, opened the door and bolted for the house, but Linda and Shirley stayed seated a moment, absorbing what they'd just heard. Hack apologized if he'd talked too much. I just sat there. I don't remember much of what he said before he left, or that I said a word at all in response.

THE GOLF SEASON TOOK OVER after that, interrupted only by my occasional fishing breaks to the Coronado Islands. We didn't see Hack again until the Sahara Open in October in Las Vegas, where we had dinner at the Flamingo and Barbara Miller gave Shirley that copy of "Meet the Mormons" in the casino. Hack said the book was especially for me, because it was full of pictures and I didn't read books.

I finished the season two weeks later in early November at the Hawaiian Open, the first time the PGA Tour had stopped there in seventeen years. One afternoon, Shirley and I went to the north side of Oahu and visited the Polynesian Cultural Center, which is owned and operated by the Church of Jesus Christ of Latter-day Saints. We sat on the steps of the nearby Mormon Temple and I asked my friend Wally Dill to take a picture of us, joking that it was as close as we'd ever get to being Mormons.

But wherever we went it seemed we couldn't avoid something associated with the church and its members. Soon after we returned to San Diego, Shirley was invited to a political function where George Romney, the governor of Michigan who would run later run for President (Mitt's father), and his wife Lenore were invited guests. The Romneys captivated Shirley with their poise, style and candor—and they were Mormon. Afterward she asked Cliff Wallace, a San Diego lawyer who she knew to be some sort of local Mormon leader (he was a stake president, in charge of several congregations known as wards), if he might have the phone number for the fulltime missionaries.

You do not have to ask a Mormon such a thing twice.

Two young missionaries on their two-year assignments knocked on our door just a couple of nights later. But Shirley didn't feel well and she asked them to come back. The very next night there was another knock. This time it was two older men who weren't fulltime missionaries but stake missionaries—local members who proselyte in their spare time. They introduced themselves as Noel Bake and Ed White and said they were "Seventies," an office in the priesthood.

My ears perked up. Seventy was an important number to me. I liked seventy! It was a good golf score. We invited the men in and called the kids to come into the living room.

They asked if we'd like to hear a lesson about the church. We had plenty of time that night so they ended up giving us several lessons. A few nights later they were back with more. In just a couple of weeks we received a crash course in Mormonism. The men explained the Word of Wisdom, the church's health code that prohibits such things as coffee, tea, alcohol, tobacco and overeating. That's a big hurdle for a lot of people but it hardly affected us. Shirley and I were never big drinkers. I could remember only a handful of times when we had drunk alcohol. We didn't smoke and even before I began my buffalo diet, which I'd been on for over a year, I'd given up coffee because I noticed it made me jittery and affected my putting. They explained the law of tithing—paying a tenth of your increase to the church, as outlined in the Bible. That one got my attention. I'd just made $100,000 playing golf in 1965; the math was easy. God would get the same as my caddy. But they pointed out that everything comes from God and we are only required to give back a small portion in gratitude and to help His cause. Most important to us, they explained the concept of families being the central unit in Heavenly Father's plan and that families are eternal. For Shirley and me, two people raised as single kids who never wanted to be alone again, that hit home.

After less than a month, the missionaries asked me during a subsequent lesson when I'd like the family to be baptized. They said it in a matter-of-fact way, as if they were asking what kind of golf ball I'd be playing that day. I looked around the room at the kids and Shirley. I could see there was no opposition from them. If I was good with this, everyone was good with this.

I knew Shirley had been ready for years. I recognized it was not an easy religion to follow. The standards were high, the expectations great. It was like a difficult golf course; but I liked a difficult golf course. Without dwelling on it any longer than a four-foot putt, I looked at a calendar and chose Sunday, December 26, the day after Christmas, as our baptismal date.

Only after the missionaries left did I realize I had a serious conflict. The San Diego Chargers were playing the Buffalo Bills in the American Football League championship game at Balboa Stadium on Sunday, December 26. I was a huge Chargers fan—still am—and never missed a game if I could help it. I did not want to break the commandment about the Sabbath Day the very day I became a Mormon, but I wanted to see that game. I called the missionaries and explained to them my problem. Could we postpone until the following Saturday? They said yes of course. It was settled. The Casper family would begin the New Year by being baptized on January 1, 1966.

The first person I called was Hack Miller in Salt Lake. I asked the man who must have wondered if I'd even been listening that night in the car ten months before if he would be willing to come to San Diego and baptize me into the church; and not just me, but Shirley, Linda and Billy also. He said yes immediately. On Sunday, December 26, I went to the Chargers game (they lost 23-0 to the Buffalo Bills). The next Saturday, Hack and Barbara came to San Diego and Hack baptized everyone but Bobby, who hadn't yet reached eight—the "age of accountability." The following day at services in the Chula Vista Ward we were confirmed members of the Church of Jesus Christ of Latter-day Saints. The world's newest Mormons.

For two months golf had been on the back burner, nothing more than an afterthought, so naturally I started off my eleventh full year on tour, and first as a Mormon, with a win in the San Diego Open, the tournament I'd been trying to win since 1952.

The fifteenth time was a charm. I was four shots behind going into the final round when a burst of very un-San Diego-like weather blew in, bringing rain and stiff winds. Brutal as they were, such conditions were a blessing for someone with allergies. The first hole was side-wind and I birdied it, the second hole was downwind and I birdied it, the third hole was stiff against the wind and I parred it, and then I birdied the fourth hole going downwind again. I was three-under after four holes. On the ninth hole I had a drive and 3-iron when normally it would be a 6- or 7-iron and I holed the putt for another birdie to go out four-under. On the back I started with a birdie downwind on ten, parred eleven, twelve and thirteen and birdied fourteen against the wind, hitting a 4-iron where I would normally hit a 9-iron. I made another birdie at sixteen against the wind and added another birdie on seventeen. All day, I kept my head down and concentrated on battling the elements. As I approached the eighteenth tee I saw my friend Jim Fox, who always followed me when I played in San Diego, and asked him how I stood. He said, "You have a four-shot lead." I said "What?!" I parred the last hole for 64 and won by four shots over Tommy Aaron and a new long-hitter on tour, Tom Weiskopf. To this day I consider that the finest round of golf I've ever shot in my life.

Two weeks after that I played in the Bob Hope Desert Classic, where I was defending champion. I finished seventh, and then, largely because of Bob Hope, left to entertain the troops in Vietnam.

Bob Hope had been my good friend for some time, and he was also my hero. Over the years we got to know each other by playing golf together in pro-ams, and every now and then he invited me to appear on his TV specials. His writers got a lot of mileage out of me when I went on my new diet. He joked, "San Diego has one of the nicest zoos in the world; every time Casper is around they have to equip him with a muzzle." And, "You know Casper eats buffalo. I tried buffalo and the only thing it did for me was I burped nickels." I found him to be as funny and gracious in person as he was on the air and I always admired the way he entertained soldiers with his USO shows, something he started in World War II and continued in every war the United States had been in since.

At church they emphasized the importance of Christian service. Just a few days after we became Mormons we went to the Bishop's Storehouse, the church's welfare depository in San Diego, and cleaned toilets, stacked shelves with food for the poor, and canned tuna. Trust me, canning tuna is a stinky job. I learned that was one way to do service. But it didn't have to be organized by anyone else. True service was doing something entirely out of the goodness of your heart and your desire to help somebody else, not something you got paid for.

I thought now was the time—the Tour was heading to Florida and it was the height of spraying season—and Bob Hope was the example. I volunteered to go to Vietnam.

The State Department was all for it. The war needed all the positive PR it could get. They set up a sixteen-day tour for me to visit the troops. The plan was that I would give golf clinics, visit the injured and in general do what I could to boost morale with a celebrity visit from back home.

I flew first to the Philippines where I played in the Philippine Open, gave clinics for Air Force personnel stationed there and visited the hospitals where they brought in the wounded from Vietnam. I also played several six a.m. rounds of golf at the Wack Wack Country Club in Manila with the brand new president of the Philippines, Ferdinand Marcos. He had been voted into office just two months earlier (and would be ousted

twenty years later for corruption). In the Philippines I began to understand just how fast the news had spread about my joining the Mormon
Church. When Shirley and I appeared on Dindo Gonzales's national TV
show, Dindo, the Walter Cronkite of the Philippines, talked about the
church I had just joined and encouraged everybody listening to let in the
Mormon missionaries when they knocked on their doors.

Hack Miller, who had spent time in Vietnam reporting on the war
for his newspaper the year before, accompanied me on the trip. It was
just the two of us—and my supply of buffalo meat—so unlike a big Bob
Hope show, we could move around the country much more freely. One
of our first stops was north of Saigon at a Marine camp near Danang.
They'd set up a tractor tire as a target for hitting shots out of the sand.
In anticipation of my arrival the colonel had been practicing and he beat
me. Welcome to the war zone.

From there we flew by helicopter to a camp where they had lost one
of their men on patrol that morning. We could hear rifle shots in the
background when we landed. I got off the helicopter wearing a white hat
and white shirt and the commanding officer who greeted us wondered
why I didn't also paint a big bulls-eye on my back. We didn't spend
much time there. On our next stop, in Dalat, I played the only golf
course I've ever seen that was entirely dirt—tees, fairways, rough, greens,
all dirt. We were hustled out of there as soon as we putted out on the
ninth "green." They explained that South Vietnam controlled the golf
course during the day but the Viet Cong controlled it at night.

I played another golf course in Saigon but mostly I spent my time
signing autographs, passing out pictures and hitting hundreds of golf
balls. I hit them off aircraft carriers, along sandy beaches, into rice pad-
dies and jungles. At one clinic, after hitting a bunch of shots into the
countryside, I told the soldiers they could retrieve the balls, and they
said, "Naw, you just hit them into our mine field." In the Tonkin Gulf, I
gave clinics on four aircraft carriers—the *Kitty Hawk, Ranger, Yorktown
and Enterprise*. Twelve years after leaving the Navy I finally boarded an
aircraft carrier. On the *Enterprise*, the men pointed me in the direction

of a Russian trawler and asked me to hit at that. The trawler was right off the bow and never left their side. If they went port, the trawler went port. If they went starboard, the trawler went starboard. I started hitting golf balls in the trawler's direction and it promptly left. Apparently the ship's radar picked up the balls coming at it. The Russians didn't know what was shooting at them but they knew they'd better leave. The sailors particularly enjoyed that part of the exhibition.

We flew around Vietnam in helicopters and light aircraft. We got shot at once when we went on a supply mission. We visited several remote Special Forces camps. At one of the larger camps we sat down to dinner and a soldier at the next table was a major from Utah named Bernie Fisher, who recognized Hack Miller from his newspaper column. Bernie proceeded to tell us that he had just returned from rescuing a downed pilot in the A Shau Valley after an intense battle that killed hundreds of Americans. He told us about landing his plane in the middle of the enemy, while U.S. fighter jets provided cover from above. He had just a one-seat plane and threw the injured pilot on his lap and somehow managed to take off and fly away again without getting shot down. Major Fisher was later awarded the Congressional Medal of Honor for his heroism and we were the first ones to hear about what he had done to earn it.

I remember Hack was frustrated because he had this major scoop and there were no phones available to get the story out. It would be five days before he could file his story and by then the rescue had been all over the news. I asked Bernie Fisher, a good Mormon boy, why he risked his life and he said he never even thought about it until he was finished. In the back of his mind he said he remembered his Patriarchal blessing, a personal revelation Mormons receive through the priesthood, that promised him if he served God then God would serve him. From where I sat he had miracle written all over him. That really strengthened my own testimony about God and His hand in all things. Two months earlier I had hardly ever prayed in my entire life, now I'm sitting in a mess hall talking about spiritual things with a man who had just risked his life to save someone else's. In my own life I'd always sensed that someone and something besides me was really in control. Now I felt I was beginning to understand what it was.

By the time we were airlifted from Saigon to the *Kitty Hawk* for transport to Hong Kong I had a new perspective on life, death, and the subtle secret to happiness that is Christian service. In a war that was far from universally popular, I saw a lot of brave, uncomplaining men keeping their heads down and doing their duty. I went over to inspire the troops and came away inspired by them. Even though I was still hitting golf balls every day, it was the longest I'd been truly separated from my golf game since I was fifteen years old. Golf wasn't any less important to me after Vietnam, but along the way a lot of other important things elbowed in for a place at the table.

It was certainly a unique way to prepare for the Masters. I came back from Asia just in time for my tenth attempt at the green jacket and finished in tenth place behind the winner, Jack Nicklaus. He became the first man to win back-to-back titles at Augusta. I finished third at the Tournament of Champions in Las Vegas before returning to San Diego, gathering up the family, and flying to the U.S. Open at The Olympic Club in San Francisco, of all places. In the epicenter of the hippie summer of free love and war protests, I showed up, just back from Vietnam and a newly baptized member of the Mormon Church. I was counter-culture to the counter-culture.

I came to San Francisco feeling fresh and ready for the game's biggest test. It didn't make sense on paper, but my focus on things non-golf increased my ability to focus on golf.

On a demanding, unforgiving course, through the Open's first three and a half rounds, I played as well as I ever had.

Arnold Palmer played just a little better.

But then came his bogey and my birdie at fifteen in the final round, and on the par-five sixteenth he was buried in the sand lying four while I was lying two with a straight shot to the green and a 5-iron in my hands . . .

13

The Playoff

14

After making a 40-foot birdie putt on the thirteenth hole of
the playoff, I finally had the lead in the U.S. Open.

San Francisco, California
June 20, 1966

The ball clicked cleanly off the blade of the 5-iron, landed on the front of the green, bit slightly, and checked up thirteen feet from the hole.

Before it stopped rolling spectators behind me were already on the run, breaking past the marshals to secure a good spot to witness the next shot. By the time Arnold got to his ball in the trap and I walked onto the putting surface, the gallery had the upper part of the sixteenth hole entirely surrounded.

I lay three with a putter in my hands, staring at the distinct possibility of a birdie. Arnold lay four with a sand iron in his hands, staring at the distinct possibility of a double-bogey.

He went first. He dug in his heels and executed a picture-perfect sand shot that ran to within three feet of the hole; a tremendous effort under the circumstances.

Then he marked and watched me roll in my thirteen-footer for a birdie four.

If he missed his putt, we were tied. He wasted no time, stepped up, and stroked the ball into the hole.

"Best six I ever made in my life," he later called it.

He was still leading the U.S. Open—one stroke up with two holes to play.

The 443-yard par-four seventeenth had played the toughest at Olympic all week, averaging 4.61 strokes for the tournament. The fairway is uphill, allowing for little or no roll, and the narrow, tiny green also slants sharply upward. I hit first and my drive bent right, but fortunately way right. All the trouble in Open courses is from the edge of the fairway to the gallery ropes because that's where the heavy rough is. Beyond the ropes the gallery walks and tramples down the grass. By Sunday afternoon, that's a lot of trampling. My ball was beyond the ropes, sitting on a patch of bare dirt, still a good distance from the green but playable.

Arnold's drive, on the other hand, veered left and ducked into the heavy, five-inch-deep rough.

I hit first, a 3-iron off the dirt that landed to the side of the green but still in the edge of the rough.

Arnold over-corrected on his approach shot and landed in the right rough, forty yards short of the green and still buried in the rough. From the shaggy grass alongside the fringe, I pitched to three feet above the hole.

Arnold recovered by hitting a wonderful pitch that came to rest ten feet below the hole.

He lined up his putt, made a beautiful stroke and the ball headed straight for the cup—only to run out of speed and turn off at the last second. Arnold tapped in for his bogey.

I faced a slippery downhill three-footer for my par. I stood over it no longer than normal—and I holed it.

We were tied.

I had picked up seven shots in eight holes and five shots over the last three—from Arnold Palmer.

In all three previous rounds, I used a 4-wood off the tee at the short par-four eighteenth and made two bogeys and a par. I decided to leave the 4-wood in the bag and took out the driver. I finally found the fairway, my ball coming to rest on the short grass three feet from the right edge.

After using his driver all week, Arnold took out his 1-iron. By this point we had completely traded personalities. And even the 1-iron didn't go straight. His tee shot veered left, settling out of sight in the heavy rough, very near where Ben Hogan hit his drive in the 1955 playoff against Jack Fleck and needed three blows to get it back on the fairway, ending his Open chances then and there.

Palmer wasn't about to let history repeat itself. He must have taken a swatch of grass three feet long. Somewhere amid all that flying sod was his ball, and after the ground stopped shaking it exploded high into the air and didn't come down until it found the upper edge of the tiny, tilting green, thirty feet beyond the hole.

I was just 105 yards from the flag, but the angle from the right side of the fairway brought a leaning cypress tree near the green into play. I had to get the ball up quickly and keep it high, an interesting challenge under the circumstances. I put a little extra loft on my wedge and managed to clear the tree and land safely on the green, fifteen feet above and to the right of the hole.

Arnold putted first, straight downhill. It was a birdie putt that could win the Open, but it was frighteningly quick.

He barely touched the ball and it still carried all the way to the hole, but it broke wide to the right, coming to rest six feet away, pin high. We were playing the continuous putting rule that year because the USGA thought it would speed up play (And it did. Rounds averaged an hour less than the 1965 Open.) As he passed me, Arnold said, "Cass, do you want me to mark it?" I said, "No Arnold, you're warm, go ahead and knock it in." He had a side-hill leaner with the U.S. Open on the line— but Arnold being Arnold, he walked right up and slammed it in the back of the hole. Then he stepped aside to see if I was going to make my putt and win the U.S. Open.

After lining up my downhill fifteen-footer I realized it wasn't a putt I wanted to try to make. My goal was to get it close enough so the second putt wouldn't be a problem. There are birdie putts and there are putts where you should two putt for a par and this was definitely a two-putt-for-a-par situation. If I tried to hole it, the ball could easily run toward the front of the green, well beyond the hole, and put me in jeopardy of a three-putt. While it was awfully tempting to go for the hole and win the U.S. Open then and there, that was not the smart play and I knew it. If the putt dropped, great, but success would be anything inside a foot.

I barely nudged the ball to get it started. It ran out of steam six inches from the cup. I tapped in, and after seventy-two holes, the last thirty-six together, Arnold Palmer and I were right back where we had started, still tied for the lead in the U.S. Open. I shot 36-32—68 and he shot 32-39—71. Not too many players leading the Open on the final day fail to win by shooting 71.

At 278 we were the only players under par for the tournament, seven shots ahead of third-place finisher Jack Nicklaus and nine strokes better than the 287 Jack Fleck and Ben Hogan had shot to set up their own playoff eleven years earlier. (Hogan's 1948 Open record of 276 was still safe, by two shots.)

Our eighteen-hole playoff was scheduled to begin at 10:30 the next morning.

AS IMPRESSIVE AS ANYTHING Arnold Palmer did in his entire career was the way he handled the press conference that followed. Over the years, as I have watched countless heartbreaking losses at sporting events, live and on television, and sometimes seen the victims of those losses skip out on press conferences or give surly one-word responses to the media, I think of Arnold that day at Olympic. Both of us were ushered into the media room where hundreds of reporters were much more interested in what went wrong than what went right. For almost an hour they grilled Palmer about this shot and that shot and this decision and that decision. He sat there and took it until the last question was asked. When it was over, a USGA official asked him if he wanted to exit by a side door so he could avoid the crowds out front. "Naw," he said, "The way I played, I deserve whatever they do to me."

After the postmortem, we went to our separate corners, Arnold to his friends' home in the city, where he and Winnie had a quiet dinner with, among others, Mark and Nancy McCormack; me to a Mormon meeting house to give a talk.

Long before I knew I would tie for the lead in the U.S. Open, and be in a lengthy press conference afterward, and that I would be playing another eighteen holes the next day, I had agreed to give a Sunday night fireside talk at seven o'clock in Petaluma, forty miles north of the city.

A deal's a deal. I changed and drove straight to the church, arriving almost an hour late. The chapel was full. No one had left. I can remember the length of every putt and exactly what club I hit on every shot that Sunday, but to this day the most I can remember about that fireside is talking about my trip to Vietnam. But I must have said something mildly interesting because it was after eleven o'clock when the meeting ended. I returned to the Leininger's home in Greenbrae. I hadn't eaten anything since lunch. Shirley turned on the grill and I had a late, late dinner of pork chops, green beans and salad. Then I went to bed and slept like a man with nothing to lose.

ALTHOUGH WE HAD BOTH WON one U.S. Open in our parallel decade as professionals, and lost the other nine, Arnold's history with the tournament was much more tortured than mine. In 1962 at Oakmont, just an hour's drive from his hometown of Latrobe, Pennsylvania, he missed a ten-foot putt on the final green of regulation to fall into a tie with Jack Nicklaus, and lost in the playoff the next day, 71 to 74. The next year at Brookline he finished regulation play tied with Julius Boros and Jacky Cupit. In the playoff he tried to hit his ball out of a rotted tree stump on the eleventh hole, made double-bogey, and never recovered. He finished with a 76 to Cupit's 73 and Boros's winning 70.

Along with the new memory of losing a seven-stroke advantage the previous day on the back nine, Arnold had to haul that baggage with him to the first tee Monday morning. It was his third playoff for the U.S. Open in five years. And before that he had to endure about two hundred newsmen waiting for him in the locker room, where they asked the same questions they'd asked the night before. One or two of the reporters wandered over to my locker for a comment, but I was largely left to myself.

OLYMPIC'S FIRST FAIRWAY WAS LINED from tee to green. It looked as if all of San Francisco decided to take the day off to watch a golf tournament. (The official attendance was 12,059, compared to 17,265 the day before. This time, they were all lining the same hole.) I opened with four straight pars, followed with a bogey, and found myself quickly down two shots. I closed the gap with birdies on seven and eight but on the ninth green I did something I hadn't done all tournament—three-putted from the right edge, which led to another bogey.

The front nine was nearly a rerun from Sunday. Palmer made the turn in 33, two under, and I was at even par 35—compared to our scores of 32-36 on Sunday.

But there was a back nine still to play.

On the par-four tenth, Arnold maintained his two-shot lead when we both parred. On eleven, each of us drove in the fairway. I then hit a 3-iron that bounced barely onto the green. Arnold hit a 4-iron that settled in the rough just short of the green. He hit a tremendous chip to fifteen feet as I sized up my putt, a looping thirty-five-footer that would break at least eight feet in the direction of Lake Merced, depending on the speed. I struck it square, watched it arc wide right toward the lake, and drop dead center.

When Arnold missed his putt and made bogey we were once again, after eighty-three holes, back to where we started—dead even.

After matching pars on the par-four twelfth we both hit the green on the par-three thirteenth. I was a little farther away, forty feet from the hole. This putt had a break of about a foot and a half. It also went into the heart of the cup for a birdie two. When Arnold two-putted for par, for the first time in four days he was not tied or in the lead of the U.S. Open.

As we stood on the fourteenth tee no one needed to tell me that anything could still happen. At this same point a day earlier I had trailed by five strokes. I could not relax. I could not afford to think about anything but the next shot. But for the first time in five long days it was finally my tournament to win or lose, and I sensed that those combined seventy-five feet of putts on eleven and thirteen had done a mental number on my opponent. He had played well. He was one-under par through thirteen holes—and even par over the past two tension-filled days—and still he was behind.

I made par on fourteen to Arnold's bogey. I made par on fifteen, again to Arnold's bogey. On the long sixteenth, the site of so much drama the day before, I played so careful I made a bogey six. But Arnold made seven.

Now I was up five shots with two to play. For the first time, I bogeyed the hard, uphill seventeenth and dropped a stroke to Arnold's par, but got it back when I finally made birdie on the eighteenth to score

35-34—69 for the playoff to Arnold's 33-40—73. In two days on the Lake Course's back nine I shot 66 and Palmer shot 79. (On the front I shot 71 to his 65.)

After I putted out Arnold graciously congratulated me and then he quickly started to walk off the green. I caught up with him. "I'm sorry Arnie," I said and put my arm over his shoulder. I wasn't sorry for winning; we were both there to compete and neither of us would have had it any other way. I was sorry because I understood how devastating it can be to play that well, climb that high, and fall just short.

So often in a major championship when a player catches fire and runs away from the field—Ben Hogan in the 1953 U.S. Open; Tiger Woods and Rory McIlroy in later U.S. Opens; Arnold himself with six-shot wins in the 1962 British Open and the 1964 Masters—it's just one player surging away. But this time there were two of us, and while Palmer played superb golf all week on a very difficult course, where eleven over par made the cut, I played superb golf as well. For the last fifty-four holes it was just the two of us.

From the first tee to the last, I felt better than at any other time in my career. My mind felt right, my body felt right, my heart felt right. Spiritually I had a new eternal perspective; and when you think in terms of eternity it tends to put a single U.S. Open in its proper place.

The Lake Course puts a premium on putting and my putting, while much less publicized, was as good or better than when I won the Open at Winged Foot. In that Open I had 114 putts. At Olympic I had 117 putts in regulation, and 28 putts in the playoff. (My "hot" putter in '66 was a Wilson Billy Casper model.) Out of 440 rounds played that week at Olympic, just fifteen were in the 60s—and I had four of them. It was as well as I ever played, as well as I was capable of playing, and it came in the biggest setting in golf.

It was destined to go down in history as the Open Arnold Palmer blew—a bookend to his seven-stroke come-from-behind charge to win in 1960—but to my mind, and this is how I suspect Arnold would prefer to view it as well, it will always be the Open I won.

ARNOLD RECEIVED PLENTY OF CRITICISM for his bold play in the final round of regulation, when he continued to shoot at the pins and didn't play it safe off the tee. But to go about it any other way wouldn't have been Arnie. In his memoir, "A Golfer's Life," he talks about always aiming at the pin and how well he understood his own golf game:

> *"There's no question that my refusal to play safe or lay up cost me the opportunity to win scores of tournaments, including, by my calculation, three or four U.S. Opens, perhaps a Masters or two, and the PGA Championship on at least two occasions. Critics who have said that a safer shot here or there would undoubtedly have won me a few more tournaments are probably correct.*
>
> *"But the other side of that proposition—seldom mentioned by some of those critics—is equally true: if I hadn't had the instinctive desire to attempt those shots, regardless of the outcome, almost without thinking, I wouldn't have won half the tournaments I did win."*

WALTER HAGEN ONCE SAID A man is lucky to win the U.S. Open once, but if he wins it twice it's not luck. Maybe that's because in 1914 and again in 1919 The Haig won it two times himself. But as I joined a rather exclusive group that at the time included eleven multiple winners (ten more players have since joined the club) I knew what he meant. It was hard enough to win the Open one time. Doing it again felt almost ridiculous.

IN THE PRESS CONFERENCE THAT followed, the reporters wondered, now that I was a Mormon, if I would pay a tithe on my winnings of $25,000. "Ten percent of it will go to the Mormon Church," I told them, "right off the top." At that remark, Palmer leaned toward me and whispered that Mark McCormack would be getting his ten percent. When the press asked what he'd said, he told them, "Ten percent of mine will go to my business manager, right off the top." Then Arnold leaned back to me and whispered, "I think you got the best deal."

At the victory ceremony I met the low amateur and eighth place overall finisher—Johnny Miller, the nineteen-year-old college kid whose mother I met at the Tuesday night church fireside before the tournament began. His mom was right; her son could play a little bit. I think Johnny was even more astonished at how the week turned out than I was. He had planned to caddy in the tournament until he finished third in the local San Francisco qualifier. Standing side by side, the low pro and the low amateur, we introduced ourselves, shook hands, and a cherished lifetime friendship began.

Reporters asked what I thought of my chances in the next major, the British Open the following month at Muirfield. I said I wouldn't be going. I would be in Salt Lake City that week for the All-Church golf tournament. They'd never heard of it. Neither had I until a couple of months earlier.

Although it has since been discontinued, every year back then the LDS Church would hold sectional tournaments throughout the United States and the winners would come to Salt Lake City for the finals. When I joined the church I was asked if I would play a few holes with the winners in the various flights and hand out trophies and I agreed. While I'm aware circumstances can change, I believe in keeping my commitments whenever possible. It probably goes back to the instability of my youth, but I like to be able to count on people and I like people to be able to count on me. After all that had gone right in 1966, I wasn't going to take any chances. I wouldn't be backing out. I was going to Utah instead of Scotland.

14

Good as it Gets

15

Shirley and I were happy to pose for the press
after I became the second man in history
to win a million dollars playing golf.

Western Open, Chicago
June 26, 1966

The day after the playoff for the U.S. Open in San Francisco I flew to Chicago for the Western Open, played that year at Medinah Country Club on the course where Cary Middlecoff won the U.S. Open in 1949. Conditions were equally as difficult as at The Olympic Club. I was the only player under par for the tournament and won by three shots over Gay Brewer to repeat as Western Open champion.

So much for the Open jinx.

My life was never busier. If you don't want to feel ignored, win a U.S. Open. Everywhere I went, people wanted to rehash what happened at The Olympic Club, and that didn't let up all year. There wasn't a tournament I entered that the media didn't ask me to sit down for a press conference, followed by one-on-one interviews. My fireside talks at Mormon churches became a weekly event, and while I was on the road, the church asked me to call alumni of Brigham Young University to help with fundraising. Who would turn down the U.S. Open winner?

The busy life didn't hurt my golf game. I won again at the end of July at the 500 Festival in Indianapolis, where I'd also won in 1962, making it four wins for the season. By the time the year ended I was leading money winner with $121,944.02, and I collected my fourth Vardon Trophy with a stroke average of 70.27. When the members of the PGA Tour cast their votes for Player of the Year, for the first time in my career I was the recipient.

FOR OBVIOUS REASONS I TRIED not to change anything in 1967. I called the State Department and again volunteered to travel to Vietnam and entertain the troops. But by now the war had heated up considerably and they thought it might be too dangerous—not just for me, but for the officers. General William Westmoreland, the commander in Vietnam who I met on my previous tour, called me on the phone and told me personally, "Billy, you appeal to the officers more than the enlisted men and we're at the height of the Tet offensive over here and I don't want a lot of my officers standing around all in one place, where Charlie can lob something in there and we lose a lot of officers."

Then he added, "and the U.S. Open champion."

I said, "Thank you, General, thank you."

I went to Thailand instead and conducted clinics for Air Force personnel who were stationed there and flying sorties into South and North Vietnam. There I got a chance to see Bernie Fisher again. He had been promoted to colonel and by now he was officially a hero. Just weeks earlier, President Johnson had presented him with the Congressional Medal of Honor for his intrepid rescue in the A Shau Valley the previous year.

I never did get back to Vietnam. The next year I did one more tour of the troops. I went to the Philippines, Thailand and Okinawa. The low point was in the Philippines when I swung my trusty Strata-bloc driver and the shaft broke. For thirteen years I'd used that driver exclusively, I knew it better than the back of my hand. Wilson sent me dozens of new drivers that they swore were identical, but I never found a club that felt the same.

The high point was a clinic I gave at a new golf course the Japanese had built in the highlands of Okinawa. The wind was blowing at least thirty-five miles an hour. I stood on the first tee, a par-three, and went through all the clubs, talking about grip and stance, until I got to an iron I could hit to the green about 175 yards away. Through an interpreter, I told the crowd that if I were playing the hole for real I'd start the ball way out over the right hand trap and let the wind blow it back onto the green and up to the hole. With that I hit the shot. Just like I said, the ball went toward the trap, drifted on the wind back to the left, landed on the green and rolled toward the hole . . . and kept rolling . . . until it dropped right in. With that, the clinic was over. The Japanese people broke through the ropes and carried me into the clubhouse as if I'd just won a major championship.

IN 1967 I WON TWO tournaments, both by playoffs and both in Canada. The first win came at the Canadian Open in Montreal, where I shot a course record 65 in an eighteen-hole playoff against Art Wall.

The second win was at the Carling World Open outside Toronto at the Board of Trades Golf Course. Al Geiberger and I tied at the end of seventy-two holes and went into sudden death. I drove first and hit in the fairway and Allen drove in the right rough. He played his second shot to about thirty yards short of the green, still in the right rough, and I hit a 7-iron just off the front of the green. He chipped to about twenty-five feet and I chipped within three feet of the hole. He putted and missed, scored five, leaving me with a three-foot putt for the win. As I sized up my putt I started thinking about the money at stake. First place was $35,000, more money than I'd ever won in a golf tournament. Second place was $17,000. I did the math in my head. That meant this three-foot putt was worth $18,000 if I made it—$6,000 a foot! Suddenly, my knees started knocking.

I had to back away and force myself to stop thinking about the money and focus on the fundamentals I used on the practice green. Then I stepped over the putt, which wasn't at all difficult, and holed it and won the tournament. Afterward, I thought about the comment President Eisenhower had made—"You sure made a knee-knocker there"—after I'd won the Bob Hope in 1965 by sinking a similar length putt. At the time, I hadn't appreciated his meaning. It took me two and a half years to experience what a knee-knocker was—and money was the reason.

The Tour was getting to be downright affluent. Big prize money was becoming the norm. Purses climbed every year. In 1963 prize money for the season cleared $2 million for the first time. In 1967 it hit $4 million. In 1968 it went to $5 million. Jack Nicklaus won the 1967 money race with a record $188,998.08. I placed third, but the $129,423.23 I won was nearly $10,000 more than the amount I'd won the previous year when I led the money list.

I GOT TO PLAY FOR Ben Hogan that year in the Ryder Cup. The competition was held at Champions Golf Club in Houston, Texas. Hogan was non-playing captain of the U.S. team. It was the last time teams could choose between using the standard American ball or the smaller British ball, which was easier to control in the wind. Hogan sent a letter to all the players that he wanted us to get there early so we could practice with the ball we decided to use. Everyone arrived on Monday or Tuesday with the exception of Arnold Palmer, who didn't show up until Wednesday evening. Thursday was our last practice round and as our team meeting was winding down that morning, Palmer said to Hogan, "Hey Cap, what ball are we using this week?" To which Hogan replied, "Well, Mr. Palmer, I have no idea what ball you'll be using this week. The team is going to use the small ball and you haven't made the team yet."

Hogan then sent Palmer out in the first practice group—his tryout, I guess. I went out in the last group and by the time I was on the seventeenth fairway I heard a loud buzz that sounded like it was right over my head.

I looked up and directly above me was Arnold in his Aero Commander airplane. After his round he'd taken Tony Jacklin and George Will of the British team up for a ride. He decided to give them a show and buzz the golf course. He swooped in over the fairway so low I could have hit a golf ball over the plane's wing. He scared George Will so bad he wet himself. The Brits never had a chance after that. They lost 23½-8½. I played in five matches, won four and halved one for 4½ points. It was never clear whether Palmer got out of Hogan's doghouse that week, but something motivated him. He played in five matches and won every one of them.

THE YEAR 1968 WAS A time of great discontent. It was the year Robert Kennedy and Martin Luther King Jr. were assassinated, the year civil rights and Vietnam war protests hit their height. And in golf it was the year civil war erupted on the Tour between the PGA of America and touring pros who felt that too much of the revenue coming in—

especially TV money—was being kept by the organization instead of being put into tournament purses. The Tour almost disintegrated over the conflict until a last-minute compromise laid the groundwork for what we know today as the PGA Tour.

But for me personally, it was a year of content.

I opened the season in January with a three-stroke win over Arnold Palmer at the Los Angeles Open when the tournament was played at the Brookside Course next to the Rose Bowl. In April I won the Greater Greensboro Open by four strokes. In May I won the Colonial by five. In June I got a one-stroke win at the 500 Festival Open.

Then I went to Scotland and fell in love with the British Open.

After thirteen full seasons on Tour I finally played in my first British Open—officially The Open Championship—at Carnoustie in Scotland, the course where Ben Hogan won in 1953. After opening with an even-par 72 I shot 68 in round two, tying the course record set fifteen years earlier by Hogan. At 140 I led by four shots. I faltered a bit in the third round with a 74 but still held a one-shot lead over Bob Charles and two over Gary Player. On Sunday I hung on in classic blustery "British Open" weather and was tied for the lead with Gary with just five holes to play.

The fourteenth at Carnoustie is a par five and Gary was playing in the group directly in front so I had a good view when he reached the green in two and, just as I was about to hit my drive, ran in his putt for eagle. The British fans, who adored Gary, broke through the ropes and swarmed across the fairway and down to the green to celebrate. It took several minutes for the stewards to clear people off the fairway. I had to wait and wait and wait. When I finally hit my drive I was too quick, hooked it left, and it went out of bounds. I re-loaded and made four on my second ball but the two-stroke OB penalty gave me a bogey six—exactly double what Gary made on the hole. That quickly, Gary had a three-shot lead.

I got back a stroke on the next three holes and trailed by two when I arrived at the eighteenth, another par five. I was just short of the green in two and knew I had to hole my chip shot for an eagle to tie Gary, already in the clubhouse. I knocked the ball over the green aggressively going for the pin and wound up with a bogey six. Gary's closing 73 earned him a two-shot win over Jack Nicklaus, who also shot 73 in the final round, and Bob Charles, who shot 76. My 78 backed me a shot behind them to fourth place at 292. In the difficult playing conditions, only one man in the field, Brian Barnes, shot under par at Carnoustie that day.

It was a disappointing loss, but no more disappointing than the realization of just how much I had missed by not coming over earlier in my career. I generally played well in the wind and weather, I had a good imagination for trouble shots, and I was basically a ground player—all the things that lent themselves to feeling comfortable in Great Britain.

Later that season I returned to Scotland and for the first time played the Old Course at St. Andrews. Again, the unpredictable rough, the ever-changing weather, the au naturel conditions, the need to manufacture shots, all agreed with me. And as an added bonus, they didn't spray petrochemicals in Scotland.

We played the Alcan at St. Andrews. The winner got $50,000 and second-place dropped all the way to $15,000. I was tied with Gay Brewer, the 1967 Masters champion and my close friend, at the end of seventy-two holes. We played an eighteen-hole playoff the following day to see who would take home the $50,000. Gay was on top of his game and shot 68 to my 72. I still left with more than enough to cover my expenses. Going to England had not been a money-loser, after all.

I returned to play four more times in the British Open but felt like I missed out. I could have won there earlier in my career.

AFTER THE ALCAN THE FOCUS was on the money race, or rather *my* money race. After I won the Greater Hartford Open in September, the press picked up on the angle that I was in position to become the first golfer to make over $200,000 in winnings in a single year. It looked like I wouldn't make it until I got to the aptly named Lucky International in San Francisco in November. The tournament was played at Harding

Park, the public course that sits across Lake Merced from The Olympic Club. I started the last day by missing the first two greens and chipping in both times for birdie. I closed with a 66 to win by four strokes over Raymond Floyd and Don Massengale.

The win raised my total money for the year to $205,168.67, a figure widely reported in newspapers and on telecasts from coast to coast as the big sports story of the day. Later on, for reasons that were never explained to me, and might have had something to do with PGA infighting that year, the number was adjusted in the record book to $181,438. All I know is that in 1968 I reported $205,168.67 to the IRS.

As in 1966, I won both the money title and the Vardon Trophy, this time with a 69.82 stroke average, the lowest of my career and the lowest on Tour since 1951. My six victories were a personal high and the most by far on Tour and although none was a major I was considered a shoo-in for Player of the Year (the majors that year were spread out between Bob Goalby at the Masters, Lee Trevino at the U.S. Open, Gary Player at the British Open and 48-year-old Julius Boros at the PGA Championship). But because of the political disputes on the Tour, for the first time since the award began in 1948, no vote was held of the members and the PGA Player of the Year award was not given.

THE YEAR WAS EQUALLY MOMENTOUS at home as on the golf course. Nineteen sixty-eight was the year the size of our family doubled. We went from three kids to six. In three months. And we did not have triplets.

Ever since joining the LDS Church we'd talked about adopting children. The church teaches that we all come to earth after an earlier, pre-mortal existence, and both Shirley and I felt strongly that there were spirits coming that for one reason or another didn't have homes and we should bring them into ours. For years we'd tried to add to our family, but Shirley had several miscarriages since Bobby's birth seven years earlier. Three doctors told her she couldn't have any more children.

Life for us had always been a family affair. If anything, Shirley and I overcompensated for our being raised without much of a family structure at all. To us, the fuller the house, the better. And our place at the top of the hill in Bonita, the old Spreckels mansion, had plenty of bedrooms. If we'd still been in the trailer we might have had a problem, but now we had the room. More importantly, we had the help. Shirley's mother, Dorothy, had her own separate quarters in the house, where she lived with her two younger children, Margee and John. Dorothy organized and ran the house when Shirley wasn't there, making it possible for her to travel with me during the school year. Dorothy did it in a style any admiral or general would have admired. In addition to that, during a trip to the United Kingdom in 1966 we found a wonderful nanny in Ireland, Ann Moffett, who we helped immigrate to America. Ann became like one of the family. She later married another member of the "family," Jerry Elwell, a young man from Ontario, California, who we met in England when he was serving a Mormon mission and we hired him upon his return to help drive the kids and do odd jobs around the house.

So we already resembled a hotel—and that's without mentioning the various "foster" kids we were constantly taking in. For us it was always the more the merrier. The electric company loved us.

After we prayed about it and consulted our bishop, Shirley and I felt good about adopting. The kids were all for it too. We asked them what they wanted. Linda said she wanted a sister, Billy said he wanted a brother, and Bobby said, I don't care, just get one.

In late February, while I was overseas visiting the troops, Dr. Charles Franklin, Shirley's gynecologist, called with the news that a baby boy had just been born in La Mesa that they were putting up for adoption. It happened that fast. Shirley went straight to the hospital and brought home our son Byron, named after the kindly gentleman golfer I got to know when he captained our Ryder Cup team in 1965. I didn't get to meet my son for another three weeks. And not long after that, just as we were getting used to having a baby brother in the house, Dr. Franklin called again in April and said he was about to deliver twin girls who needed a home. We said we'd take them too, and that's how we got our twins, Judith and Jennifer, but we've always called them Judi and Jeni.

Two years later we adopted Charlie and the year after that David and then Julia. In six years we went from three children to nine.

I RARELY DID ANYTHING OUT of the spotlight in those days. I was playing the best golf of my career and people were trying to figure me out. I was the story that hadn't been told, the personality that hadn't been probed. A writer from *Sports Illustrated* flew to San Diego and spent a week with me on a fishing trip to the Coronado Islands.

At the 1968 U.S. Open held at Oak Hill in Rochester, New York—Lee Trevino's coming-out party, when he made the U.S. Open his first win on the PGA Tour—I planned a side trip to nearby Palmyra to see the Sacred Grove where Joseph Smith received the First Vision. Jim Murray, the syndicated columnist for the *Los Angeles Times*, tagged along—and he didn't make fun of Mormons in the column he wrote about our visit.

Gary Player also came on that trip. Gary was always interested in everything and everyone, and was a fascinating person himself. I always thought he would make a great president of the world. He was a natural diplomat. I remember one time he was introducing a new player around the locker room and when he got to me—this was in my heavier days—he said, "This is Billy Casper. He'll probably out-live me." One of history's great injustices was when anti-apartheid protestors singled out Gary Player, of all people, for his country's racist policies. He was a man who had as much compassion and tolerance for his fellow human beings as anyone I ever met.

One offseason Gary invited me to South Africa for a series of exhibitions. I stayed at his home and we played matches in Johannesburg, Cape Town, Durbin, Pretoria, Salisbury, Rhodesia, which is now Zimbabwe. and then he said, "Now we're going to the second windiest place in the world." I said, "Where's the windiest place?" and he said. "It blew away." The second windiest place turned out to be Port Elizabeth, where it was actually quite mild the day we played.

While we were in Johannesburg we visited an animal park where they let you walk right into the lions' den. The handlers said to go ahead and pet the lions, you could even put your hand in their mouth. I walked over and started petting some lions and they got quite frisky. I had to pull my arm away from one that I thought was getting a little too interested. I looked over at Gary and noticed that he wasn't getting anywhere near the animals.

I STARTED THE 1969 SEASON with my second win at the Bob Hope Desert Classic. I knew things were going my way the first day of the tournament. My playing partner in the pro-am was Andy Williams, the entertainer and sponsor of the San Diego Open, and a good friend. There was always a wait at the eleventh hole at Tamarask, a 210-yard par-three across a lake, and while we were waiting for the green to clear, Andy said, "Billy, let's see you make a birdie here." When it was our turn, I hit a 2-iron that cleared the lake, hit the front part of the green and rolled straight into the hole. Andy was so excited he grabbed me and started jumping up and down. I said, "Andy, I'm sorry I didn't make a birdie for you."

I also thought things were going my way at the Masters, where I opened with a 66, my lowest round ever at Augusta National, and held onto the lead for three rounds, coming into Sunday with a one-shot advantage over 6-foot-5 George Archer. Most of the top contenders had faded. Nicklaus, Palmer and Player were all well back in the pack. It was clearly my best opportunity to win the green jacket. But I shot 40 on the front nine on Sunday to fall well behind Archer, and made bogey on ten. I was five over par after ten holes.

Then I went three under par over the last eight holes to finish with a 74. It wasn't enough. Archer played steadily all day, shot 72, and beat me by one to become the tallest champion in Masters history. I left bitterly disappointed, but encouraged by the way I turned things around and played down the stretch.

AFTER WINNING THE WESTERN OPEN in June for the third time, I got the most unlikely victory of my career, and my biggest check, at the Alcan in Portland. It was yet another reminder that no lead in golf should ever be considered safe.

We played at the Portland Golf Club, where I'd won two Portland Opens as well as my first check on Tour. In all the tournaments I played there, I never had a score over 72, so I'm sure that helped my frame of mind when I came to the last three holes six shots behind Lee Trevino.

After making birdie on the par-five fifteenth hole I was standing on the sixteenth tee and watched Trevino, who was playing in the final group right behind me, roll in an eagle putt on the fifteenth green to go up by six. As I prepared to tee off I thought to myself, let's finish birdie, birdie, birdie and see what happens. I proceeded to roll in three straight one-putts for consecutive birdies. While I was doing this, Trevino made bogey on sixteen to give back two shots; then on the par-three seventeenth, where the pin was cut in the very front of the green, he let his caddy talk him into using a 9-iron, shaved it too close and landed in the front sand trap. That left him with a very delicate trap shot. He blasted out, the ball rolled up the bank toward the green . . . and then rolled right back down. He had to jump out of the way so the ball wouldn't hit him. It landed in his footprint. He hit his next shot to the back of the green and three putted for a triple bogey six. In two holes I'd made up six shots. After I made my final birdie by sinking a five-foot putt on the eighteenth green I saw Punch Green, a friend from the early days of the Portland Open, and asked him how I stood. "Trevino needs a birdie to tie," he said. When Trevino parred eighteen I won my first $55,000 check in golf—more money than I'd made my first two and a half years on Tour combined.

THE RYDER CUP IN 1969 was among my most memorable events in golf. I doubt that anyone who was there will ever forget it.

The competition started out more tense than usual. Two years earlier, at Champions in Houston, our 23½-8½ win was one of the soundest thrashings in Cup history. For two years the Brits stewed on that defeat and had their collective jaw set for the rematch, which was played at Royal Birkdale Golf Club in Southport, England. That summer, when Tony Jacklin became the first Englishman to win the British Open in eighteen years, it only heightened their resolve.

On opening morning, the British team won three of the four foursomes matches and halved the other to take a quick 3½-½ lead. I teamed with Frank Beard and our tie with Christy O'Connor and Peter Alliss accounted for the only American points. In the afternoon foursomes, the results were reversed. Beard and I lost to Tony Jacklin and Peter Townsend, 1 up. But every other American team won. In the next day's four-ball matches, Frank and I got a point back with a 2-up win over Peter Butler and Townsend but it was one of only three triumphs for the Americans. Going into Saturday's singles matches, the score was tied 8-8. It was the closest Cup in thirty-five years.

Great Britain took a two-point advantage with five wins in the eight singles matches in the morning session. I won my match with Brian Barnes, and Lee Trevino and Dave Hill also got victories to keep the U.S. hopes alive. But still they were fading. In the afternoon, Dave Hill went off first and defeated Barnes, followed by more American victories from Miller Barber, Dan Sikes and Gene Littler. Sandwiched in between, however, Bernard Gallacher defeated Lee Trevino, and Peter Butler beat Dale Douglass, bringing the score back to dead even, 15-15, with two matches still to conclude—me against Brian Huggett and Jack Nicklaus against Tony Jacklin.

Huggett and I went shot-for-shot for the entire eighteen holes and he secured a tie with a clutch five-foot putt on the final green. Just as the ovation for his putt was dying down at eighteen a roar went up from seventeen. I knew that kind of cheer wasn't for Nicklaus, and so did Huggett. Assuming Jacklin had won the Cup, Huggett was so overwhelmed with joy he grabbed me in an embrace. I was hugging Huggett.

What he didn't know is that the roar was because Jacklin had holed a long putt to get back to even with Nicklaus.

They came to the final hole with still nothing decided and the Ryder Cup on the line.

Both players made it to the par-five eighteenth green in three shots. Nicklaus faced about a four-foot putt on one side of the hole, Jacklin about a four-footer on the opposite side. The putts were close enough to the same distance that the officials had to measure to determine who was away. It was Jack, by about an inch, so he putted first . . . and dropped the ball dead center. Now the pressure shifted to the Englishman, the weight of the Ryder Cup on his shoulders. If he made his putt, the Cup would end in a 16-16 tie. If he missed, the U.S. would win yet again.

But before Jacklin could putt, Nicklaus stepped across his line and picked up Jacklin's ball marker. He conceded the putt. Tie game. The U.S. kept the Cup because in the event of a tie the side with possession keeps the trophy.

A tremendous cheer went up from the British crowd, celebrating what could only be considered a victory. On the U.S. side, however, the reaction from the players shifted from shock to irritation that Nicklaus had done such a thing. Jacklin's putt was hardly a gimmee, and after all, Tony hadn't given Jack his putt. I was good friends with members of the British team and, in addition, was a member of the British PGA. That night I went to their "victory" party and celebrated with them. But I remember at the time none of us cared for what Jack had done. Sam Snead was our non-playing captain and he was particularly incensed. We had worked so hard to get that far and Jack just gave it away. I flew back to America frustrated by the whole episode.

It was only later, as time passed and my perspective broadened, that my feelings changed. The more I thought about it, the more I began to appreciate what Jack Nicklaus had done and why he'd done it. He wasn't thinking about just a golf match, he was thinking in terms of compassion, camaraderie, friendship—human values that are at the core of the Ryder Cup competition. I came to regard what Jack did that day at Royal Birkdale as the greatest gesture of sportsmanship I have seen in my life.

I STARTED MY THIRD DECADE of play on the PGA Tour in 1970 by be-coming golf's second millionaire. Arnold Palmer was the first. But I was right behind him.

As was often the case, I didn't know I'd done it until the press told me.

We were playing the Los Angeles Open at Rancho Park the second week of January. Hale Irwin, a new player on Tour, and I tied at the end of regulation at 276 and headed back to the fifteenth hole to start our sudden-death playoff. Less than an hour earlier I'd played the fifteenth, a four-par. I'd hit driver to the center of the fairway, 143 yards from the hole. My next shot was slightly uphill with just a little wind in my face. I hit 7-iron three feet off line and two feet short, and made the five-foot putt for birdie. In the playoff my drive landed nine inches from my pre-vious divot. I knew I had 143 yards to the hole. I took out my 7-iron and this time hit it on line, but again two feet short. I tapped the putt in for birdie to Irwin's par and won the tournament. At the press conference afterward the media informed me I'd just cleared the million mark in of-ficial career earnings. With the $20,000 first prize my lifetime total was $1,001,924.48 (we still counted the pennies back then). Arnold Palmer, that other millionaire, finished fortieth in L.A. and won $390 to push his career total to $1,121,946.17. He was still ahead but I was gaining.

I played steady golf but didn't win another tournament by the time the calendar turned to April and all golfers lucky enough to be invited assembled once again in Georgia to vie not for a million dollars, but for something far more valuable in the universe of golf—the green jacket.

15

Augusta

16

The hardest part about winning my first green jacket was not being able to share it with Gene Littler. John Winters is in the middle.

Augusta, Georgia
April 12, 1970

I suppose it only made sense that to win the tournament I could never seem to win I would have to beat the man I could never seem to beat.

But before the Masters golf tournament of 1970 evolved into what the press called "The San Diego City Championship" between Gene Littler and me, we first had to get clear of the other eighty-one masters of golf invited that year to the Augusta National Golf Club.

And before that I had to answer for last year.

Wherever I went, the questions were the same. How would my loss to George Archer in the 1969 Masters, when I had the lead going into the final round and lost it with a 40 on the front nine, affect me on my return? Could I mentally recover from the defeat? Would I change my conservative game plan?

More to the point, would I go for the par fives in two?

The media had analyzed and re-analyzed my tournament from the year before and the statistic that stuck out was my play on the par-five holes, where I typically laid up instead of trying to hit the green in two. In 1969 I did this through three and a half rounds, until the back nine on Sunday after I had fallen out of the lead. I then hit the green in two on both thirteen and fifteen and made birdie each time. That accounted for two of the four strokes I was under par on the fives for the entire tournament. Archer, on the other hand, had scored eleven-under on the par fives by constantly going for the green.

The statistics made for good newspaper copy, but I had no intention of changing how I played Augusta National. I'd been around the course too many times—this was my fourteenth straight appearance—and I knew my game and myself. Being consistently aggressive only hurt my score. If I was behind on Sunday, I would attack, otherwise I'd mostly try for birdies on the fives the old fashioned way, by chipping and putting. I knew it wasn't the par fives that cost me in 1969; it was shooting 40 on the opening nine on Sunday. That's what I couldn't do again. I also knew one factor that contributed to shooting that 40 was all the energy I wasted just getting to the first tee. I'd never led the Masters before on Saturday night and I didn't realize just how much demand that puts on your time. Long interviews with the print media were followed by more long interviews with the broadcast media and after that there were all sorts of people tugging and pulling and wanting autographs or just to talk. I resolved that if I ever had the lead again on Saturday night, I would make as quick a getaway as possible.

I DID COME TO AUGUSTA with some different weapons. Wilson had developed a new lightweight shaft that I was using on my irons. And one big positive I was bringing back from the previous year was the way I hit my driver. I still missed my old fade driver that I had broken in the Philippines in 1968, but I put a natural draw on the ball with its replacement. And hitting from right to left at Augusta, where a majority of the fairways bend in that direction, is not a bad thing. I didn't necessarily believe that faders couldn't win at the Masters. Some good left-to-right players had won the tournament. Jimmy Demaret faded the ball and he won at Augusta three times. I had five top-tens when I faded the ball. But there was no question that the course was much kinder to hooks than it was to slices.

I CAME INTO THE TOURNAMENT well rested. I didn't go with the Tour to Florida during the pesticide-spraying season in March. I stayed home and did some fishing and welcomed the newest member of the Casper family into the world, our son Charles Franklin, who we called Charlie. I didn't play again until a week before the Masters at the Greater Greensboro Open in North Carolina, where I tried out my new lightweight irons. I liked the feel of them, but I finished eleven shots back of the winner, Gary Player, who was at the top of his game.

I hadn't won since the L.A. Open in early January, the tournament that made me a millionaire. At the end of that month I went to the Monterey Peninsula for the Bing Crosby and didn't hit a single shot. I scored a zero. Del Taylor, my caddy, was given the wrong starting time and wasn't there when it was time for me to tee off. More significantly, neither were my golf clubs. It wasn't Del's fault, but just the same I was disqualified from the tournament.

Del wasn't with me at the Masters, but it had nothing to do with the Crosby. In 1970 you were still assigned a caddy by the club (1982 was the first year the Masters permitted outside caddies). I had a regular Masters caddy who'd been carrying my bag for several years. His name was Mathew Palmer. He worked as a short-order cook when he wasn't caddying at Augusta. He was a little guy, about five-foot-six, and the other caddies called him "Shorty." Shorty insisted he knew Augusta's greens like the back of his hand, but I didn't trust him and year after year didn't solicit his advice. Finally in 1969 I asked him to help me read the greens, and I nearly won the tournament. He was right. He did know Augusta's greens like the back of his hand. I planned to draw on his expertise again in 1970.

Shirley and I were joined in Georgia by our son Billy, who was then in eighth grade. He didn't seem to have a problem with missing school. Billy had been coming to the Masters for the past four years and had formed a fast friendship with Freddy, the caddy master. They worked a deal. Freddy would tell Billy where the fish were biting on the lakes around the par-three course, and in exchange Billy would bring Freddy a nice, fat bass. During the practice rounds Billy fished the lakes with Sam Snead and Julius Boros and brought home some nice fish every night, even after he'd given Freddy his cut. The tournament hadn't even started and it was already going great.

THE FIRST DAY DAWNED HOT, windy and dry, the kind of conditions that can turn Augusta's lightning-quick greens into something close to un-puttable. The usual 30,000 spectators were on hand, along with 150 extra Pinkerton Guards brought in because of rumors that demonstrators might try to hassle the two South African players in the field, Gary Player and Harold Henning, because of their country's policy of apartheid. At the most recent major, the PGA Championship, protestors had thrown ice in Player's face and shouted in his backswing. (He still placed second.) The Masters, long a bastion of decorum and Southern hospitality, was determined not to have a similar display and stationed guards at every hole. Either the show of force, or the threat of being expelled from the world's most popular golf tournament, worked. Player and Henning were not hassled the entire week.

Tommy Aaron, a native Georgian accustomed to the weather, took the first round lead with a four-under-par 68, one of just three rounds in the 60s. The two 69s belonged to Gene Littler and Bert Yancey, who had won at the Crosby that year. Yancey was obsessed with Augusta to the extent that he had built a scale model of the golf course in his basement at his home in Atlanta. It seemed to help him. I was impressed by anyone who went under par in Thursday's difficult conditions. I shot even-par 72 and was glad for it.

On Friday the winds calmed and the humidity returned, softening the greens. I shot 68 to move into a tie for third place with Bob Lunn, a shot behind Littler and Yancey, who each shot 70. On Saturday I added another 68 for 208 while Littler shot 70 for 209, Gary Player came through with his second straight 68 to move into contention at 210, and Yancey shot 72 for 211.

After three rounds I had a one-stroke lead going into the final day of the Masters—exactly where I'd stood a year earlier. But this time I knew what was coming. I made quick work of the Saturday night media sessions and hurried off to the house we were renting near the golf course as quickly as I could.

THE MASTERS PAIRED ONE AND three together back then, and two and four, which meant Player and I went out as the last twosome on Sunday, with Littler and Yancey directly in front of us.

I held onto my slim lead through seven holes, making six pars and a birdie at the par-three fourth hole. Then, semi-disaster struck. My drive on the long, bending par-five eighth hole landed in a fairway bunker. To play it safe, I selected a 5-iron, but hit it fat and landed only halfway up the hill, still far from the green. I took out a 2-iron for my third shot and made a terrible swing. The ball hit a tree and bounced onto an asphalt maintenance road, stopping in some pine needles next to the curb. I got a free drop onto the road, but when I dropped my ball my caddy had to run to catch it as it rolled down the hill back toward the tee. After two drops I was allowed to place the ball because I couldn't make it stay. If my original shot hadn't somehow got caught up in those pine needles it would have rolled two hundred yards or more away from the green. As it was, I was able to advance the ball back toward the fairway, where I lay four. I finally found the green in five and two-putted for seven, but a really lucky seven. It cost me the lead but I got back into a tie with Littler and Yancey when I birdied the ninth hole to make the turn in 36, not 40. Gary was one shot behind.

Whoever coined the phrase "The Masters doesn't begin until the back nine on Sunday" could use the 1970 tournament as Exhibit A. Half-a-dozen players had legitimate shots at winning on the final nine, including a charging Jack Nicklaus, who shot 69 to finish eighth. I miss-hit a 5-iron to bogey the par-four eleventh to again fall out of the lead, and when I parred the par-three twelfth and Player made a terrific twenty-foot putt for birdie he pulled into a tie with Littler and Yancey, the three of them ahead of me by a stroke.

My game plan called for going for the par fives in two if I was behind on Sunday—and I was behind on Sunday. On the thirteenth, facing a 240-yard second shot. I pulled out my 4-wood and aimed to the left of the green, allowing for as much room as possible to clear Rae's Creek as the stream angles past the sloping putting surface above. The ball hit on the top slope of the green, forty-five feet above the hole. I two-putted for four, matching Gene and Gary's birdies. Yancey had parred the hole, and that put the two of us a stroke behind the leaders.

Gary missed the green and made bogey on fourteen while I parred. Now we were all chasing Littler, who, playing ahead of us, laid up and made birdie at the par-five fifteenth to stay in front by one. Gary and

I both went for the green on fifteen, where they'd extended the tee by forty yards since the previous year and added mounds in the landing area to discourage such a thing. I hit another 4-wood. This one landed in the sand trap to the right of the green. If I'd hit the same shot toward the flag I'd have been in the lake and effectively out of the tournament. As it was I hit a bunker shot to four feet—probably my best shot of the tournament—and made the putt, matching birdies with Player. At this point Littler had the lead and it was his tournament to win or lose, but he missed the green at the par-three sixteenth, flew into a bunker and made bogey four. When Player and I followed with pars, the three of us were deadlocked with two holes to play.

Gene finished par-par and was in the clubhouse with a nine-under 279 when Gary and I, after both making pars on seventeen—I missed a six-foot putt by inches—hit our drives on eighteen. Each ball landed safely in the fairway, almost the same distance from the green. I hit first, a 6-iron, dead at the flag, and ended right of the hole, pin-high, fifteen feet from the pin. Gary pulled out a 7-iron and I remember thinking he couldn't get there with a 7-iron. He didn't get there. He hit in the front trap and blasted out to ten feet. I stood over my putt. I had fifteen feet to win the Masters. I made a beautiful stroke, at what I thought was perfect speed and on a perfect line. For a moment I thought I'd won. The ball was headed straight for the hole. But at the last second it lost pace on the low side, hit the edge, and spun around the lip, overhanging the hole.

I tapped in so Gary could concentrate on his ten-footer, which he needed to remain in a tie for the lead. He missed; a crushing finish for Player, who'd never even gone to the restroom all week without a Pinkerton Guard following him. But he always kept his class. "My father always told me to be humble in victory and smile in defeat," he said to the press. "Well, fellows, here are my teeth. I'm smiling at you."

All that was left were the two guys from San Diego. The next day we would have an eighteen-hole playoff to determine the Masters champion.

IT WASN'T THE FIRST TIME two men from the same hometown met in a playoff at the Masters. Byron Nelson and Ben Hogan tied at the end of regulation in 1942 and played eighteen holes the next day to settle a winner. Byron and Ben grew up caddying at the same country club in Fort Worth. They had their first match against each other in the caddy tournament when they were just kids. They were within six months of each other in age (Nelson was older). They turned pro within a year of each other, and they traveled together on the Tour when they were just starting out. (Nelson won their Masters playoff, 69 to 70.)

People figured that would never happen again. What were the odds?

But twenty-eight years later, here were Littler and I with lives every bit as interconnected and a friendship and roots that went just as deep. We'd first met when we were junior golfers in San Diego. He was just eleven months older than I was. We had our first competitive match in the county amateur when I was fifteen and he was sixteen. (He won.) We joined the Navy at the same time and ended up playing on the golf team together. We turned pro the same year and traveled together on Tour when we were just starting out.

On the PGA Tour, our careers went on different trajectories. He won more at the beginning and then tailed off; I did just the opposite. By the time of the 1970 Masters I'd won forty-four times on Tour and Gene had won twenty-two. But despite all these wins, and the hundreds of golf tournaments we'd been in together over the years, for one reason or another we'd never had a one-on-one showdown on the Tour. We were in a three-way sudden death playoff that also included Jack Nicklaus in the 1966 World Series of Golf. But the event was only a four-man exhibition to begin with. Gene won, by the way.

For twenty-four years, more than half our lives, Gene and I had known each other, and for fifteen years we traveled the same routes on the PGA Tour. We played on Ryder Cup teams together. We watched each other win national championships (Gene won the 1961 U.S. Open at Oakland Hills.) We even both had problems with allergies. Our homes remained in San Diego, about twenty-five miles apart. Our families were friends. We were friends. There was no one in golf I liked or respected more than Gene Littler.

And, of course, our parallel lives became the storyline for the play-off. The press wanted details and we obliged, talking about our growing-up days in San Diego, about playing together in the Navy and the trip we took to Oklahoma to play in the 1954 U.S. Amateur ("You think he's good now," I said to the writers, "you should have seen him when he was nineteen.") We reminisced about pulling trailers on the early Tour, about how close our families remained, about our many battles. The more we talked, I had the unsettling realization that I couldn't remember a single time that I had beaten Gene Littler head-to-head.

THE PLAYOFF BEGAN IN WARM, overcast, muggy weather. The gallery was estimated at 15,000. That's a lot of people when they're all following the same twosome. I wore a red cashmere sweater, about the only person on the golf course not in short sleeves. But I wanted to make sure I stayed warm—I often wore sweaters, even in hotter temperatures, to help keep my back muscles loose—and I wasn't about to take it off when I hit my approach close on the first hole and made a four-foot putt for birdie. Gene parred and just like that I had a one-shot lead.

On the par-five second hole, Gene's drive was dead center while I duck-hooked into the pines and deflected into a water hazard. At the beginning of the week the grass where my ball came to rest was about three feet tall, but over the course of the week the gallery had mashed it down. My ball was sitting on flat grass in front of a small, loose tree branch that was about half the height of the ball. The only shot I had was to take a 9-iron and make sure I missed the branch on my downswing and then get the club underneath the ball in a hurry so I could get it over the pine trees and carry the 120 yards I needed to get back to the fairway. I couldn't ground my club because I was in a water hazard. I had almost no margin for error. It was maybe the most perfect shot I ever hit in my life. I caught the ball clean with the blade of the 9-iron and it arced back to the safe short grass of the fairway.

It left me with about 175 yards for my third shot and I hit 5-iron to just off the back of the green. Meanwhile, Gene was only twenty yards short of the green in two. He was in the driver's seat. But his ball had come to rest in a repaired divot and when he hit a rather indifferent chip the clubface sank underneath the ball and he chili-dipped the shot maybe twenty feet into the bunker guarding the green. From there he blasted out and two-putted for a six. I chipped to three feet and made the putt for my par. Instead of being back to even, which is the best I was hoping for off the tee, I was up by two.

All week long I'd putted well. For the tournament proper I had 117 putts—29 in each of the first two rounds, 28 in the third round and 31 in the final round—and no three-putts. In the playoff the putter heated up even more. After making the four-footer on one and the three-footer on two, I made a thirty-footer on three for a birdie, a four-footer on four for a par, a five-footer on six for another par and a ten-footer on seven for a birdie—six one-putt greens in the first seven holes and a quick five-shot lead.

When I birdied the eleventh hole with another one-putt, my lead was seven shots with seven holes to play.

Hmm, that had a familiar ring to it.

So did my dropping a shot at the delicate par-three twelfth with a bogey to Gene's par . . . and another on thirteen with a par to his birdie . . . and another on fourteen with a bogey to his par . . . and yet another on fifteen with a par to his birdie.

I dropped four shots in four holes. Standing on the tee of the par-three sixteenth, my lead was three with three to play.

Gene had honors and placed his tee shot in good position on the green, fifteen feet from the cup, a makeable putt.

I had to respond with my tee shot. I was in the same situation Arnold Palmer had been in at The Olympic Club in the '66 Open. He had a seven shot lead over me on the back nine that seemed insurmountable, but I made up four shots by the sixteenth tee to cut the lead to three and I had honors. I split the fairway with my drive, Arnold hit into the rough, I went on to make birdie, he made bogey, and the momentum of the match changed completely.

For me, the Masters came down to the tee shot on sixteen. I didn't hurry, but I didn't dawdle either. I went through my usual pre-shot routine and hit a 5-iron to seven feet.

Gene putted first and just missed on the high side, having to settle for par. My ball was sitting on a side-hill. I turned to Mathew Palmer, who I trusted completely by now, and asked what it would do. He said it's straight. So I putted it straight and it went straight in.

Now I could breathe easier. My lead was four with two to play. I finished birdie-par and Gene went bogey-birdie, making a long putt for the first time all day on the last green. He shot 74 to my 69.

The first person to reach me after I signed my scorecard was Cliff Roberts, the personification of the event now that Bobby Jones could no longer attend because of health problems (Jones died a year later). Cliff extended his hand, but instead of saying "Congratulations" he said, "Thank you." We'd become such good friends over the years and we both knew how badly I yearned to win his tournament and how much he was pulling for me to some day win it. Still, I thought I was supposed to be thanking him.

As he was packing up my bag, my trusty caddy turned to me and said he was thinking of changing his name from Palmer to Casper. I told him fine by me. At the press conference, the writers asked how many greens he had helped on. "All of them," I said. The last time I saw him, Shorty was being interviewed by as many writers as I was.

THERE WAS ONLY ONE GLITCH, and it was a small one but a big one. At the ceremony where the champion from the year before drapes the green jacket over the newest winner, George Archer placed the coat on my shoulders and it almost drowned me. I figured it was because they'd measured me when I first came to Augusta in 1958. That coat said a lot. In many ways I was the same person I was back then. But in so many other ways I was a different person entirely.

16

Fifty-one

17

The King and I: His Majesty Hassan II, King of Morocco,
is on my right; on my far left is Claude Harmon.

New Orleans, Louisiana
May 18, 1975

Win the Masters and immediately you are the member of a very exclusive club—the only person left on earth with a chance to win the yearly Grand Slam.

Asked over and over what I thought my chances were of winning the rest of the majors in 1970, I couldn't come up with a definitive answer until the U.S. Open in June, where I finished eighth. That answered that.

The Open was held that year at Hazeltine National Golf Club in Minnesota, a course so new the trees hadn't had time to grow up and there was hardly anything to break the strong winds that blew in for the opening round. Jack Nicklaus shot 81 and Arnold Palmer shot 79—and they made the cut. I opened with 75 on my way to 294 for the week. That was good for eighth place and was only six shots out of second place, but still thirteen behind Tony Jacklin, who played like he was back home in England.

As to whether anyone will ever win all the majors—the Masters, U.S. Open, British Open and PGA Championship—in a single season, I believe someday it will happen. It could be in a hundred years, or it could be next year. But I believe to do it a golfer will have to focus on the majors at the expense of all else—something I was never interested in doing.

Grand Slam or no Grand Slam, I'd planned all along to play in the British Open in 1970. It was my third trip to the world's oldest golf tournament and my first chance to play the Open Championship at St. Andrews, the birthplace of golf. I was still in the mix after an opening 71 but never made any more headway and finished tied for seventeenth.

I returned from Scotland and won the IVB-Philadelphia Golf Classic the very next week. A month later I opened with a 64 at the AVCO Golf Classic in Massachusetts and won by one over Bruce Crampton and Tom Weiskopf. That gave me four wins for the 1970 season, the seventh year in my career I'd won four tournaments or more. I played in sixteen events, the fewest since I'd joined the Tour, but still won $140,667, a total that wound up second on the money list that year to Lee Trevino.

I might have played more events in the fall but I was eager to return to Morocco.

I'd made my first trip there in 1969, when Claude Harmon, the 1948 Masters champion and longtime head professional at Winged Foot, called and asked if I'd be interested in playing golf with Hassan II, the King of Morocco. Claude had been giving the King lessons and, as often happens, the King had turned into a golf nut. As also often happens, he was looking for guys to play with.

Hassan II was just two years older than I was, and a fairly new King in a fairly new kingdom, at least in its present incarnation. He'd taken over the throne in 1961 upon the death of his father, Mohammed V, the man who had restored the monarchy in 1956 after nearly fifty years of French and Spanish occupation.

Ours was an unlikely friendship—an English-speaking Mormon from San Diego and a French/Arab-speaking Muslim from Rabat—but a true friendship it became. The King and I meshed. He was as interested in where I came from as I was interested in where he came from. And he was crazy about golf. He not only loved to play the game, he also saw it as a way of attracting tourism to his country. He told me time and time again how much he wanted to do business with the West, particularly the United States, but that ninety-nine percent of Morocco's population was Arabic and Muslim so he had to walk a fine line.

We actually got off to a rough start. I'd never met a king before and when we were first introduced, I said through a translator, "It's a pleasure to meet you, Your Highness." He looked at me and didn't say a word. Even in a different language, I knew I'd committed some kind of blunder. I was pulled aside and told that the term "Your Highness" wasn't considered royal in Moroccan culture. It translated to something more along the lines of "Mister." I was supposed to say "Your Majesty."

50

This shot was snapped after I holed a sand shot at the seventeenth
green of The Olympic Club during the second round of the
1966 U.S. Open. It became the signature photograph
of my career and the logo for Billy Casper Golf.

51

That's Arnold and me AFTER he lost a seven-shot lead
at the U.S. Open. His sportsmanship was
above reproach. He took it like the gentleman he is.

52

When this putt dropped on the eighteenth at The Olympic Club,
I was officially the U.S. Open winner of 1966.

53

Nineteen-year-old Johnny Miller gives his speech after finishing in
eighth place and low amateur in the '66 Open. He was always
comfortable around a microphone. I'm in the bottom left corner,
trying to decide what I'll say when it's my turn.

54

For the second time in my career, the USGA let me hold the U.S. Open Cup.

55

The winner's check for the '66 Open didn't stay in my hand very long.

A week after winning the
U.S. Open in 1966, I won the
Western Open in Chicago.

56

57

Shell's Wonderful World of Golf got me to some faraway places.
Here, we're in Caracas, Venezuela, at the Lagunita Country Club. That's Jimmy Demaret
interviewing Argentine pro Miguel Sala while I stand by with Gene Sarazen.

58

A fearsome foursome: Al Geiberger, me, Jack Nicklaus and Gene Littler prior to teeing off in the 1966 World Series of Golf. Gene went on to the win.

59

That's Jack Nicklaus and me having a heart-to-heart talk prior to the 1968 Masters. My son Billy is between us.

When I kept my head down, good things happened.

Within three months in 1968, our family doubled in size from three children to six.
Here I'm holding our twins, Judi and Jeni.

When my good friend Gary Player invited me to South Africa for a series of golf exhibitions, we took a side trip to an animal park, where he encouraged me to get up close and personal with the lions.

63

If this putt had fallen on the final green at the Masters in 1970,
I would have avoided the next day's playoff with Gene Littler.
That's my caddy, Mathew Palmer, twisting in agony.

64

George Archer, the 1969 Masters champion, helps me into my green jacket.
It was a bit roomy, but I wasn't complaining.

At the White House, President Richard Nixon presented me
with a Presidential golf ball.

After winning the 1973
Ryder Cup at Muirfield
in Scotland, I joined with
Lou Graham, left,
Lee Trevino, and Dave
Hill to hoist our captain,
Jack Burke, Jr. J.C. Snead
is on the far right.

A colorful foursome: The other men wearing the pants
are Gerald Ford, Bob Hope and Jackie Gleason.

Bob Hope could make anyone laugh, anywhere—even when he
gives you a check for fourteen dollars and twenty-nine cents.
This was at the pro-am during the 1974 San Diego Open.

69

Johnny Miller became a cherished friend, on and off the golf course.
This is in 1974, when he won eight tournaments
and was PGA Player of the Year.

70

I didn't realize it at the time, but this check for $30,000 at the 1975
New Orleans Open was the fifty-first and final time I would be
awarded first-place money on the regular Tour.

Making it into the World Golf Hall of Fame in 1978 was special; receiving the award from longtime friend and Hall of Fame President Don Collett was priceless.

71

Winning the 1979 Ryder Cup as captain of the U.S. team was just as big a thrill as winning as a player.

72

73

A golf course developer in Guam was responsible for this group getting together. We each designed two holes for the course. In the back row that's Orville Moody, left, Gene Littler, Bob Toski, Doug Ford, Chi Chi Rodriguez and me. We decided it was only right that Sam Snead, left, Gene Sarazen and Ben Hogan should get the chairs.

74

She's letting me take the wheel here, but in truth Shirley has always been in the driver's seat.

A couple of old San Diego sailors enjoying the sunset: Gene Littler and I have seen a lot together.

Above the hearth at the San Diego Country Club, my home away from home, they've hoisted a plaque commemorating my career victories.

To celebrate my 80th birthday, the family got together at my daughter Linda and son-in-law Kim Henrie's home in Park City, Utah. That's not quite all of us, but it's close.

The King—His Majesty—started building golf courses all around the country. He tore up gardens at his palaces and replaced them with fairways and greens. He built a course at his palace in Rabat, the capital. He built another on the road to Casablanca, and another inside the palace walls in a city called Fes. He hired Robert Trent Jones to design three beautiful eighteen-hole courses out of a cork forest that became the Dar Es Salam Royal Golf Club. The King put lights up so he could play during Ramadan, the Muslim holy month when they fast from sunup to sundown. He'd send a jet for me and we'd tee off at eleven o'clock at night and finish around two the next morning. One time we were playing at night and I was five under through seven holes and I said, "Your Majesty I've been playing at the wrong time of the day," and he laughed like mad. He was a great guy, the King, very easy to get along with. And money was no object. I made multiple trips to play with him and his sons, who were also avid golfers, and after several visits I said, "Your Majesty, you don't have to pay me every time I come over here. Just cover my expenses." The King replied, "Monsieur Billy, that's for you to say, but it's for me to do what I want to do."

In 1971 the King decided to throw a party to christen the Dar Es Salam complex and asked me if I'd see if some of my friends on the Tour would like to come over and play for the Hassan II Trophy. It wasn't a hard sell. The king offered a guaranteed appearance fee, all expenses paid for the player and his wife, a week of banquets and parties in 300-year-old palaces, and it was after the Tour's season had ended. Orville Moody, the 1969 U.S. Open winner, won the inaugural Hassan II Trophy. I won it in 1973 and again in 1975, but in the early years the tournament was never as much about the competition as it was about camaraderie and enjoying a completely different cultural experience.

Trips to Morocco became a family thing for us. I took my son Bobby over several times when he was a youngster, the first when he was ten years old. I'd partner with the King and Bobby would partner with one of the generals. We often played in a sixsome with another member of the military, Colonel Spai, and Hassan El Glaoui, a world-renowned artist the King enjoyed playing with. The King loved to arrange the matches and he always figured out the bisques (strokes). One day Bobby was playing like mad, well beyond what you'd expect from a ten-year-old. I said Bobby, "If you make any more birdies you'll be going back to Rabat by camel." The King overheard us and added, "Yes, and it takes fourteen days to get there by camel."

In 1972 I just missed being in the country when the government was threatened with a coup. I was playing in the British Open at Muirfield and ticketed to travel to Morocco once the tournament was over. Luckily, I made the cut that weekend in Scotland, otherwise I'd have been in Morocco and in the thick of the revolt. Rebel forces wound up killing nine generals and the King barely escaped with his life.

Nine days later the King sent word that order had been restored and asked me to make my visit. It so happened that I was in the palace with the King and his ministers when word came that Spiro Agnew, Vice President of the United States, was coming to pay a State visit. We postponed our golf game that morning and the King asked me to attend lunch with the ministers. Coincidentally, I had played golf with Vice President Agnew earlier that year at the Bob Hope Classic. When the U.S. ambassador was introducing all the ministers and telling the Vice President their titles, when he got to me he didn't know what to say. The King stepped in and said, "Minister du Golf, Billy Casper."

I said, "Mr. Vice President, I'll bet you're surprised I'm here." He said, "Yes, Billy, I am."

We played golf later that day and it was almost like we were in a Tour event with all of the Vice President's secret service men watching us play. The King marveled at the size of Agnew's security detail—and it was the King who'd just gone through a coup attempt.

Hassan II was a direct descendent of the Prophet Muhammad so besides being King he was also the people's spiritual leader. On one occasion we went with the royal caravan that traveled over the Atlas Mountains to dedicate a dam. For three days we journeyed through the countryside and every town or village we went through had Moroccan carpets on the road so the King didn't have to drive over the dirt as he passed through. People by the thousands stood along the roadside and waved and the women made musical clicking sounds to serenade the royalty. We went through places where their King hadn't been seen for hundreds of years.

I CAME HOME FROM MOROCCO to hear some very welcome news: I'd been voted the PGA's Player of the Year by the Tour membership. Soon after that I was invited to Los Angeles for a "Tribute to Billy Casper" night at the Century Plaza Hotel, a fundraiser for the City of Hope Medical Center sponsored by the Los Angeles Junior Chamber of Commerce. It was a black tie event where they recognized my visits to the servicemen in Asia, service to the community, and my golf accomplishments. Bob Hope was the master of ceremonies. The guest list included Richard Nixon and Ronald Reagan. What a year it had been. I'd become a millionaire, Masters champion, Player of the Year, and dined with kings and presidents and movie stars, all because of a simple game I learned to play in my grandfather's pasture. I sat on the dais in my tuxedo with Shirley at my side and listened as my hero, Bob Hope, read a laudatory letter from another hero, Ben Hogan. He wrote, "I want to be included among your friends who honor you. Thank you for simply being a person of compassion, unselfishness, dignity and success." I hadn't yet turned forty and was already hearing my eulogy.

Such events, and the realization of how much others had done for me, prompted me to start my summer youth golf camps. For twenty-two years, from 1970 through 1992, we enrolled about two hundred kids a summer, almost four thousand in all. A youngster could sign up for anywhere from one to six weeks. I stressed two fundamentals with my instructors: one, get their hands on the club properly, and two, make sure they get aligned correctly. I always felt the swing sort of fell into place if you got those two things right. I made it a point to spend personal time with each player. I'd play at least one hole with every kid in camp. I gave away signed golf balls for a par and if someone did something special, such as make an eagle or a birdie, I gave him or her a signed glove or cap. To this day, I continually run into people who went through my golf camps; they'll show me the signed ball or the cap that they still have all these years later.

IN AN EXPERIMENT THAT DIDN'T last, they played the 1971 PGA Championship in February, instead of its usual August date, at the PGA National Golf Club in Palm Beach Gardens, Florida. I made an exception to my no-Florida policy and entered the tournament, and for the third time in my career finished second at the PGA. My 283 total was two behind the winner, Jack Nicklaus, who had a four-shot lead over his closest pursuer, Gary Player, and a seven-shot lead over me after three rounds. I shot 68 on the final day and Jack shot 73, but he could afford to.

At the Masters that year I got to do something every golfer dreams of: choose the menu for the champions dinner held Tuesday night in the upper room of the clubhouse. The tradition started in 1952 when Ben Hogan, after winning his first green jacket in 1951 (the green jacket tradition had begun in 1949), invited all previous winners to be his guests for dinner. Hogan was a regular at the dinner every year until 1967, when he stopped coming to Augusta altogether, so, unfortunately, I won three years too late to be able to dine with him. I think many of the players were expecting buffalo or rhino for the main course but I went with basic prime rib and didn't hear any complaints. At the end of the week I draped the green jacket on the shoulders of Charles Coody, who won by two shots over Johnny Miller and Jack Nicklaus. I finished in a tie for thirteenth. In another close bid for the green jacket, Gene Littler was fourth that year, just four shots back.

I MISSED THE CUT IN the U.S. Open at Merion five days before my birthday, a cruel introduction to turning forty. But I made a better showing at the British Open at Royal Birkdale, an English course I knew from Ryder Cups there in 1965 and 1969. I closed with a 67 in the final round, the best score of the field, although it wasn't enough to catch

Lee Trevino, and I placed seventh—another indication rather late in the game that British courses suited me. In four straight trips to golf's oldest tournament, I'd finished in the top ten twice and in the top twenty-five all four times.

While in Europe I played in the Swiss Open at the Crans-sur-Sierre Golf Club. I didn't win the tournament, but I did something more rare when my second shot climbed onto the green and rolled into the cup for a two on the par-five fourteenth hole: a double eagle, or albatross. Mathematicians figure the odds of getting a double eagle are a million to one, about one hundred times as rare as a hole in one. The Swiss put a plaque next to the tee box to commemorate the shot.

For the first time in my career, I came to October without a Tour victory all season, but I averted a shutout when I went nineteen under par at the Kaiser International in Napa, California, to win by four strokes over Fred Marti. It was the sixteenth straight season I'd registered a victory on the PGA Tour, a streak exceeded in history only by the seventeen straight by Arnold Palmer, who got started a year ahead of me and also saw his streak come to an end in 1971. (Jack Nicklaus would later also win seventeen years in a row.)

SHIRLEY AND I EXPANDED OUR family again in 1970 when we adopted our son David, named after David O. McKay, the president of the Church of Jesus Christ of Latter-day Saints. That gave us five adopted children to go along with our three biological children. Our oldest was sixteen and we had five under the age of three. This did not escape the attention of The American Mothers Association in Washington, D.C., who named Shirley its California and National Young Mother of the Year for 1971—in recognition of what she had accomplished and, I suppose, for what lay ahead. No one knew better than I just how richly Shirley deserved the honor. All those years I was collecting trophies and paychecks at the golf course she was making sure there was a home to bring them to. She was tireless in her support of me and the children. You couldn't find a CEO in America who wouldn't envy the way Shirley

Casper managed her home, her children and me. We went to New York City for the ceremony where she received the award at the Waldorf Astoria Hotel. We Caspers made up a gallery all by ourselves.

FOR THE FIRST FULL SEASON in my career, I went winless in 1972, and to add injury to insult, when I returned to San Diego for the offseason I tore a muscle in my back. I was playing at the club in a fivesome with my usual gang—Harry Lebaron, Tom Huist, Frank Fornaca and Doug Price. It was a cold, blustery November day with a little bit of rain. On the fifteenth tee my foot slipped after I'd swung a new graphite driver I was trying out and I tore a muscle in the lower left-hand side of my back. I knew it immediately. It sent me right down to the ground. The next morning when I woke up my back hurt so badly I could barely make it out of bed.

I tried every back remedy and stretch I could think of and that anyone recommended. I went to see Dr. Stillman, the man who worked wonders with my hand injury in 1963, and he did some manipulations, but without much relief. Through Thanksgiving and Christmas I mostly sat around the house, hoping rest would do the trick. When the Tour was ready to start up again in January at the Los Angeles Open, I went to Riviera Country Club in L.A. for a practice round and couldn't make it through the full eighteen. I threw the clubs in the trunk and drove back to San Diego.

I was beginning to have genuine concerns about my future. Was this it? Back problems have been the end of many a golf career. This time I forced myself to be more disciplined than ever, stretching constantly and strengthening my stomach muscles. And I prayed; I mean I really prayed. I begged the good Lord for help.

And then, bit by bit, I noticed what felt like improvement. By February I was confident enough to again give the Tour a try, but this time I brought along a portable seat that fit in my golf bag. While I was waiting on shots I could sit down and give my back a rest. It wasn't until April, about the time of the Masters (I finished seventeenth), that I felt close to full strength again. Ever since, whenever I see anyone with a back problem, I don't just have sympathy, I have empathy. It literally stops you in your tracks.

WE SENT OUR OLDEST DAUGHTER Linda off to college at Brigham Young University in Provo, Utah, and in 1973, about the time of the first oil energy crisis, we decided to join her in Utah. We left San Diego and moved to Mapleton, just south of Provo. A farm with one hundred and sixteen acres, six thousand fruit trees and a small brick house was for sale. We bought it and lived in that small farmhouse while we built a bigger one up on the bench. We made it large enough for one more and added our daughter Julia to our family. She would be the last of our adopted children.

There was lots of fresh air and room for the kids to roam—and in Utah a big family wasn't unusual. We fit right in. I partnered with a friend from California, George Wright, and hired a fellow by the name of Rex Jensen to run the orchard. We raised peaches, cherries and pears, with no pesticides. Organic farming would become popular later, but we were definitely ahead of the curve. Because of our association with Dr. Randolph in Chicago we had a ready-made clientele for our produce. Once Rex got the operation up and running, we had a truck going every day to the airport all summer long.

BETWEEN THE MOVE, THE BACK problem, the adoptions, and the trips to Morocco, I hadn't won a golf tournament in twenty months when I flew to Chicago for the Western Open in the summer of 1973. I needed a win for more reasons than my ego and to pay for the new house. My Ryder Cup points were low and I had to place in the top three in the tournament or I'd miss making the team for the first time since I'd become eligible in 1960. It was just the incentive I needed. I stroked in a little downhill slice putt on the last hole to win the tournament by a shot over Hale Irwin and Larry Hinson and make the Ryder Cup. I wasn't normally one for a lot of outward expressions of emotion, but this time I let it go. I jumped up and down like it was Christmas morning and did a little dance in the middle of the green. Later I got a letter from Elder Robert Simpson, one of the leaders in the Mormon Church. He'd watched my dance on television and he wrote, "I know the Lord probably can use the tithing, but I don't know about that dancing on Sunday."

For a further Ryder Cup tune-up I went to Hartford and won the Sammy Davis Jr. Greater Hartford Open. Three cities were very, very good to me in my golf career: Portland, where I won my first check, three Portland Opens and the Alcan; Chicago, where I won four Western Opens; and Hartford, where I also won four times. Indianapolis was another sanctuary city for me. I won the 500 Festival tournament there three times.

The Ryder Cup was held that year at Muirfield in Scotland, home of the Honourable Company of Edinburgh Golfers. I played in every match, split four doubles matches, won both my singles matches, and contributed four points as the U.S. retained the Cup over the team from Great Britain and Ireland, 19-11.

THE BIGGEST SURPRISE OF 1974 didn't come on a golf course. It came at a hotel in Paris as I was preparing to play in the Trophee Lancome, a new event in France that was backed by Mark McCormack and brought in a number of top players from around the world. I had played in an exhibition in Sweden and then flew to Paris and got in a practice round before checking into our hotel to wait for Shirley, who was flying in from the States. I was in the shower when she got to our room. After she put down her luggage, she said she had an announcement to make.

"Well, what is it?" I said.

She said, "I'm pregnant."

It's a wonder I didn't break my neck falling in the tub.

For years, Shirley had been assured she couldn't have any more children. Now, at the age of forty, she was pregnant again.

I was so shook up I went out and won the tournament.

Our Sarah came along the next year and two years later, to make sure no one got lonely, we had our last child, a boy we named Tommy. He was born on Christmas Day in Utah in 1977.

MY HOUSE WASN'T THE ONLY place seeing a youth movement. It dawned on me that the players now winning a majority of the tournaments on tour were much younger than I was. Among them were Johnny Miller, Raymond Floyd, Tom Watson, Hale Irwin, Tom Weiskopf, Lanny Wadkins and a bunch of other fresh faces. Johnny Miller, still a college kid when I met him at The Olympic Club in 1966, won the U.S. Open in 1973, when he shot his Open-record 63 in the final round, and another eight tournaments in 1974 alone—more than Gary Player, Jack Nicklaus, Arnold Palmer and me combined!

By 1975 I was getting more selective about my schedule. I had a top ten at the Masters where I finished sixth behind Jack Nicklaus, who held off Johnny Miller and Tom Weiskopf by a shot for his fifth green jacket, but played sparingly after that.

In May I was scheduled to play in the New Orleans Open, but on Monday of tournament week the entire Casper household came down with a stomach virus. I called Jack Weiss, the tournament director, and pulled out because of illness. I hated to make that call. New Orleans was one of the greatest food towns, if not THE greatest food town on Tour, and we always looked forward to going there. Shirley and I stayed with friends and every night we would eat at a different restaurant. One of our favorites was Minali's. It was located away from Bourbon Street and the tourist restaurants, the kind of place all the natives go. We'd come in with maybe eight or ten people from the tournament and they'd have a table for us and bring out a platter of crawdads piled high and wide. After that they'd bring us barbecued shrimp and it was just fabulous. Ruth's Chris, the steakhouse, started in New Orleans and that was another favorite of ours.

I guess thinking about all that great food gave me a change of heart. Whatever was bothering my stomach, the cuisine in New Orleans could probably cure it. On Tuesday, two days before the tournament was to begin, I started feeling a bit better and called Jack and asked if there was any way I could get back in. He said, "I never heard you say that you weren't coming." Personal relationships like that were the lifeblood of the Tour.

So it was that in the middle of May, one month before I would turn forty-four, that I played in the First NBC New Orleans Open at Lakewood Country Club. I opened with a 67 on an upset stomach to take the first-round lead, followed that with 68, then 66 and closed with a 70 for 271, two strokes better than Peter Oosterhuis, the runnerup. Seventeen years after winning a first prize in New Orleans of $2,800 I won a first prize of $30,000—as good a barometer as any of just how far and how fast the Tour had developed during my career. It was my fifty-first win. I had no idea as we made our way to Minali's to celebrate that it would be my final victory on the regular PGA Tour.

Of much more immediate impact was that the New Orleans win all but guaranteed me a spot in that fall's Ryder Cup, scheduled for Laurel Valley Golf Club in Ligonier, Pennsylvania, just down the road from Arnold Palmer's home town of Latrobe. That was no coincidence. Arnold had been chosen as captain of the U.S. team and that's why Laurel Valley got the nod. When he didn't compile enough points during the year to make the team, Arnold became a non-playing captain.

It was quite a lineup. In his memoir Arnold calls it the Dream Team. It included Jack Nicklaus, Lee Trevino, Gene Littler, Johnny Miller, Tom Weiskopf, Raymond Floyd, Hale Irwin, J.C. Snead, Al Geiberger, Lou Graham, Bob Murphy and me. The U.S. team won easily, 21-11, and after opening with a four-ball loss and halving a foursomes match with Johnny Miller, I teamed with Hale Irwin for a four-ball win over Peter Oosterhuis and Maurice Bembridge, despite the fact we hit only one fairway, and on the final day I finished with a 3 and 2 singles win over Eamonn Darcy.

That last win gave me 23½ points for my Ryder Cup career, surpassing Arnold Palmer's 23 points as the most ever scored by an American, a record that remained on the books through 2010.

I FINISHED 1975 WITH A win at the Italian Open at the Monticello Golf Club, near Milan, my first and only official triumph on the European PGA Tour. My son Billy caddied for me. He was eighteen and it was the first time he carried my bag in a competitive tournament. I wasn't playing particularly well during the first three rounds but in the final round I was paired with a young Spaniard, Severiano Ballesteros, who was only eighteen himself, and was making birdies all over the place. Then I started making birdies and before I knew it, I'd won the tournament. "Dad," Billy said, "I could get to liking this."

I added a second Hassan II Trophy in Morocco later in 1975 and in 1977 I went to Chiluca and won the Mexican Open, becoming the second man in history to win the national championships of Canada, the United States, and Mexico (Lee Trevino was the first). But if I was winning in other countries, I hadn't won on the American Tour for two years, and for the first time since 1961 I did not make the Ryder Cup team.

Golf is a cruel mistress. Unlike team sports like baseball, football and basketball, there is no front office man to inform you that your contract hasn't been picked up for next season, no general manager or coach to break the news to you that you're off the roster or you've been bumped from the starting lineup. You have to do it yourself, and after years of convincing yourself that you *can* do it, it's not an easy thing to convince yourself that you can't. On one level you recognize your skills are diminishing, your focus is faltering, your energy isn't quite what it once was, but on another level you look away and don't recognize it until a couple of years after everyone else.

I could still hit the shots. A young boy in Boise could attest to that. I was playing in a cancer benefit event with Tom Watson and Lawrence Welk at Hillcrest Country Club in Boise, Idaho, in 1979 when we came to the thirteenth hole, a par three with a lake from tee to green. "This is the way you play this hole," I said, playing to the crowd, and then, spotting a youngster on the tee box, I added, "and for you I'll have to put it in the hole." I took out a 3-iron, hit the ball on a low trajectory purposely toward the lake. It skipped twice on the water, hopped onto the green, and rolled straight into the hole. The gallery reacted as if I'd won the U.S. Open *and* the British Open.

But if the good shots were still good, the injuries were more frequent and took longer to heal, and like it or not my concentration would sometimes lag. Not to any noticeable extent, but in a game as demanding as championship golf, any lapse is too much. The margins are so thin, shooting an average of just one additional stroke per round can mean the difference between making a comfortable living and going broke.

A PLEASANT REMINDER THAT I was getting up there came from the Hall of Fame in 1978. The caller had a familiar voice. My longtime friend Don Collett had moved to Pinehurst, North Carolina, and was in charge of the World Golf Hall of Fame, which had recently been established there. He was the first to tell me the good news that I would be entering the Hall that fall along with Harold Hilton, Clifford Roberts and Bing Crosby. Harold Hilton was one of the early English champions. He won two British Opens in 1892 and 1897, four British Amateurs and when he was forty-two years old came to America and won the 1911 U.S. Amateur. Clifford Roberts, of course, was co-founder of the Augusta National Golf Club and the Masters Tournament and a very close friend, and Bing Crosby, besides being an avid golfer, was an important and tremendous contributor to the game through his annual clambake tournament.

Bing and Cliff had died within two weeks of each other in the fall of 1977 and were honored posthumously, as was Harold Hilton. In my acceptance speech, I was able to pay a personal tribute to Bing and Cliff and talk about the special relationship I had with each of them because of the great game of golf.

IN 1979 I WAS GIVEN the signal honor of captaining the U.S. Ryder Cup team at The Greenbrier in White Sulphur Springs, West Virginia, the course Sam Snead used to sneak onto when he was a kid and play with a hickory stick. It was a historic Ryder Cup in the sense that the rules were changed to allow players from continental Europe to be added to the team from Great Britain and Ireland. The move, strongly advocated by Jack Nicklaus at the 1977 Ryder Cup matches, was designed to make the biennial competition more competitive as America had won sixteen of the last eighteen contests and nine of the last ten.

It had only been four years since my last appearance as a player, but reflecting just how fast the face of competitive golf can change, the U.S. lineup included just two of my teammates from that 1975 team—Hale Irwin and Lee Trevino. They were joined by Lanny Wadkins, Larry Nelson, Tom Kite, Tom Watson, Andy Bean, John Mahaffey, Lee Elder, Hubert Green, Fuzzy Zoeller and Gil Morgan. Jack Nicklaus hadn't compiled enough points to qualify and at the time the rosters were determined strictly on points. Mark Hayes was next in line.

There was an easy, loose camaraderie on that team. The first practice round I played with Hale Irwin and Andy Bean. On the tenth hole Hale hit his ball into the creek that crosses the fairway. We all went down to look for his ball, but everyone was being extra careful because there were water moccasins and copperheads in that stream. I turned around and saw Andy with a club in his hands going after a snake. I said, "Andy, don't hit that snake with that club, you'll need it during the week." He shook his head and said he wouldn't need that club. I asked how could he be so sure. "Because it's your 3-iron," he said.

As captain, the most important part of your job comes before the competition starts. The whole idea is to unify the players, who are used to playing as individuals, and make them feel like they're all part of a team. And you have to do your best to decide what players team best together. I had a good feel for my lineup. I especially liked the chemistry between Tom Watson and Lanny Wadkins, and I wanted to team Lee Trevino with Fuzzy Zoeller because I believed the two of them could talk their way into winning the match no matter how they were playing.

But my best-laid plans went out the window on Wednesday night when Tom Watson's wife, Linda, went into labor with their first child.

Tom withdrew, as he should have, and Mark Hayes took his place. I could have simply penciled in Hayes as Lanny's new partner, but on the spur of the moment I got the bright idea of putting Larry Nelson with Lanny Wadkins. Thursday morning they practiced together for the first time and had a best-ball score of 59.

The next morning Nelson and Wadkins played their four-ball match against the two Spaniards on the European team, Antonio Garrido and the young phenom Severiano Ballesteros, fresh off a win in the British Open. Nelson and Wadkins won the match, 2 and 1. They followed that with a 4 and 3 win over Bernard Gallacher and Brian Barnes in the foursomes matches that afternoon. The following day I paired Nelson and Wadkins again and in both their foursomes and four-ball matches the blind draw matched them each time against, you guessed it, Garrido and Ballesteros. Nelson and Wadkins won both matches.

Meanwhile, the Fuzzy-Trevino pairing, after opening with a foursomes win over Mark James and Ken Brown, lost their next match to Gallacher and Barnes. I'm convinced the reason they lost is because they relaxed the European team so much with their chitchat.

We had a bare 8½-7½ lead going into Sunday's singles matches. As it turned out, the blind draw matched Nelson against Ballesteros, who had been quoted in the newspapers that morning that he considered Nelson was "lucky" in the doubles matches. Well, guess who won? Nelson, 3 and 2. Larry didn't lose a match all week. He went 5-0 in his first Ryder Cup. Lanny won all of his matches but one and the United States prevailed in the first competition with Europe, 17-11. And I looked like a genius for just pulling something out of the woodwork.

I left Ryder Cup competition with eight team wins and one tie in nine appearances as player and captain.

The Ryder Cup may have been a grand finale but it was still a finale. I was about to turn fifty, and face a life without competitive golf. I had six thousand fruit trees on a 110-acre farm in Utah, and eleven kids, but I was losing the element that kept it all glued together. I wasn't sure what to do next. I could become a full-time fruit farmer. I could design golf courses, something I'd already started to do. I could probably find a club that would hire me as their golf professional. But whatever it was, I wasn't going to be playing golf anymore for my living. That much was certain.

And then, like a roar from the other side of the course, I heard echoes about the possibility of something called a Senior Tour.

17

Mulligans

18

When I joined the Senior (now Champions) Tour I started
wearing knickers; they are very comfortable.

The Senior Tour
1981

I n the 1960s the Shell Oil Company had sponsored a made-for-televi-
sion golf series and a film producer named Fred Raphael asked me if
I'd like to participate. Little did I realize at the time that I was looking
at my retirement plan.

Shell's Wonderful World of Golf was a huge hit. It featured matches
between two, and sometimes three, players at exotic locations all over the
world. The series ran during the prime of my career from 1962 through
1970, and again in a revival from 1994 through 2003. I was invited to
play in six of the matches, in Brazil, Ireland, Venezuela, the Philippines,
Massachusetts and Florida.

But it wasn't the exhibitions that set up my retirement plan—and
the retirement plan for hundreds of other golfers who had always assumed the Tour competition ended sometime before they turned fifty. It
was an idea Fred Raphael got while he was producing the shows.

One of the stars of *Shell's Wonderful World of Golf* was Gene Sarazen, the first man to win all four professional majors—the career Grand
Slam—and a natural as the expert analyst on the telecast. In 1963, Fred
Raphael was at the Masters and watched Gene, who was in the field as
a former champion, play the opening two rounds of the tournament
paired with Arnold Palmer. Palmer was thirty-three at the time and Sarazen was sixty-one, but at the end of thirty-six holes they had the same
score—147. Two thoughts struck Fred. One was that a so-called old man
could match strokes with the best current player in golf. The other was
that not many people got to see Sarazen or others of his vintage compete
because television wasn't around when they were in their prime. Why
not, thought Fred, produce a TV series along the order of *Shell's Wonderful World of Golf* that featured the living legends of the game?

He held onto that thought until the Shell series ran its course and
then went to work on his next idea, which in 1978 became a reality when
the *Liberty Mutual Legends of Golf* was played at Onion Creek Country

Club in Austin, Texas. Fred brought in sixteen legendary players for the made-for-TV event and paired them in teams for a three-round best-ball tournament. Included were the likes of Gene Sarazen, Jimmy Demaret, Paul Runyan and Ralph Guldahl from the old old days, and players from more recent old days like Sam Snead, Jay Hebert, Cary Middlecoff and Bob Rosburg, all of whom I had competed against many times.

Sixty-six-year-old Sam Snead and fifty-year-old Gardner Dickinson won the inaugural *Legends*, with Snead contributing fourteen of the team's eighteen birdies. The team of seventy-year-old Paul Runyan and sixty-one-year-old Lew Worsham finished last (with a score of just three-over-par 213) and split $20,000. Runyan's $10,000 share was more money than he made as the PGA tour's leading money-winner in 1934. TV ratings exceeded expectations, and were even better the next year when Roberto De Vicenzo and Julius Boros defeated Tommy Bolt and Art Wall in a sudden death playoff that lasted six holes, with a birdie on every hole. The implication was clear: these guys could *still* play.

The event caught the attention of commissioner Deane Beman and others at the PGA Tour, leading to a meeting at Tour headquarters on January 16, 1980 that formally organized what was at first known as the Senior Tour and today is called the Champions Tour—a place where players over the age of fifty can keep playing.

Two tournaments were held on the Senior Tour in 1980 and while I wasn't old enough to play in them they had my undivided attention. For several years I'd reconciled myself to the fact that my playing days were all but over. Every year the number of Tour events I entered had declined, and most of the tournaments I did attend were because of previous commitments or sponsor obligations. Now, a year from turning fifty, a reprieve!

The timing for me was extraordinary. I had been fortunate to see the birth of what could be called the modern Tour, with its corporate sponsors, television coverage, and purses large enough to allow players to make a living without something on the side. And now I was witnessing the birth of a competitive arena for players in their so-called retirement.

Not everyone was ready to play it again. For some players, the regular Tour had been plenty. But I was eager for more. It wasn't that I didn't have other options. I was involved in a golf course design company that could have occupied all my time. (I designed twenty-five courses in the late 1970s, with an emphasis on playability for the recreational player.) I had my fruit farm in Mapleton that could have occupied all my time and then some. I'd bought a sportfishing business in San Diego. And there were always a variety of business and real estate offers promising to make me rich beyond my wildest dreams. But playing competitive golf was what I preferred, especially against guys my own age. On the new Senior Tour there would be no more battling players ten to thirty years younger. I wouldn't have to worry about the youth movement. I *was* the youth movement.

But first, I had to get my game back in shape.

OVER THE YEARS, AGE AND gravity had taken their toll. I'd lost much of the elasticity of my younger days, which greatly affected my swing. I'd always had a strong grip with my left hand over the top and my right hand underneath, but I had such a good lateral movement with my hips that I came through the ball fine. But as I got older I couldn't do that. My lateral movement diminished and I was blocking the ball, costing me both distance and direction.

To get ready for the Senior Tour I left the Utah winter and went back to San Diego. At the San Diego Country Club I bumped into my friend, Frank Verna, who impressed me with his improved golf game. I asked him what he'd done and he said he'd been working with Phil Rodgers.

I'd known Phil ever since he started tearing up the junior golf tournaments in San Diego as a teenager. He was seven years younger than I was so our paths didn't cross competitively until he turned pro in 1961 and came out on Tour. He won five times on the PGA Tour and nearly won the British Open in 1963, when he lost the Claret Jug in a playoff with Bob Charles. After his playing career, Phil found his calling as a teacher. He had a gifted eye that could see the intricacies of the golf swing. Shortly before I went to see him he'd worked with Jack Nicklaus on a major swing overhaul, one Jack credited for allowing him to win both the U.S. Open and the PGA Championship in 1980 after he turned forty.

Phil Rodgers gave me the second formal golf lesson of my life—and the first since Charlie Heaney at the San Diego Country Club taught me the Vardon grip in 1947.

Phil changed both my grip and my swing. Because I couldn't move my hips like I once did, he had me start my backswing on the inside and then stay inside on my downswing. That way I could release properly through impact. But there was a side effect. I was now hooking the ball. I'd come full circle back to my youth, when my trademark off the tee was a hook. But this wasn't any old hook. This was a big sweeping, hide-the-women-and-children hook.

When I showed up with my new swing, the players on the Senior Tour—many of whom I hadn't played with in years—couldn't quite believe the wild hooks I was hitting. After spending eighteen holes with me, Don January described my shot trajectory: "You start it in the right rough, it goes over the entire fairway, and winds up in the left rough. You're the only golfer I've ever seen who covers the entire hole with one shot." I was playing with Jim Ferree in Syracuse, where almost all the holes are doglegs to the right. I started all my tee shots directly in the direction of the rough and trees, counting on the right-to-left trajectory that would eventually bring them back to the fairway. After about eight holes, Jim said, "Cass, damn, you play exciting golf." Doug Sanders said, "You're all mixed up Casper; you're hooking in the day and fading at night." At the *Golf Digest* tournament in Newport, Rhode Island, I won a four-hole playoff against Bob Toski, who had become a noted teacher of the golf swing. Toski was amazed at the transformation I'd made, and that I was winning with a completely revamped swing. But I knew it was what I had to do to be successful. I didn't try to go against it. I went with it.

THE SENIOR TOUR STARTED WITH just two events in 1980, one in Atlantic City, New Jersey, and another, the Suntree Classic, in Melbourne, Florida, for a combined purse of $250,000. The next year, when I joined, there were seven tournaments and the purse was $1 million. I couldn't wait to get started. The week I turned fifty I went to Massachusetts for the Marlboro tournament. On June 23, 1981, the night before my birthday, Toney Penna and Billy Maxwell took me to dinner. The next day I played in the pro-am. It was exactly twenty-six years and a day since I teed it up in my very first official PGA Tour event at the Western Open in Portland, Oregon.

I guess it should come as no surprise that my first flirtation with a victory in the over-fifty club came later that summer in the company of a very familiar name. At the 1981 U.S. Senior Open at Oakland Hills Country Club in Michigan, I found myself tied for the lead at the end of regulation play with Arnold Palmer and Bob Stone.

Fifteen years after The Olympic Club, Arnold and I were back at it. But in the eighteen-hole playoff the next day, this time there was no fading by Arnie. He grabbed the lead early and never let go, shooting 70 to Bob Stone's 74 and my 77. Two years later I would join Palmer as a winner of both the U.S. Open and the U.S. Senior Open when I outlasted Rod Funseth for the title at Hazeltine. And outlasted is the right word. We tied at the end of regulation and were still tied after our eighteen-hole playoff the next day. Finally, on the ninety-first hole, I hit an 8-iron to fourteen feet and made the putt for a birdie that secured the win, my first of two senior majors. (I also won the Mazda Senior Tournament Players Championship in 1988.)

THE SENIOR TOUR HAD ITS growing pains, and I suppose it also fits that Arnie and I were often in the thick of the battles, and on opposite sides. One thing we fought tooth and nail over were golf carts. Palmer was a member of the divisional board of the Senior Tour and didn't want carts. He wanted everyone to walk just like on the regular Tour. I was chairman of the players' committee and knew we had a number of players the public wanted to see but who couldn't get around unless they used carts. I took an informal poll of the Senior Tour membership to gauge how the majority felt and the vote was something like forty-six to nine in favor of carts. It was that lopsided. I turned those results in to Deane Beman and when it came time for the board to rule, they made the decision to allow carts. I looked over at Arnold—we were both at the meeting—and he almost slid under the table. After the meeting he said, "Casper, every time you take a cart I hope you get it stuck in the mud up to the axle."

There were other issues concerning concessions for age, such as shorter tees on some holes, which Arnold didn't want either. His reputation for railing against the "panty-waists" of the Senior Tour was well known. When we got to the Tournament of Champions, where they had established a senior division, I had breakfast one morning with Dave Hill, Lee Elder and Chi Chi Rodriguez, when Chi Chi had a suggestion. "Fellas," he said, "what we ought to do is put on a skirt, stand by our carts, have a picture taken and give it to Arnold." I thought it was Chi Chi just talking, but after breakfast I saw him in the parking lot and he said, "I got one." I said, "Got one what?" and he said, "I got one of my wife's petticoats," and he pulled out this pink petticoat and wrapped it around his waist twice. He'd just finished cinching it up when Arnold came walking by. Chi Chi put a foot up on the cart and sang out in his highest falsetto voice, "Hi, Arnie old buddy." Arnie had to laugh. That's all he could do.

I said, "Arnie, if I could have found one to fit me I'd have worn one too."

Two days later, we played the final round of the tournament. I shot 68 and Palmer shot 77, which didn't help matters much. Two weeks later, Palmer, Chi Chi, Gary Player and I were playing in a foursome at the Merrill Lynch Shootout at La Costa. On the first tee, Player had honors and he hit his ball into the left trap. Chi Chi went next and hit into the weeds on the right. I said, "Arnold, it's somewhere between those two." He looked at me and said, "You're right Cass, and that's the first time we've agreed in years."

BUT FOR ALL THAT, THE great bonus of the Senior Tour was being able to play and compete—and associate with one another—without the kind of pressure that exists on the regular Tour. Everyone still wanted to win and do well; there was still plenty of pride and ego. But as was repeated over and over in the locker room, this was a mulligan, a do-over, a complete gift. And we all knew it. As much as I still enjoyed bearing down and competing, I was a different player on the Senior Tour and so were most of the other guys. I wore knickers and dressed in wild colors. In the 1983 Senior Open at Hazeltine, when Rod Funseth and I tied at the end of regulation, the media asked me if I had clothes for the playoff. I said I had tan knickers with a brown shirt, or powder blue knickers with a bright blue shirt, or pink knickers with a cherry shirt and matching argyle socks. "Why don't you select?" They picked the pink and cherry, of course. That would never have happened on the regular Tour, but with this new lease on life, I joked with the galleries and tried my best to give something back to the game that had given me so much.

By 1987, the Senior Tour had expanded to thirty-two events and a purse of nearly $9 million (by 2012 it was over $50 million). It was clearly here to stay. After several years of spending much of each winter away from the family in Utah so I could practice in warm weather, we packed up, sold our Utah ranch house to Johnny Miller, and moved back to San Diego.

I won nine times on the Senior Tour in less than a decade and collected more in official winnings than I did my entire career on the regular Tour—$1,718,672 to $1,691,583. My final victory came in 1989 when I was fifty-eight years old. We were playing the inaugural Transamerica Senior Golf Championship at the Silverado Country Club in Napa, California. I was staying in a room at Silverado next to the golf course. I could walk out my door and putt on the putting green. Several nights that week I took my putter to the green and practiced in the dark. It was like old times. I was a teenager again, putting at night at the San Diego Country Club after everyone else had gone home. Sunday afternoon I sank a putt on the eighteenth green and walked away with the tournament trophy.

And the wins and the money pale compared to the fringe benefits from this fabulous mulligan. At stop after stop, people would come up to talk. They had seen me in the playoff with Palmer in '66, or they had watched the Masters in '70, or I had given them a golf ball in one of my golf camps, or I had spoken at a church fireside that they remembered. How many athletes in any other sport get that kind of opportunity for what amounts to a victory lap?

The biggest fringe benefit of all for me was getting to spend time with my sons as they caddied for me on the Senior Tour. When the kids were younger we'd made it a point to travel on the Tour as a family, but this was a chance for quality, one-on-one time. Each son and I wound up spending days and weeks together, just the two of us, and it was tremendous the rapport and relationship that built. Billy actually started caddying for me occasionally while I was still competing on the regular Tour; after that, Bobby, Byron, Charlie and Tommy all took their turns, and all did a fine job—and made good money, I might add. The only exception was our son David. When it was David's turn to caddy, we were on the first hole at San Diego Country Club, the place where I'd started caddying. Before we began I went over a checklist about what he'd packed in the bag, making sure we were ready to go. It was the same kind of questions I asked all the boys when they started out. When he said he didn't have some of the items I reminded him that it was his responsibility to have everything ready, that he had a job to do, and he was getting paid well to do it. He said, "This isn't for me" and walked off the course.

I wish the incident had been a surprise, an aberration, but it wasn't. For years Shirley and I had worried about the choices David, an extremely intelligent and charming but also very willful young man, was making. We racked our brains, trying to understand why, constantly questioning where we had gone wrong with our parenting. We raised him no differently than the other kids; we tried to teach them all the same values and standards of respect.

We had moved to Utah right after David was born. His formative years were spent on a farm next to a forest, fresh air and trout streams. He didn't grow up around nearly as many so-called worldly distractions and temptations as his older brothers and sisters. But just the same, at a fairly early age he got involved with drugs and alcohol, and the crowd that goes along with them. That led to lying and stealing and scrapes with the law. All the talking and worrying in the world is no match for drug addiction, and by the time he was twenty-two—just a few years after the caddying incident—David was sentenced to three years hard jail time for burglary and parole violation.

Shirley and I spent countless nights crying for him and praying for help from above. When he was released we brought him home, got him back on his feet and drove him to his Alcoholics Anonymous and Narcotics Anonymous meetings. While he was in jail we investigated a variety of programs that might move him beyond his addictions and help him find stability in his life. The best one, we felt, was the Delancey Street Foundation in Los Angeles. Delancey Street is a wonderful program that takes you in with the clothes on your back and for the next two years weans you off your addictions and teaches you a skill, or a trade, that you can use the rest of your life. After the two years you commit to work in that trade for two more years to pay them back. At the end of the four years you are free and clear—and better equipped to handle what the world throws at you.

But David decided Delancey Street wasn't for him. He said it sounded too much like prison all over again. He didn't like the time commitment; he wanted to do it himself, on his own. After three months we helped him move into an apartment so he could do just that.

His crime spree started almost immediately. During a forty-day stretch in late 1999, in Southern California and Nevada, David committed thirty-five armed robberies and hijacked two cars, all at gunpoint. As an indicator of how clouded and disaffected his judgment had become, he used no disguise whatsoever as he waved his gun and threatened the people he robbed. He was caught and eventually sent to prison for 105 years, a virtual life sentence. When David got out of jail the first time I asked him to name the most important thing to him in life and he answered, "Freedom." I said, "Then don't let anything take that away from you." But his addictions did just that.

At his sentencing, David stood up and told the judge how sorry he was for what he had done to his family. He looked at us sitting in the courtroom and said, "I want them to know I take responsibility for all that has happened. I would change everything if I could. It's not their fault." It was the good we had always seen in David speaking, and there is so much goodness in him. It broke our hearts to hear him say that, and to see where he was headed because we were powerless to change what had happened.

No one in the family gave up on David then, and no one ever will. In our faith we are taught that families are forever and so is forgiveness. Whatever David has to answer for in this life he must answer for, but our love and hope for him is unconditional and everlasting and goes infinitely beyond any life sentence.

All our children have had their ups and downs, as have their parents, but Shirley and I have so much to be grateful for with them all. They have brought us more joy than we could ever have imagined or are capable of expressing.

None of us are perfect or immune from temptation. As the scripture says, this life is a time to prepare to meet God. We are all here to be tested. I know that I've failed my share of tests. I thank Almighty God for His Son, the Savior of the World, whose mercy lets us all re-tee when we need to.

LIFE IS A LONG AND patient teacher. Before they died, I had a reconciliation of sorts with both of my parents. My father all but disappeared from my life after we parted ways in San Francisco when I was fifteen years old. He remained in the diamond-drilling business and his work took him to Alaska and then to Puerto Rico, where he remarried, settled down, and raised a stepdaughter. In his retirement he moved to Long

Island in New York. Although I carried his name throughout my career, the man who first put a golf club in my hands never came to see me play on the regular Tour. He didn't explain why and I didn't ask. We finally got together a few times when I was playing on the Senior Tour. But by then we had gone our separate ways for so long that it wasn't possible to resurrect much out of our relationship. William Earl Casper died in 1990, of emphysema. I went to the funeral in Long Island but did not speak.

My mother retired and moved to Mexico with her husband. After he passed away she eventually returned to her family roots in southwest New Mexico. I went to see her at her home in Silver City and we began to re-kindle our relationship. The golf course in Silver City had expanded to eighteen holes, with grass on the greens, and the pro, Jim Smith, invited me to attend a tournament there in my honor. The affair was a success and I suggested it become an annual event to benefit a local charity. Of course it would also allow me to see my mother. For several years we held the tournament and raised in the neighborhood of $750,000 for the Gila Regional Hospital in Silver City. Coming "home" always felt good and comfortable to me. Just after I turned sixty, very near the pasture where I first played golf, I shot 61 at the Silver City municipal golf course. I'd have shot my age, for the first time, but I missed a twenty-five-foot putt on the last green.

Over time, my mother and I developed a closeness we'd never experienced before. One day she was driving in Silver City and passed out at the wheel. I was the first person she called when she came to in the hospital. My oldest son Billy and I went to visit her and talked her into moving to Southern California, so she could be near us and we could take care of her. For the last seven years of her life, Isabel Williams lived in San Diego. We moved her into Frederica Manor, where she could feel the ocean breeze and look out and see Point Loma. After she got used to it, which did not take long, she said she wished she would have come much earlier. She really enjoyed her life there. She ran the place. She took charge of the bingo games and she'd sit in the front office and make sure everything was organized and running smoothly. That's the kind of person she was.

Her one wish was that she wouldn't become a burden, that when she went she'd go quickly. She got her wish. One day she had a stroke, lapsed into a coma, and passed away the next morning. She was ninety-one years old and alert and active right to the end. Her body was cremated. She'd asked that her ashes be dropped into the Pacific Ocean, where she enjoyed fishing so much. We chartered a fishing boat out of Mission Bay and took the family out to sea, where we said a prayer and lowered her ashes over the side. They went down about twenty feet and exploded in every direction. We returned to the bay and had a big picnic to celebrate her life. I think my mother was embarrassed she wasn't more of a mother, but she started out hard in life and did the best she could, and in the end she became the mother I always hoped I would have.

18

A Golfer Looks at 80

19

Every year at Augusta I camp out under the umbrellas
by the first tee, where I can visit with all
my friends from all areas of the golfing world.

Springville, Utah
2011

I discovered the same thing when I turned eighty that I discovered when I turned fifty, sixty, and seventy: it wasn't nearly as old as I thought it was going to be.

And I discovered something else: When I look back, my vision keeps getting better. The longer I live the clearer I can see and appreciate where my life has taken me and all the wonderful things I've been able to experience.

I can't imagine being born at a better time to watch the grand parade of golf. It's like someone set me down in the middle of the show and gave me a ringside seat. So many of the greats who added so much to golf added to my own life and career. When Shirley and I take cruises I give an onboard presentation called "Golfers I Have Known." I start with Walter Hagen and move on down through the years to Tiger and Phil. I shook hands with Hagen. I became good friends with Gene Sarazen. For years I was able to enjoy a conversation every April with Bobby Jones at the Masters. I played for the incomparable Byron Nelson in the Ryder Cup. I got to know Lloyd Mangrum and Doug Ford and Jimmy Demaret and Julius Boros and Cary Middlecoff and a hundred other early legends of the game when they were still competing. I saw the picture-perfect swing of Tommy Bolt, and what could happen when the ball didn't go where it was supposed to. I played alongside Ben Hogan and Sam Snead. It never fails to make me smile when I recall the trip I took through Italy and France with Snead. This is when we were Seniors. He was in his 70s, I was in my 50s, and we were invited to play several exhibitions with two European pros. Sam is a story-teller and we spent three weeks traveling together. During those three weeks I must have heard Snead tell the same stories a hundred times. And I laughed every time he told them. He'd get this twinkle in his eye and start to grin even before he began, and it didn't matter how many times you'd already heard it you still had to laugh.

Another talk I give on the cruise ships is entitled "Golf Yesterday and Today," subtitled "From House Trailers to Jets." I tell about watching the Tour evolve from the era of Snead, Hogan and Nelson through the era of Palmer, Nicklaus, Player and myself, then Watson, Trevino, Miller and the rest, right up to the present.

The Tour has grown by leaps and bounds. It's a big business. It's now in phenomenal, unbelievable shape. The purse for the entire year was $750,000 in 1955 when I started; in 1975, the year I won my last tournament, it was $8,000,000; in 2011 it was $280,000,000.

But while money has made the Tour I think it has also brought its own set of problems. The reward for winning just one tournament is so great that it can turn a player into a pin-seeker, someone who constantly aims for the flag to try to make birdies, willing to take enormous risks because if you can catch lightning in a bottle just once you'll make a million dollars in four days and you'll be set. As a consequence, shot-making and course-management—the skills that generate a consistently solid golf game that is able to hold up in all conditions and situations—often take a backseat, hurting a player's overall development. What is beneficial short-term can often backfire long-term.

Another consequence that comes with the enormous prize money is that it dilutes the quality of play in the regular events. The top players can afford to skip tournaments right and left and concentrate on the majors, which many of them do, a situation that often leaves fields full of players the galleries have barely heard of.

Speaking of money and the golf Tour, it's a shame that as the Tour found its stride and became extremely profitable, no provision was made to provide a pension fund for the older generation of players who helped build it. A profit-sharing plan was put into place in the 1970s when Deane Beman was PGA Tour commissioner, with players given credit according to how they finished in tournaments, but nothing was grandfathered in for players from earlier eras. Some older players who were still young enough when the Senior Tour came along got a small pension from that Tour, but nothing from the regular Tour. Snead, Hogan, Nelson, Palmer, Player, all those guys and hundreds of others, including me, never have participated in profit sharing on the regular PGA Tour. Beman later started a program called the Grand Champions that is strictly for players over seventy, who are eligible to receive compensation for playing in as many as four pro-amateur events a year on the Champions Tour. We have around fifteen or so who participate in that program, but the reality is that many of the real pioneers of the modern Tour, men who played back when tournaments only paid through twenty or thirty places and slept four to a motel room to cut down on expenses, have had to watch the Tour soar to runaway wealth while receiving no compensation for helping lay the foundation.

I STAY CONNECTED TO THE past, present and future of golf each year in April when I spend a week in Augusta at the Masters—the game's great worldwide family reunion. We rent houses near the golf course and catch up with old friends and make new ones. What a reward it has been to do that, and to attend the champions dinner on the Tuesday before the tournament begins and be able to rub shoulders with the green jacket fraternity called the Masters Club.

It used to be I couldn't wait to get to Augusta and play the golf course. Now I can't wait to get there and sit next to the golf course. Every day I make my way to the umbrellas east of the big oak tree in front of the trophy room near the first tee. There are about thirty to forty tables under the umbrellas. I arrive about ten in the morning, secure a table, and stay until three or four in the afternoon. I get to meet all kinds of people that are involved with the game of golf. The parade never ends. I plan to keep coming back till I die and probably even after that. Last year I was sitting at my usual spot, under the umbrella, and a little fog bank came floating down the first fairway, and I thought maybe that was all the spirits of the past champions coming to the Masters.

I GOT A LOT OF attention the last time I played in the Masters in 2005, the year Tiger shot 12-under to win the tournament. I was seventy-three years old and recently recovered from hip surgery and shot 106. In hindsight, it probably wasn't the best decision I ever made. But after three years of not being able to play because of my hip, I wanted to give my grandchildren, many of whom were there, a chance to see me in the tournament. My Waterloo, as fate would have it, was the par-three sixteenth, where I splashed five balls into the pond before hitting the green and three-putting for a 14. The irony is that if it hadn't been for the birdie I made on sixteen in the 1970 playoff with Gene Littler, I would have never gotten my lifetime exemption that made shooting that 14 possible!

Not a single member of the media made that comparison after the round. But my impromptu press conference after shooting 106 attracted more reporters than when I won the tournament.

Officially, the score didn't count because instead of turning in my card I put it in my back pocket and withdrew from the tournament. When I got home to Utah I had the scorecard framed and hung it on the wall next to my Masters trophy, a reminder to me, and to my grandchildren, that things don't always go exactly as planned. But you don't up and quit when that happens. You don't pick up your ball and go home. I have no regrets about my last round in the Masters, or anything to do with that wonderful tournament. Given the chance to do it all over again, I'd do it all over again.

I HAVE FEW REGRETS FROM my lifetime in golf, but if I could have mulligans in my career, I would use them on these:

- I would play in the British Open much earlier and much more often.
- I would take Ben Hogan up on that open invitation for lunch in Fort Worth.
- I would play that round of golf with President Eisenhower we always promised each other we'd play and never quite got around to.

My dream foursome—let's make it a fivesome—would include the incomparable Bob Hope, Gene Littler and two of my closest friends on Tour, Ken Still and Gay Brewer. At Cypress Point.

When it comes to momentous decisions in my life, two stand out that relate to golf. The first was deciding to caddy at the age of eleven. Caddying allowed me to learn to take care of myself at an early age and placed me in the world of golf. It opened all the doors that followed.

The second was laying up on the par-three third hole at Winged Foot in 1959. That decision paved the way for my first U.S. Open win and my first major championship—a victory that gave me the confidence I needed to take my game to the next level, and it also opened the gate to the rest of my life.

IN 1987 I STARTED A golf course management company, Billy Casper Golf, with Peter Hill and Bob Morris. We had a hard time getting clients in the beginning, but over time we caught momentum and the company now owns and manages more than 130 golf courses, both private and public, all around the country. We're the second largest golf management company in the United States and fourth largest in the world, and still growing. Every day, more than twelve thousands rounds are played on a Billy Casper Golf-managed course; over four million rounds a year. I take a lot of pride in that.

I don't take the responsibility of having my name on the company masthead lightly. While I leave the business details to the businessmen— Peter Hill, our CEO, is consistently ranked as one of the most influential people in the golf world—I take a hands-on approach in ensuring that the values and standards associated with Billy Casper Golf reflect my own values and standards. We stress a positive, family-oriented, guest-friendly atmosphere, and that begins with hiring positive, family-oriented, guest-friendly employees. Our starting point isn't profit, it's people. We never want to forget that it's people who are playing the golf courses, not dollars, and it's our people who are enhancing that experience. Peter often states that our ambition is to become the best management company in the history of golf. That's not an immodest goal, but I know it's reachable if you keep your head down and concentrate on getting a little better every day. We started out with five employees and now we have over six thousand.

My primary role with the company could best be described as ambassador-at-large. I'm the company diplomat. I make periodic appearances at the courses, meet with public and private decision-makers, and in general lend a hand wherever and whenever I can. What gives me as much pleasure as anything is interacting with the staff at our annual meetings. I often see tears in the eyes of employees when they talk about their experiences in helping people through the great game of golf. So many people have so much passion for what they do and how much they care. That inspires me. And I'm convinced it's the secret to our growth and success. Quality people get quality results. The company history is filled with stories of facilities that were losing significant money, and in danger of being closed, when Billy Casper Golf took over, and now they're thriving. A good example is the Chicago area, where Billy Casper Golf was called in to take over the operation of ten courses and two driving ranges for Cook County Forest Reserve. The courses were losing well over $1 million a year. In the first six months under Billy Casper Golf they made a profit of over $250,000. We now operate twenty-three facilities in the Chicago area.

THE GAME KEEPS GIVING BACK to me in so many unexpected ways. One summer the city of Chula Vista named the entrance to the municipal golf course "Billy Casper Way." In 1996 I was overwhelmed when Jack Nicklaus invited me to his tournament in Dublin, Ohio, the Memorial, and singled me out as that year's Memorial Honoree. I joined a long list that stretched from Old Tom Morris to Bobby Jones and dozens of others. I will never forget Jack's graciousness on that occasion. For so many years we had circled each other as competitive rivals, keeping our professional distance; now we were able to develop a relationship of deep warmth and respect that continues to grow.

In the early spring of 2010 I was in Idaho, doing some fishing and relaxing at the cabin that belongs to our daughter Linda and son-in-law Kim Henrie, when the phone rang. An official with the Moroccan Golf Association was on the line with news that they were making the Hassan II Golf Trophy an official stop on the European Tour. He wanted to invite me to be there for the signing of the contract.

I packed a bag, drove from Idaho to Salt Lake City, caught a plane to New York and was in Rabat the next morning.

They asked me to speak at the ceremony and I told the audience how much Morocco means to me and reminisced about all the wonderful times I'd experienced there. I recalled that when King Hassan first invited me in 1969 there were only a handful of golf courses in the entire country. Now there are dozens of them, including the beautiful Royal Dar Es Salam Club, site of the new European Tour event. I had a hard time keeping my emotions in check, and when I returned to my seat I sat down next to the director of the golf tournament, a Moroccan friend. He was crying like a baby. I asked him to stop crying, I was crying enough for both of us.

Later that same year, I received another call. This one was from the PGA of America informing me that I'd been selected to receive the 2010 PGA Distinguished Service Award, the organization's highest honor. For a moment Jim Remy, the PGA president, didn't hear anything from my end of the line. That's because I was speechless. It was such a great and humbling honor to be the recipient of an award previously given to Byron Nelson, George H.W. Bush, Gerald Ford, Bob Hope, Patty Berg, Arnold Palmer, Jack Nicklaus and so many others I admire. I honestly didn't know what to say.

I was invited to the 92nd PGA Championship at Whistling Straits in Wisconsin for the ceremony, where I had a chance to address the audience on the Tuesday before the tournament began. I had a hard time getting through that speech as well, but I welcomed the opportunity to talk about the importance of service and giving back after all I had been given.

NOT LONG AGO, I WAS asked to give the keynote speech to open the Huntsman World Senior Games, a competition sponsored by my friend Jon Huntsman for athletes fifty-and-over that is held every summer in St. George, Utah. Two men came up to me afterward and asked a question. They wanted to know how I would like to be remembered. I'd never really thought about that but I found out I didn't need to think very long. After only a second or two I knew my answer. I told them I would like to be remembered as a person who had a great love for his fellow man.

I'm not sure that's how I will be remembered, that's not for me to say. But it is my goal.

I try to do just that as I travel, as I sit on airplanes, as Shirley and I enjoy our cruises, as I recline under the umbrella at Augusta National, as I visit golf courses and meet with old acquaintances and make new ones. I don't want to detract, I don't want to be negative. I want to be someone who adds to the lives and aspirations of others. I recently read that Arnold Palmer expressed a similar sentiment. After all that life has given him he wants to give back as much as he possibly can. That is no surprise, coming from the ultimate people person, and I have the same hope and desire. It's the best way I can think of to repay the many kindnesses I have received.

Shirley and I became very close over the years with Jim Huber, the talented writer and TV commentator and great friend to golf, and Jim's wife Carol. We went on several cruises together and enjoyed each other's company tremendously. Jim and I would often follow one another giving onboard lectures. I appreciated so much something Jim wrote about me in one of his last "Sense of Huber" columns before a very untimely and unexpected death due to leukemia.

"No man I've ever known with his kind of credentials," he wrote, "has ever been more eager to hug and be hugged, to give until it runs out. To travel with him is to walk the world with the Dalai Lama of Golf."

Contrary to what we might think when we are young, none of us will live forever. I was recently diagnosed with a rare slow-moving disease called amyloid cardiomyopathy. It's a condition where the body doesn't consume all the protein it produces; instead, it stores the unused protein, called amyloid, in one of the organs. Mine is the left ventricle of the heart. Consequently, it's twice as big as it should be. Mostly it affects my breathing. I take longer to go upstairs or walk up a hill now. I'm constantly having to catch my breath. I need a cart to get around a golf course. There is no cure for this disease, but in the form I have they tell me you can live with it for a good, long time.

MY GREATEST REWARD IN LIFE is, has been, and always will be, my family. Nothing has brought me more joy and satisfaction. At last count our eleven children had expanded to include thirty-four grandchildren and fifteen great-grandchildren. Family is indeed the gift that keeps on giving.

Being a parent is life's highest calling and biggest challenge. We want more for our children than we do for ourselves. I've found it's much easier to handle my own highs and lows than those of my children. When my son Bob, a fine professional golfer in his own right, decided he wanted to attend the PGA Tour Qualifying Tournament, known as Q-school, and see if he could get his Tour card, I thought I could help him and signed on as his caddy for the event at the Fort Ord course in California. Bob was in the thick of the competition, where more than a hundred and fifty golfers compete for a very limited number of spots. After the first day carrying his bag I got so nervous I came down with shingles and was forced to leave the tournament. I had to go home and recover. In fifty years playing competitive golf I didn't drop out of a single tournament because of nerves, but watching Bob and not being able to do anything other than hand him a club was more than I could handle.

EACH OF OUR CHILDREN HAS made their own way and found their own niche. They like to do it their way (I wonder where that comes from?) Linda, the little girl who wondered why daddies didn't go to church, is a homemaker who devotes considerable time and energy to church and community service and looking after others. After many years in the sportfishing business, Billy is currently an investment counselor and consultant. Bob is co-host with Brian Taylor of the nationally syndicated radio show, "Real Golf Radio." Byron is one of the top teachers for the nationwide golf instruction company, GolfTEC. Judi and Jeni, our identical twins, live a state apart, in California and Arizona, but they still talk daily. Judi is a mother to five, helps run our Billy's Kids tournament in San Diego, and is an accomplished graphic artist. Jeni is a mother to one and also a skilled artist and homemaker. Charlie is co-owner of a youth corrections facility who spends weeks at a time at camps helping kids find their way. In his incarceration, we are aware David is using the caring side of his nature to help others. Julia is a compassionate health care worker. Sarah is a single mom who returned to college for her bachelor's degree and finished near the top of her class. Tommy is in charge of season ticket sales for Canyons Resort in Park City, Utah.

Shirley and I are proud of all of them. But as much as we share in our children's accomplishments and achievements, we try to remember an important truth we've learned from the church, and that is that we are instruments in the lives of our children for a finite period of time here on earth and it's our responsibility to give them what they need so they can return to their Father in Heaven. Our children are His children, just as we are His children, and He gives us all the freedom to make our own choices.

I find great comfort in my faith. Nothing in my life has meant more to me than my membership in the Church of Jesus Christ of Latter-day Saints. From the gospel I learn why I'm here, where I came from, and where I'm going. This eternal perspective changed my life from the day I was baptized and has influenced my actions ever since. I was pretty selfish when I joined the church and over time my eyes were opened to just how much I could do for others if I could learn to forget myself. The church has given me tremendous examples to follow. I've been fortunate to meet modern-day apostles and prophets on a personal level. On numerous occasions I've been able to travel to Israel in the company of church leaders and walk where Jesus walked. The last time we traveled there we went to Caesarea Phillipi on the northern edge of Israel, on the headwaters of the Jordan River. The water comes out of Mount Hermon and it fills the beautiful pools. It was one of Jesus's favorite places and in Matthew you read about Him talking to the multitude and asking the people who they say He is. Then Jesus asks Peter the same question and Peter declares that Jesus is the Son of the Living God. Jesus blesses Peter and tells him no man has told him this, only his Father in Heaven. And then Jesus says that upon this rock He will build His church. The rock is revelation. Revelation from Heavenly Father is the cornerstone of my religion. He gives revelation to the church leaders to guide the church and He gives individual revelation for each of us to guide our own lives. There is no doubt in my mind that I've been guided and directed. But I've had to make the choices to receive and act on that direction. It was never forced on me; the decision has always been mine and mine alone.

THROUGH IT ALL, THERE HAS been one immovable constant: my wife Shirley. No golfer has had a better companion. Ever. Shirley never swung a club but she was behind every shot I hit. Of the more than three thousand rounds of golf I played as a professional on the regular and senior Tours, Shirley walked at least eighty-five percent of them, and that's a conservative estimate. She was always there. From the beginning, when we pulled out of San Diego together on our big wild dream, she said we were going to make it. She never once asked to go home. She had more confidence in me than I had in myself. She handled the money, ran the home, and looked out for everyone. In the early days on Tour, when our kids were small, we'd arrive at a tournament site and she'd have already planned several outings for the family while I was at the golf course practicing. They'd see a museum or some historical site or the zoo. I remember one year in Mobile, Alabama. We played over the Thanksgiving weekend, and there was Shirley, organizing a big turkey dinner for everyone in the tournament. She talked to the people at the club and they let her use their big ovens in the kitchen. Several more wives got involved and over two hundred of us sat down together for Thanksgiving. None of it would have happened without Shirley.

Not long ago, Shirley asked me why I didn't have a psychologist while I was playing like everybody has today and I said, "Honey, you handled all that stuff." If a Hall of Fame for golf wives existed, and it should, Shirley Casper would be a charter member. I'd match her up against any Tour wife that ever lived.

IN 2004 WE MOVED AGAIN to Utah, where much of our family is now located. I bid another farewell to the San Diego Country Club, and my almost daily rounds there with Irv Sommers, but in truth we have never completely left San Diego. Each spring Shirley and I go back for two months to run the Billy's Kids tournament that we host every May at San Diego Country Club. We rent a place next to the ocean in Imperial Beach not more than a par-five from the trailer park we lived in when I was in the Navy.

We started the Billy Casper Youth Foundation in 1992 and organized the golf tournament as a fundraiser to benefit Junior Achievement, the national group that helps young people acquire skills that will enable them to be economically successful in life. Shortly thereafter, we added the Boys and Girls Clubs of San Diego and the Music Machine, an award-winning traveling singing group at Bonita Vista High School that our daughter Sarah was involved with, as good causes for young people we wanted to give assistance to. Helping out youngsters, especially those who start life with huge disadvantages, has always been the top priority for Shirley and me. It is where our heart is. Over the years Billy's Kids has raised nearly $3 million for the Boys and Girls Clubs and Junior Achievement. In addition to that, we have helped any number of other causes, including the Music Machine, junior golf groups, hospitals, colleges, the Down Syndrome Connection, the Boy Scouts and Girl Scouts of America, the Primary Children's Medical Center, and the Champions Tour Wives Youth Dental Clinic.

It brings me enormous satisfaction to be able to return every year and put on an event to help kids at the place that helped me so much when I was a kid. I hesitate to think what I might have otherwise amounted to and where I might have ended up if not for that sanctuary.

During our annual stay in San Diego in the spring, Shirley and Judi organize the tournament while I talk to sponsors, line up players and make the pairings. I'm continually impressed by how many companies and individuals open up their pocketbooks, even in tough economic times, to give to these important causes.

But I also get the chance to slip away almost every day to the San Diego Country Club, where I'm surrounded by so many wonderful friends, reminders and memories.

The club has gone through many changes since I first laid eyes on it in 1939. There's a completely new clubhouse and facilities. What was once the caddy shed is now the cart garage. The surrounding area has also changed dramatically. There are no more lemon groves in Chula Vista, I can tell you that. If I tried to hit a golf ball today from the course to Chub's Pool Hall I'd be arrested for trespassing before I made it half a block, and Chub's isn't there any longer anyway.

But the golf course I remember from my youth—the tees, greens and fairways—remains remarkably the same, an oasis of green tucked in behind the traffic, taco stands, check-cashing places and fast-food franchises that have sprung up on every outside corner. I can still walk out the back of the clubhouse and in my mind's eye see Ben Hogan hitting those shots from the fairway on five. I can envision the countless hours I spent walking every inch of the course, caddying and playing, the times spent putting after dark, playing cards in the caddy shed. Those Tonk games are long gone, but every spring when I arrive the ladies at the club are waiting for me to join them in their bridge games. They ask Shirley if Billy can come out and play.

In the clubhouse foyer, next to the Mickey Wright Lounge and the Billy Casper Grille, they've framed the scorecard showing the course-record 60 I shot in 1978. Next to that there's a selection of cups and trophies from my career, and above the mantel there's a plaque with a golf ball representing each of my wins on the PGA Tour, fifty-one of them in all.

To this day I have a hard time believing it all happened. More than anything, when I was young I wanted to be a professional golfer, but I had no grand scheme in mind, no set number of victories I wanted to win. Not for a single moment during my career did I stop to tally up my wins or my statistics. I never kept score when I was keeping score.

But others did—the caretakers of the game who understand that golf's past creates its present and shapes its future.

As I write this, the phone has already started to ring (and if I had email I'm sure the emails would already be flying). With the United States Open returning to The Olympic Club in 2012, reporters want to talk about what happened there in 1966. They want to hear about Arnold Palmer and me. That's almost half-a-century ago now. But that's all right. I can remember every shot.

EPILOGUE

Closing Statement

20

Returning to The Olympic Club in 2011; it's
hard to believe forty-five summers have passed
since the memorable U.S. Open in 1966.

San Francisco, California
August 9, 2011

By JAMES PARKINSON

On a foggy San Francisco morning, I watch as Billy Casper returns to The Olympic Club.

Mists roll in off the Pacific, half obscuring the classic old golf course as we pull off Skyline Boulevard and drive down the lane past the driving range toward the nearly century-old clubhouse.

The weather isn't appreciably different than it was when he won the National Open. It might be the same day, except for the fact that forty-five summers have somehow slipped by since then.

It's my idea that we've come. I want to see if we can pick up some details and jar a few more memories loose for this book. Plus, I couldn't think of anything much more thrilling than returning with Billy Casper to the scene of Billy Casper's greatest triumph.

The huge galleries that witnessed the comeback in sixty-six are long gone, but even before we stop the car, someone who was there is at the passenger door. Pat Murphy, an Olympic Club member who is on the committee that is helping to coordinate the U.S. Open's return to the Lake Course in 2012, was a seventeen-year-old kid in 1966. He carried the scoring placard during the Casper-Palmer playoff.

"I'll never forget your putt on eleven," Pat says after welcoming Billy back with open arms. "There was no way you could make it from there."

Everywhere you look in the clubhouse are reminders that Billy Casper once spent a remarkable week here, making all sorts of shots he wasn't supposed to be able to make. Photographs of the 1966 Open line the walls. At the entrance to the men's locker room there's a life-sized mural showing Casper with his arms raised in jubilation and a dejected Arnold Palmer in the background. In the world of golf at large

Billy Casper may be unheralded, under-appreciated and unsung. But at Olympic he reigns supreme.

Assistant pro Willie Toney trots over to say hello and Chris Stein, the head pro, personally escorts Mr. Casper to the first tee of the Lake Course, where another longtime Olympic Club member, Steve Gregoire, on his way to tee it up on the adjoining Ocean Course, makes a detour to come over and give the champ a hug.

Once on the course, surveying the landscape from the driver's seat of a golf cart, Billy's first reaction is, "What happened to the trees? It used to be a forest out here."

Olympic, it turns out, is a victim of its own longevity. When the course was built in the 1920s there was hardly a tree to be seen, just sand dunes and scrub growth. Back then you could see all the way to the Golden Gate Bridge. Then Sam Whiting, the architect, planted his reputed 40,000 trees, most of them dark cypress and Monterey pine. The problem is that Monterey pine have a lifespan of eighty to one hundred-twenty years. Those that aren't dead yet soon will be. Hundreds of trees, mostly cypress, have been planted to help stem the tide, but Olympic is considerably less forested than it was in 1966. The reconfigured par-three eighth hole occupies land that used to be all cypress and pine.

Casper notes that the course is much longer than the one he remembers. Tees have been stretched on virtually every hole, and traps have been added to catch big-hitters.

But underneath, the tricky contours of the course remain, all the uneven lies, sharp elevation changes, and shot-making demands that have been there since the beginning.

"You had to know the distances here," says Casper, taking it all back in. "You had all these swales and everything to deal with."

Rolling through those swales, he recalls how the heavy morning air knocked ten yards off your drives and forced you to use a lofted club to hit out of the wet rough.

"Golly," he adds in an aside, "I'd be lucky to break 90 now."

ON THE NINTH GREEN, CASPER pauses to remember Arnold Palmer rolling in his twenty-five-foot birdie putt on Sunday to go up by seven.

"Oh he was flying," Casper says, "I said I want to finish second and he said I'll do everything I can to help you."

To the side of the tenth green we stop at Hot Dog Bills. In 1950, a man named Bill Parrish and his wife Billie opened their refreshment stand across the street from the golf course. Their dogs and burgers proved to be so popular with the golfers, Bill and Billie were invited to set up shop right on the golf course, and they've been here ever since.

When he was making the turn in sixty-six, Casper did not so much as look at the hot dog stand, let alone eat anything that might upset his allergies. Now the allergies, like the Open, are part of his past, and after ordering one of the signature dogs with all the trimmings he signs an autograph for Linda, the woman who sold it to him, as they sink into a long conversation about their families.

"Man, that was a good hot dog. Thank you," he says as we're leaving.

WALKING THE BACK NINE OF Olympic with Billy Casper is like being with a kid at Christmas. He took 66 strokes to get around the inward nine during the final round and the playoff in '66; Arnold Palmer took 79. Everything good that happened to him, it happened here.

On the eleventh and thirteenth greens he remembers the lengthy putts he ran in for birdies in the playoff—the thirty-five-footer Pat Murphy mentioned in the parking lot and the forty-footer on thirteen that essentially slammed the door on Palmer.

This many years later, he doesn't dismiss the long putts as flukes, and he doesn't give luck much credit, either.

"If I didn't make two or three like that a round I was having a bad day," he says in the manner of a man who has arrived at the age when he knows he can tell it like it is and needn't worry about the filter.

On fourteen he remembers the uphill putt Palmer hit on Sunday that was halfway in the hole until it spun out, resulting in par instead of birdie.

"If that putt stays in," he says, "we wouldn't be here."

At the par-three fifteenth he recalls how both he and Palmer aimed for the pin on Sunday, him because he was five behind and had to, Palmer because, well, because he was Palmer. He first points to the spot on the green where his ball landed on its way to a one-putt birdie and then to the spot in the trap where Palmer's ball landed on its way to a bogey. If that didn't happen, we wouldn't be here either.

On the par-five sixteenth he walks to a patch of grass ten yards right of the present tee box—the place where the players hit their drives in 1966. From here, the tall cypress and pines on the right come more into play. They mess with your eye if not your ball flight. Palmer managed to miss the trees on the right but hooked wildly and hit the pine tree to the left. "He was having trouble breathing and swallowing," says Casper candidly. "I'd never seen him hit a shot like that in his life."

On seventeen, a par five for the members but a monstrous par four for the Open, Casper not only recalls the chip he made on Sunday that gave him a short putt for par that pulled him into a tie with Palmer, but also the two birdies he made here on Thursday and Friday. The one on Friday came after he holed a shot out of the right sand trap. Hundreds of cameras clicked when that happened. *Sports Illustrated* used one of them on its cover following the Open, his hands raised in the air after the ball disappeared into the cup, as if he's signaling a touchdown. An artist friend also snapped the photo and painted a picture from it that hangs in Billy's home. It's the signature shot of his career.

On eighteen, a 337-yard par four that takes off like a ski jump and is packed with so much history, he says, "What a great hole. I think every golf course should have a hole this length," noting how you can't see the downward slope of the fairway from the tee and motioning toward the well-trapped green above. To the left of the narrow fairway is where Palmer hit his 1-iron on Sunday, into the same rough where Ben Hogan buried his chances against Jack Fleck in their 1955 U.S. Open playoff. But Palmer fought back for a great closing par on the tilting green, which Casper notes isn't nearly as sloped as it was when they played it. Of course he's right. After the 1998 U.S. Open, there were so many complaints from players that the green was reconfigured. It still drops from back to front, just not as much.

Emily Dougherty, one of our Olympic Club hosts for the day, has played the hole, and after she putts out, Billy takes her to the edge of the green for an impromptu short-game clinic. Emily is an accomplished player. She is captain of the women's golf team at the University of Northern Colorado. But Billy has noticed she tends to hit her chip shots with a lot of loft. He drops two golf balls in the rough next to the green and discusses the merits of hitting short chip shots with a 7- or 8-iron, depending on how far you are off the green in the long grass. The idea is to position the ball well behind your back foot and stroke it like a putter, keeping the ball low to the ground. He demonstrates from about fifty feet and hits two shots, one after the other, within inches of the cup. When it's Emily's turn, she does the same. She beams and thanks Billy profusely for the tip. Another happy ending on the back nine at Olympic.

AFTER LUNCH, DANNY SINK OF the USGA invites Billy to come by USGA headquarters for a preview of what's in store when the Open returns to Olympic in June of 2012. Sink is the USGA's point person for the Open. Headquarters is the trailer the USGA rolled into the parking lot in the summer of 2010 to begin on-site preparation for the event, which is expected to attract some 200,000 spectators. He wants to make sure Billy Casper knows how important it is to the USGA that he is a part of the championship in any way he wants to be. He stresses that it is the Caspers and Palmers and other great champions of the past who built golf and made the U.S. Open the special tournament it is today, attracting turn-away crowds and offering lottery-level prize money.

"Did you play for $1.3 million?" Sink asks playfully.

"Not quite," says Casper, who collected $25,000 for winning the 1966 Open, out of a purse of $150,000. (Adjusted for inflation, that $25,000 translates to $169,500 in today's dollars; a nice paycheck but nowhere near the $1.3 million the 2012 winner gets.)

STUDENTS OF THE GAME'S HISTORY have never needed an introduction to Billy Casper's legacy. Two U.S. Open titles is preamble enough. But as dramatic as his wins were at Winged Foot and here at The Olympic Club, two legendary golf courses where he left the likes of Hogan, Snead, Palmer, Nicklaus and Player in his wake, he has always remained largely an enigma to the public at large. A public figure difficult to compartmentalize.

I thought the writer Jaime Diaz phrased it perfectly in an article he wrote in 1996:

> *"Quietly, neatly, gracefully, like a pool hustler running the table and calmly leaving with everyone's money, Billy Casper's glide through golf history was too subtle and too stoic to be properly appreciated. The truth is, the public probably had less idea who Billy Casper was than any great golfer of the second half of the century. He is arguably the best golfer who never got his due."*

BUT IF THE WORLD WAS largely unaware, the players knew. Inside the ropes they always knew.

As Lee Trevino said, "When I came on Tour in 1967 I didn't know any of the players that well. I was a laborer just out of the Marines and professional golf was new to me. I had no idea what anyone's records were or who had won what. I wanted to see for myself who the best player was and I wanted to see how hard he worked and I wanted to outwork him, and even though they pushed and promoted the Big Three, Jack Nicklaus, Arnold Palmer and Gary Player, in my opinion Billy Casper was the best player in the middle sixties. He was a magician with the golf club, he had every shot in the book. He was a great bunker player, an excellent driver of the ball, and an exceptionally good putter. I thought he was very underrated as a player; I thought he was a superstar, and the best-kept secret in golf."

In his autobiography, Jack Nicklaus echoed a similar sentiment when he wrote, "When I first went out on Tour in 1962, I would always look over the lists of who was playing in the tournaments I entered to see who my chief competition was likely to be. Arnold Palmer obviously ranked highly, as did the other member of the so-called 'Big Three,' Gary Player. Many people who knew golf at that time felt the trio should really have been a quartet—'The Big Four,' if you will. I certainly would not have argued with them, because the name Bill Casper stood right up there alongside Arnie's and Gary's as far as I was concerned. Mostly, I believe, because of his conservative playing style and unassuming manner, Bill Casper never enjoyed the recognition his record deserves, but there is no question that he is one of golf's all-time greats. There has probably never been a better wedge player, and he was also magnificent from bunkers and a great chipper. And what took the pressure off all those shots, of course, was his putting. Knowing you are rarely going to miss from inside ten feet, as he did in his prime, does wonders for your confidence about the little recovery shots."

As Chi Chi Rodriguez put it, "Billy Casper could make a forty-foot putt just by winking at it."

And Phil Rodgers: "I think Billy, along with Sam Snead and Bob Rosburg, had the greatest hand-eye coordination I ever saw."

And the inimitable Dave Marr: "He just gave you this terrible feeling he was never going to make a mistake."

In his recount of the fateful Sunday at Olympic, Arnold Palmer, in his autobiography, noted, "In all the high drama of my collapse, it's sometimes forgotten that Bill Casper played almost flawless golf down the stretch. That point can't be driven home enough. I didn't just lose the 1966 U.S. Open—Bill Casper's brilliant play won it."

The peer praise goes on and on. It is not possible to find a player who watched Casper in his prime who doesn't acknowledge his uncommon ability to tame an uncommonly difficult game. Tom Watson said watching Casper as a teenager in the gallery of the Los Angeles Open inspired him to reach higher and play better. Tom Weiskopf said playing two rounds with Casper taught him more about golf than he learned on his own in a year.

But of all the accolades, Casper might choose this one for his epitaph:

"If I had to pick a man to play one round, and my life depended on it, that man would be Billy Casper. I believe most of the modern players would agree with me. This man simply is a great player, although he never has been given credit for it."

The author was Byron Nelson, responding to a question from a reporter for the *Christian Science Monitor* in 1970.

No golfer knows Billy Casper better than Johnny Miller. From the day they met at the U.S. Open presentation ceremony at The Olympic Club in 1966, a tournament that launched both of them to greater heights, they have been fast friends. Here is Miller's summation of the man he calls his older brother:

"When I first came on Tour he really took me under his wing. We started doing a lot of practice rounds together and firesides together. I'd be the five-minute speaker and he'd be the fifty-five-minute speaker. I watched how he played and how he handled himself. He had the first dedicated pre-shot routine, it was very quick, he was like a fast robot the way he played. But if he got disturbed, he'd put the club back in the bag, put the head cover back on, walk over to Del (caddy Del Taylor), take out his yardage books, his notes, and start all over again. I thought he was nuts when I first saw him doing those things, but he had programmed how you hit a golf ball and nothing would deter it. That's one thing I learned from him. I basically did a lot of watching and learned so much more. He had the most consistent weight shift I have ever seen in my life, the way he slid that right foot down the line. And his demeanor. He didn't get real high and he didn't get real low. He learned that from Hogan.

"I could never beat the guy, he never had a bad week, he was probably the most consistent golfer who ever lived. He wouldn't do the dumb things I'd do, lifting heavy rocks, four-wheeling, hurting myself. He had so much wisdom in that area. He said it was sort of like a violin string or a guitar string, if he were to do some strange exercise like pick peaches or work in the orchard or whatever then the violin string would go out of tune. He was a wise man in so many ways. He was the first guy to anchor the top of that putter on the inside of the left thigh. When he putted he would leave it there. Every time the putter handle would be in the same spot. I won a couple of tournaments doing that same thing. He had a great impact on my game. He was huge to me in my career, we had kinda an older brother, younger brother relationship. He made the comment that if he won that Open (in '66) he would sort of consecrate his time and talents to further the work and he did not turn down any firesides and he set the example for me. I sort of picked up the slack with Mike Reid and other Mormon guys on tour. I followed his example in so many ways."

"Another thing I learned from Billy is how he would hit whatever shot he wanted, low cuts, high cuts, whatever, he wasn't stuck with one flight. The only thing Billy lacked was ten to twenty yards. If he'd had ten to twenty yards he'd have been the greatest golfer who ever lived. He was pretty close anyway. He did it with precision, like Ben Hogan, not with the long cherry bomb like Jack Nicklaus or even Arnie. Like Clint Eastwood said, a man's got to know his limitations. He knew what he could do, what he couldn't do, and he didn't try to hit a shot he couldn't hit. He had to be top three in history in shot-making. He didn't do it with long drives all the time, just paper cuts, pretty soon you're shredded up and it's the fourteenth hole. And he didn't choke. Ever. Look at his match play record, his play in the Ryder Cup. In match play you've got to have the right stuff to make the important putts at the right time. He was the greatest lag putter I've ever seen in my life. His average second putt was ten to fifteen inches. Every single hole was a tap-in. You could tell when he putted he couldn't wait to putt. Most guys, 'I hope I make it.' He couldn't wait to make it. Billy never worked on his swing per se, he'd just look at impact, at those six inches, and keep that left knuckle aimed at the target. He was emotional but you never knew he was emotional. He didn't use any demonstrative gestures. He had his way of doing it but I always say the greatest entertainment is not a guy like Chi Chi, it's a guy who can play perfect golf. Billy wasn't flash and dash, he was more like Jack and Ben Hogan, he didn't get the gallery involved. Then Arnie came along. Arnie was a tough guy to compare yourself to."

MAYBE, AT THE END OF the day, that's the most accurate answer to the riddle of Casper's unsungness: Arnie.

It was his fate to play parallel to the most popular player in the history of golf.

Even in his finest hour, when he subdued an incredibly difficult golf course with four rounds in the 60s and mounted the greatest comeback ever seen in the United States Open, he not only had to victimize Arnie to do it, it started a downward slide for the people's champion. Palmer would win fifteen more times on Tour after that, but he never won another major.

And not only did he deny the king, he did it at the same place where Hogan was denied, thus moving into the Jack Fleck-like category of felling a legend, not becoming one.

ON THE WALL IN THE Olympic Club, a framed picture shows Casper and Palmer walking off the eighteenth green at the end of their playoff. Casper has his arm around Arnie, patting him on the back.

Asked about the photo, Casper explains, "I told him I was sorry and I meant it. He had a three-shot lead and shot 71 on Sunday—that wins the U.S. Open every time. You think about what you may have deprived someone else of. I think about what another U.S. Open would have meant to Arnold Palmer. I think about what I deprived Gene Littler of at the Masters—all the great associations and relationships I've been able to enjoy at Augusta over the years and Gene hasn't had the same opportunity. If it would have been my grandmother out there I wouldn't have played any different, but, still . . ."

He lets the thought linger as he climbs into the car.

". . . Well, anyway, that is the game," he says as he settles into the passenger seat—a man comfortable with where he's going and where he's been. I notice that he does not turn around as we drive away, and behind us The Olympic Club fades back into the mist.

Leaving the final green with Arnold, U.S. Open, 1966.

ACKNOWLEDGMENTS

The authors are indebted to an army of people without whom this project could not have been started let alone completed.

Multiple thanks and deep appreciation to:

Shirley Casper, for constant encouragement and support, meticulous fact-checking, and expert editing.

Bob Marra, Dee Benson, Eric Benson, Kerri Benson, Tanner Benson, Tori Benson, Sue Parkinson, Brett Parkinson, Dusty Heuston, "Professor" Steve Hill, Scott Thornton, Elder Craig Zwick, and the inestimable Doug Robinson, for reading the manuscript in various degrees of completion and providing valuable suggestions, corrections and input, all of it capped by a major championship performance from Deborah Schumaker, as careful and caring as editors get.

Matthew Parkinson, for his fine photography.

Bill Byrne and Irv Sommers, for pushing and pushing and pushing Billy to get this done.

The late Jim Huber, for unfailing support, kindness and encouragement.

Michael DeGroote, for valuable technical assistance.

Laury Livsey and Maureen Feeley at the PGA Tour, for research help and, Laury, for reading the manuscript on the long flight to Malaysia.

John Abendroth, Pat Murphy, Emily Dougherty, Jessica Smith, Chris Stein, Willie Toney, Steve Gregoire, and the entire friendly and accommodating staff at The Olympic Club.

David Morris and staff at San Diego Country Club.

Steve Ethun at Augusta National Golf Club.

Peter Hill, Bob Morris, and Rich Katz at Billy Casper Golf and Buffalo Communications.

Merrie Monteagudo and Tod Leonard at *The San Diego Union*.

Richard Geiger at *The San Francisco Chronicle*.

Les and Sheridan England and Richard and Mavis Parkinson, for generous assistance with lodging.

Wilbur Colom, Diane Blair, Chris Esler, Ric Kolenda, and all the great people at Genesis Press.

Susan Ramundo, for fantastic page design.

Bob Marra, again, for his marketing genius and coordinating all facets of the project from start to finish.

Linda and Kim Henrie, Billy Jr. and Karen Casper, Bob and Kelly Casper, Byron Casper, Judi and Jack Fisher, Jennifer and Jack Carpenter, Charlie and Gina Casper, Julia Casper, Sarah Casper, Tommy Casper, and Margee Rader, for sharing family insights and personal reflections.

Johnny Miller, Don Collett, Lee Trevino, Jim Nantz, and Jaime Diaz, for insightful interviews and quotes.

Barbara Nicklaus, for kind editing help; Doc Giffin and Vivian Player, for support and logistical assistance.

And a special thank-you to The Big Three, Arnold Palmer, Jack Nicklaus, and Gary Player, who, when asked if they would consider writing the book's Foreword, responded without hesitation: "Absolutely. How can we help?"

While *The Big Three and Me* is primarily an autobiography, numerous books and online sources were researched for facts, dates, statistics and what might best be described as "memory substantiation." Websites that included pgatour.com, rydercup.com, Wikipedia and the golf component of About.com made research a breeze. Also, there is a growing treasure trove on golfers and golf history out there that proved invaluable. Publications consulted include *The History of the PGA Tour*, by Ira Barkow; *The Wonderful World of Professional Golf*, by Mark H. McCormack; *My Mulligan to Golf*, by Fred Raphael with Don Wade; *The Story of American Golf*, by Herbert Warren Wind; *Arnold Palmer, A Golfer's Life*, by Arnold Palmer with James Dodson; *Jack Nicklaus, My Story*, by Jack Nicklaus with Ken Bowden; *Gary Player, World Golfer*, by Gary Player with Floyd Thatcher; *Ben Hogan, An American Life*, by James Dodson; *Slammin' Sam*, by Sam Snead and George Mendoza; *The New Billy Casper*, by Hack Miller; *A Disorderly Compendium of Golf*, by Lorne Rubenstein and Jeff Neuman; *The Eternal Summer*, by Curt Sampson; and *100 Years of Golf in San Diego County*, by Norrie West. Anyone who loves the game of golf and its rich past would do well to read the lot.

Billy Casper's Career Record

PGA Tour Victories (51) 1956–1975

1956

(1) Labatt Open, Quebec City, Canada

1957

(2) Phoenix Open Invitational, Phoenix, Arizona

(3) Kentucky Derby Open Invitational, Lexington, Kentucky

1958

(4) Bing Crosby National Pro-Am, Pebble Beach, California

(5) Greater New Orleans Open, New Orleans, Louisiana

(6) Buick Open Invitational, Flint, Michigan

1959

(7) United States Open, Mamaroneck, New York

(8) Portland Centennial Open Invitational, Portland, Oregon

(9) Lafayette Open Invitational, Lafayette, Louisiana

(10) Mobile Sertoma Open, Mobile, Alabama

1960

(11) Portland Open Invitational, Portland, Oregon

(12) Hesperia Open Invitational, Hesperia, California

(13) Orange County Open Invitational, Costa Mesa, California

1961

(14) Portland Open Invitational, Portland, Oregon

1962

(15) Doral Open Invitational, Doral, Florida

(16) Greater Greensboro Open, Greensboro, North Carolina

(17) 500 Festival Open Invitational, Indianapolis, Indiana

(18) Bakersfield Open Invitational, Bakersfield, California

1963

(19) Bing Crosby National Pro-Am, Pebble Beach, California

(20) Insurance City Open Invitational, Hartford, Connecticut

1964

(21) Doral Open Invitational, Doral, Florida

(22) Colonial National Invitational, Fort Worth, Texas

(23) Greater Seattle Open Invitational, Seattle, Washington

(24) Almaden Open Invitational, San Jose, California

1965

(25) Bob Hope Desert Classic, Bermuda Dunes, California

(26) Western Open, Niles, Illinois

(27) Insurance City Open Invitational, Hartford, Connecticut

(28) Sahara Invitational, Las Vegas, Nevada

1966

(29) San Diego Open Invitational, San Diego, California

(30) United States Open, San Francisco, California

(31) Western Open, Medinah, Illinois

(32) 500 Festival Open Invitational, Indianapolis, Indiana

1967

(33) Canadian Open, Montreal, Quebec

(34) Carling World Open, Toronto, Ontario

1968

(35) Los Angeles Open, Los Angeles, California

(36) Greater Greensboro Open, Greensboro, North Carolina

(37) Colonial National Invitational, Fort Worth, Texas

(38) 500 Festival Open Invitational, Indianapolis, Indiana

(39) Greater Hartford Open Invitational, Hartford, Connecticut

(40) Lucky International Open, San Francisco, California

1969

(41) Bob Hope Desert Classic, Bermuda Dunes, California

(42) Western Open, Midlothian, Illinois

(43) Alcan Open, Seattle, Washington

1970

(44) Los Angeles Open, Los Angeles, California

(45) Masters, Augusta, Georgia

(46) IVB-Philadelphia Golf Classic, Philadelphia, Pennsylvania

(47) AVCO Golf Classic, Sutton, Massachusetts

1971

(48) Kaiser International Open Invitational, Napa, California

1973

(49) Western Open, Midlothian, Illinois

(50) Sammy Davis, Jr. Greater Hartford Open, Hartford, Connecticut

1975
(51) First NBC New Orleans Open, New Orleans, Louisiana

- PGA Tour Player of the Year: 1966, 1970
- PGA Tour Leading Money Winner: 1966, 1968
- Vardon Trophy Winner (low scoring average): 1960, 1963, 1965, 1966, 1968

International Victories

1958
Brazilian Open
Havana Open (Cuba)

1959
Brazilian Open

1973
Hassan II Golf Trophy (Morocco)

1974
Trophee Lancome (France)
Is Molas Tournament (Italy)

1975
Hassan II Golf Trophy (Morocco)
Italian Open (Monticello)

1977
Mexican Open

1988
Urbanet International Golf Championship (Japan)

1989
Urbanet International Golf Championship (Japan)

Senior (now Champions) Tour

1982
Shootout at Jeremy Ranch, Park City, Utah
Merrill Lynch/Golf Digest Pro-Am, Newport, Rhode Island

1983
United States Senior Open, Chaska, Minnesota

1984
Liberty Mutual Legends of Golf (with Gay Brewer), Austin, Texas
Senior PGA Tour Roundup, Sun City West, Arizona

1987
Del E. Webb Arizona Classic, Sun City West, Arizona
Greater Grand Rapids Open, Grand Rapids, Michigan

1988
Vantage at The Dominion, San Antonio, Texas
Mazda Sr. Tournament Players Championship, Ponte Vedra Beach, Fl.

1989
Transamerica Senior Golf Championship, Napa, California

Ryder Cup Playing Record

1961
Royal Lytham & St. Annes Golf Course, St. Annes, England
Points scored: 3.0
Final Score: United States 14½, Great Britain 9½

1963
East Lake Country Club, Atlanta Georgia
Points scored: 4½
Final Score: United States 23, Great Britain 9

1965
Royal Birkdale Golf Course, Southport, England
Points scored: 2.0
Final score: United States 19½ Great Britain, 12½

1967
Champions Golf Course, Houston, Texas
Points scored: 4½
Final score: United States 23½, Great Britain, 8½

1969
Royal Birkdale Golf Course, Southport, England
Points scored: 3.0
Final score: United States 16, Great Britain 16

1971
Old Warson Country Club, St. Louis, Missouri
Points scored: 0
Final score: United States 18½, Great Britain 13½

1973
Muirfield Links, Gullane, Scotland
Points scored: 4.0
Final Score: United States 19, Great Britain & Ireland 13

1975
Laurel Valley Golf Course, Ligonier, Pennsylvania
Points scored: 2½
Final score: United States 21, Great Britain & Ireland 11

Player totals: 23½ points scored. Member of seven winning U.S. teams, one tie.

Ryder Cup Captain Record

1979
The Greenbrier Golf Club, White Sulphur Springs, West Virginia
Final score: United States 17, Europe 11

Ryder Cup Records Held (as of 2010)

Most points: 23½
Most appearances: 8 (tied with Raymond Floyd and Lanny Wadkins)
Most matches played: 37
Most singles points: 7 (tied with Arnold Palmer)
Most foursomes points: 9 (tied with Arnold Palmer)
Most four-ball points: 7½ (tied with Lanny Wadkins)

INDEX

PHOTO CREDITS

Biograph
Casper